A former professional cyclist, James Hamilton Hibbard studied philosophy at The University of California, Santa Cruz and DePaul University. He has received grants and been selected for workshops by PEN America and Tin House.

Also a screenwriter, James' first feature film is currently being developed. He lives with his wife and son in Northern California.

THE
ART OF
CYCLING

Philosophy,
meaning and a life
on two wheels

James Hibbard

QUERCUS

First published in Great Britain in 2021 by Quercus.
This paperback edition first published in 2022 by

QUERCUS

Quercus Editions Ltd
Carmelite House
50 Victoria Embankment
London EC4Y 0DZ

An Hachette UK company

MMP ISBN 978 1 52941 028 0
Ebook ISBN 978 1 52941 027 3
Every effort has been made to contact copyright holders.
However, the publishers will be glad to rectify in future
editions any inadvertent omissions brought to their attention.

10 9 8 7 6

Typeset by CC Book Production
Printed and bound in Great Britain by Clays Ltd, Elcograf S.p.A.

To my son, Graeme, with love beyond measure.

'There is more wisdom in your body than in your deepest philosophy.'

—Friedrich Nietzsche, *Thus Spoke Zarathustra*

Contents

Introduction

You Are Not Your Brain: On Cycling and the Transcendent

From the first time I rode my neighbor's yellow Schwinn Varsity down the street, I was determined to become a cyclist. My hands deep in the curve of the handlebars, every pedal stroke transformed into speed as the road silently retreated beneath the narrow tires of the bicycle. Like most children, I'd ridden bicycles before, but with their flat bars and knobby tires they had always seemed clunky and utilitarian. This bike was different – so fast that it felt tantalizingly close to the freedom of flying – and riding it was perhaps the most beautiful sensation I'd ever experienced.

I started racing the summer after that fateful ride on the Schwinn, just before my thirteenth birthday. Progressing quickly through the junior ranks, I moved to the U.S. Olympic Training Center while still a teenager – trading proms and homecoming for an insular world of Eastern Bloc coaches, travel, and physical pain. Turning professional with a top-ranked American team, I became just good enough to realize first-hand that my cycling heroes of the late 1990s were hiding the secret of their doping. By the time I stopped racing in my mid-twenties, I'd decided that the sport I'd once loved beyond reason was rotten to the core – comprised of people who espoused the virtues of fair play and hard work all the while doing and putting into their body whatever was necessary to win.

Now far removed from the younger version of myself who had pined after the external validation of winning, I began to ride again after not touching a bicycle for nearly a decade – discovering with each successive ride that the positive aspects of the sport had come to eclipse the toxicity of the doping era. Cycling has since regained a different sort of luster – harder won and more complex. With the perspective afforded by the passage of time, I'm able to see not just its shortcomings, but also the innumerable moments of beauty and insight which, regardless of winning or losing, came from my attempt to do something as well as I possibly could.

Every choice carries with it the sentimental shadow of everything else that might have been and I still remain uncertain about the ways in which the sport of cycling was invaluable to shaping who I am, how it deformed me, and who I might have become had I not pursued it as intensely as I did. My only response is that on some level, caring deeply about anything eventually leads to the great pain of loss – be that the loss of your sport, or the loss of self which results from becoming so identified with something that other aspects of your personality which might have flourished, wither on the vine.

Slowly, I've come to regard cycling as not simply pleasant, but even redemptive, and can reflect on how riding has always been able to return me to the realm of the embodied and physical – if only temporarily, releasing me from the egoistic striving of what Buddhism aptly terms the 'small self.'

As I write this, I've just returned from a ride. Still fresh in my mind is the feeling of my bike swaying beneath me as I climbed the same winding mountain roads I trained on when I was a racer. My breathing is more labored than it used to be, and I consciously no longer concern myself with how far or fast I've ridden. I simply try to notice the sensations; the feeling of the thick morning fog passing over my skin; the hum of my tires as they roll over the chipseal road, and the slight burning in my legs as I muscle my way over the last meters of a steep climb – my sensitivity to the innumerable inputs from my bike and body having been honed by tens of thousands of hours of training. Like a beach at low tide, words and ideas recede, and suddenly everything seems possible again.

In the pages that follow, my purpose is to address all of the 'little things' – all the aspects of the sport which at first appear superficial and banal. In dealing with the surface of things however, my aim is not to obsess endlessly over them, but rather to understand them sufficiently so that they can become so natural, so engrained in the subconscious, that they fall away – so that you're no longer merely pedaling a bicycle, but doing something far more interesting, significant, and meaningful: remembering, with every pedal stroke and heartbeat, that you truly exist.

Φ

Upon learning that I both studied philosophy and used to be a professional cyclist, people often asked me what I thought about during the many hours I spent training alone. Usually,

I'd say something about how time passed quickly, or how I occupied my mind by looking at the power meter on my handlebars. While none of these answers was untrue per se, the most compelling – even beautiful – aspect of cycling is that when riding I'm able to think about very little. Through philosophy I'd sought answers to life's mysteries – to ultimate questions of life, death, and meaning, but in Descartes and Nietzsche, Husserl and de Beauvoir, I'd only encountered its limits. Ultimate things could be approached from every direction, but like trying to learn the floor plan of a house in total darkness, there seemed no way to think or speak rationally about those things I cared about the most.

Cycling forced me to reframe the problem itself. In many ways the demands and challenges of being a cyclist were the antitheses of those I found in philosophy. With the solitude afforded by the bike, the questions remained, but I was changed. My once all-consuming desire to understand and bring words to all things evaporated – rationality itself seeming to grow silent as I pedaled. Cycling provided an escape hatch from my own head and the bicycle grew to be sacrosanct. Visceral and immediate, riding drew me back to the physical world: the play of the sunlight as it filtered through the leaves of a tree onto the surface of the dark asphalt or how the cork tape on my bicycle's handlebars felt underneath my hands – pedal, breath, pedal, breath, pedal, over and over again in an unremitting pattern of repetition which even among the cerebral and strong-willed, forces your higher-order faculties to capitulate.

Like so many others, in my attempts to outthink and somehow get ahead of life's uncertainties, I have the habit of endlessly assessing this or that idea, plan, or concept. As if I were contesting a never-ending chess match, hypothetical scenarios feverishly unfurl until my own abstractions come to eclipse all that's proximate and near. The real threat is that just often enough, this sort of thinking works – or at least it serves its ostensible purpose – and increasingly life came to feel like little more than a series of events to be dissected by the scalpel of logic. Coupled with the distracting allure of the internet at our fingertips, it's tempting to be induced to live much of your life in a trance-like state, seduced by the short-term dopamine victories provided by the consumption of easily digested bits of information. As a result of both rational thought and electronic distraction, the 'blooming and buzzing confusion' of life is tamed and held in abeyance, but with this power (and its material benefits) comes a gnawing detachment – a feeling that a basic element of what it is to be alive has been lost.

This sort of rational calculation, which reduces the real world to little more than abstraction, is so pervasive that for many it has become the default lens through which all of life is understood. From the decisions you make at work, to how you speak and present yourself, to who you choose as a partner – the operating fiction of modernity is that if you have enough information it's possible to maximize the utility of every choice and push aside misfortune for yourself and those you care about. When you're technically attuned, the world becomes a series of disembodied cost/benefit analyses – data being extracted and profits being maximized – and those who are unable to cast the world in these terms are often regarded as whimsical romantic reactionaries. However, with so many concepts of progress lacking any endgame or achievable ideal, it's neither depressive nor irrational to feel bound by a set of conceptual constraints not of one's own making and wonder what the point of it all is.

For nearly as long as I can remember, I've had the inexplicable feeling that just beyond the purview of the rational was not mere nonsense and superstition, but an alternative way of confronting existence which had become obscured – eclipsed not just by social constraints, but by my own predilection for endless thinking. In many cases, the vague sense of loss over this way of viewing the world goes back to the basic question of who you are – deep down and outside of an ever-calculating frame of mind. It's easy to conflate your very existence with the processes of your brain – ideas or symbols for reality itself – and when you do, something fundamental about what it is to be alive is bound to be lost. You're distanced not just from your own body (a sort of machine which is ultimately doomed to failure), but the particulars of the world are substituted for universal concepts – in other words, abstractions which have been drained of their vitality and dynamism. There is little doubt that abstract modes of thought which ask pointed questions about the function of the natural world have elevated vast swathes of the population from 'short, nasty and brutish' lives of superstition and premature death, into the light of reason, but it's naïve to think that this has been without cost.

These costs, and the natural and age-old conflict between the rational and romantic temperaments came to the forefront in twentieth-century philosophy with central figures making claims about what philosophy could, and perhaps more importantly, could *not* hope to make sense of. In many ways, this question as to the limits of rational thought is at the root of the division which took place between so-called 'analytic' or Anglo-American philosophy, and the school of 'Continental philosophy' which grew out of the intellectual milieu of post-war Germany and France. Attempting to delimit and circumscribe all intelligible and therefore 'legitimate' questions, Ludwig Wittgenstein – undoubtedly one of the most important philosophers of the twentieth century – begins his *Tractatus Logico-Philosophicus* with the grounding statement, 'The world is all that is the case,' proceeding, brick by brick, to construct the logical terms of the world and to police the domain of valid philosophical inquiry. But Wittgenstein was not a mere positivist or materialist. With the sense that something ineffable remains outside the scope of rational language, near the conclusion of the *Tractatus*, Wittgenstein famously writes 'There are, indeed, things that cannot be put into words. They *make themselves manifest*. They are what is mystical.'

By the time Wittgenstein was writing the *Tractatus* in the early 1920s, the West – particularly Britain and the United States – had already largely lost its taste for mystical, 'ultimate questions' about life and death, meaning and existence. Often construed as fuzzy, and conceptually sloppy, the very idea of the mystical had withered. Since the Enlightenment, progress had been the result of hard-nosed pragmatism coupled with Protestant practicality which sought to pose only the sort of questions which were amenable to empirical answers, and more often than not, that meant scientific questions. Ideas about the soul – about meaning and purpose – had necessarily retreated to art, religion, small corners of philosophy like existentialism, and, while it may at first appear unlikely, to the realm of sport. While the ascetic suffering induced by exertion and exposure to the elements is central to cycling's connection to questions of meaning and purpose, it wasn't merely the physical, experiential aspects of the sport, but also certain cultural elements which made the sport so attractive to those who remained attuned to the transcendent. Cycling has always been a bastion for romantic reactionaries – for outsiders who feel that perhaps something is amiss with modern society (or perhaps with him or herself) and it's difficult to overstate just how connected the revival of the sport was in the English-speaking world to the 1960s and '70s counterculture.

Led by loners, hippies, and oddballs, the sport's churches were cluttered bicycle shops where the grace of Tom Simpson's pedaling style and exotic Italian bicycles with names like Masi, Colnago, De Rosa and Pinarello on their down tubes were discussed along with music, philosophy, and literature. This interest in cycling wasn't merely technical or sporting, but instead spurred on by ideas of living differently and of rejecting mainstream consumer culture which for many had come to feel both ossified and vacuous. Simply put, at the time, normal gainfully employed adults didn't ride bicycles for either pleasure or enjoyment. And, though several generations removed, it was this version of cycling, rather than the hyper-competitive sport that it now is, that I was drawn to.

This convergence of cycling and the counterculture with its famous edicts to 'question reality' and 'turn on, tune in and drop out' had strong roots in the San Francisco Bay Area where I grew up. Long before sports science, and

Team Sky's 'marginal gains' approach, mid-ride stops to smoke marijuana at the top of a climb weren't uncommon, and as I experienced the solitary freedom of the bicycle the implicit message from early club mates and mentors was that spending one's life behind a desk in service of a corporation's agenda would be the worst sort of soul-crushing failure. It wasn't only the abstract and heady desire to escape the hyper-rational, but also riding and racing a bicycle in a country which had little historical ties to the sport which engendered this outsider perspective, and my first cycling club, the Garden City Wheelmen, epitomized the links between cycling and the vestiges of the sixties which still remained in the Bay Area of the 1990s.

With a distinctive jersey emblazoned with a yellow fleur-de-lis on the chest, the club was over a hundred years old and run out of a small shop in Santa Clara, California called Shaw's Lightweight Cycles. The owner, Terry Shaw, was equal parts proprietor, cycling historian, and coach. With a long, dark beard, and a reputation burnished by having had several juniors from the club go on to race professionally in Europe, Terry was a local fixture both on the road and at the velodrome. He spoke Italian, and before taking up cycling and opening the shop, had played the clarinet in the U.S. Army Band. A Bay Area baby boomer, his interests were wide-ranging, and during rides he was just as likely to quote Herman Melville or Thomas Mann as he was to talk about the technicalities of training.

Tellingly, making money never seemed to be Terry's top priority, and he would often discourage neophytes who walked into the shop from buying anything too expensive – instead suggesting that they spend a few years riding and learning the sport before purchasing such a machine. From how one navigated the peloton, to whose advice was legitimate, respect was something to be earned and not merely bought. Like music, painting, or writing, cycling was an art, and becoming skillful was a pursuit with an ever-retreating horizon of proficiency which was shrouded in mystery.

Sorely lacking in windows, the shop was dark and smelled distinctly of Phil Wood bearing grease and tubular glue. Rows of dusty frames and components hung from the ceiling and walls, interspersed with photos and jerseys of former club members who had moved successfully into the professional ranks. On the door was a large sticker from the legendary Italian component brand, Campagnolo, which seemed designed to appeal to the already initiated: 'Campagnolo spoken here.' Two books were always present on the shop counter: *The C.O.N.I. Training Manual* and *Bartlett's Familiar Quotations*. Their pages both well thumbed and black with grease, Bartlett's was employed to settle many a dispute as to the true originator of this or that memorable turn of phrase. The mostly forgotten *C.O.N.I. Training Manual* however, demands something more of an explanation as it very much speaks to what the sport was at the time.

One of the only training manuals available until the mid-1980s, *The C.O.N.I Manual* as we referred to it, was a cycling bible of sorts. First published in the late 1960s by the Italian Olympic Committee, the English version was replete with awkward syntax and questionable translations, but was one of the only available sources of information about training, tactics, diet, and the care of equipment. Tellingly, even though it was written during what is now considered the golden era of the sport, it includes an introduction from the then head of the international cycling union which romantically recalls times past and lambasts the technological advances which were taking place: 'the cold pigeon-holes of reason, allowed less and less space for the imagination. Adventurous sport, improvised and invented sport – whether we accept the fact with joy, resignation or regret – has gone for good, together with the mentality of an age past.' Like all truly great things, it seems that cycling has perennially been in a state of decline.

Beyond the typical sale of parts and servicing of bicycles, Shaw's Lightweight Cycles also served as a meeting point for numerous club rides throughout the week, and we would often ride up the Santa Clara Valley to Palo Alto, climb Alpine Road, and descend into the small, coastal town of La Honda which felt like a time capsule. Long before tech giants like Google and Apple dominated the economic and cultural landscape, the area south of San Francisco had been the epicenter of 1960s counterculture, but by the late 1990s, those wanting to think and live outside of the mainstream had for the most part been priced out of the Valley and driven to the rural mountains which separate it from the Pacific Ocean. On the narrow, deserted roads which were best for riding, one still encountered run-down mountain cabins, Volkswagen buses, and communes with Buddhist prayer flags strung across their entrances. Recounted in all of its psychedelic tumult and grand ambition in Tom Wolfe's *The Electric Kool-Aid Acid Test*, it had been La Honda where the writer Ken Kesey and his Merry Pranksters had lived and famously hosted the likes of The Grateful Dead and Hunter S. Thompson.

As I rode with my club mates along the silent, tree-lined roads, where some of my early literary and intellectual heroes had once roamed, the same sense of possibility I'd felt when reading the works of Kesey, Wolfe, Aldous Huxley, and Alan Watts, became intertwined with the version of cycling I found with Terry and the rest of the Garden City Wheelmen. Here was an alternative to the desk job of my father and my friends' fathers – something romantic, grand, and significant; simply put, something that seemed to *mean* something more than what other adults appeared to spend their lives doing.

Cycling was a way to have it both ways – to appear to be an upstanding citizen when deep down I knew I was anything but. I intuitively understood that my highest ideal wasn't mere knowledge, but to lose myself in Dionysian drunkenness – in art and thought, madness, and music. However, I was internally divided. Conservative by temperament, I also wanted to be well thought of by precisely those 'respectable' people I told myself didn't matter. Rage and pain, the breakdown of your own personality through physical exertion and sheer force of will, all played a central role in the sport and, best of all, no one else seemed to understand this – they merely took my photo for the newspaper when I won, lauding me for my hard work and dedication.

Φ

The months and years of training as an athlete are often not appreciated as the truly radical act of self-creation and will that they are. As Nietzsche said: 'We however, want to *become who we are* – human beings who are new, unique, incomparable, who give themselves laws, who create themselves!' In many ways this is the pinnacle of human will and action. Against the current of complacency and biological instinct, you impose your will and make the promise to yourself to become who you were intended to be. Every training ride was motivated by my desire to recreate myself, to adapt and change not just physically, but to mould myself into someone who could mentally endure more and more.

For years I did the vast majority of my training on the back roads of Northern California's coast, the damp salinity of the Pacific fog mingling with the sweet scent of redwoods which lined the narrow tracks of buckling pavement. At the time, I was so habituated to the geometry and fit of my road bicycle that it felt like an extension of my own body – so sensitive that I could detect a mere millimeter of change to the height of my saddle or degree of tilt of my handlebar. With my carbon fiber frame beneath me as I climbed and smoothly traced the gentle arcs of descents, my perceptions of reality would begin to shift. Progressively, over the course of a four- or five-hour ride, the thoughts would recede. A sense of not merely meaning, but of transcendence – Wittgenstein's 'mystical' – would unexpectedly overtake me. When it happened, I was nearly always riding alone, having escaped to tiny towns which still had one-room schools and general stores. My legs turning beneath me as if by their own volition, the flow of time ebbed into an eternal present, all of life's slights and failures suddenly felt insignificant and, as odd as it might sound for a professional athlete, worldly ambition suddenly seemed myopic, the winning or losing of a race of little consequence. In place of my thoughts – of my 'small self' which was striving, rational and afraid – another possibility would emerge. Ineffable, and not only beyond language, but beyond the rationally constituted idea I had of myself, suddenly I'd see the world around me as if for the first time.

Whatever 'I' was, wasn't reducible to my brain or thinking and had no purpose or intent involving me as an agent. I wasn't merely part of a culture, a sport, or a period of time, but in the most basic sense, of existence itself. Freed from my habituated thinking and analysis which placed me in an adversarial position – always trying to extract certain things from the world to meet my wants and needs – other aspects of what it is to be alive would come to the forefront, and throughout my years of training and racing one particular instance remains etched in my mind.

Once, after a point-to-point time trial, I was riding down a desolate mountain road at the base of the Sierra Nevada Mountains. A thunderstorm was fast approaching, blowing warm gusts of wind through the golden grass that blanketed the hills. As I started to make my way back down the road I'd just climbed, my lightweight racing tire went flat. With no way to fix it, I continued down the mountain slowly on the rim and waited for a support vehicle to drive by. Certain that one would eventually come, I was calm, but the air was electric. As the sky darkened, I heard the clap of thunder echo in the distance and seconds later, a flash of lightning above the mountains that made the hair on the back of my neck stand up.

As a light rain began to fall, I got off my bike and sat down in the grass by the side of the road. Silent but for the cicadas and the gentle sound of raindrops falling, I had the strangest feeling that everything was *okay*. Not merely all right – but even loving – and for perhaps the first time in my life, I realized I was truly happy to be alive. Through the discomfort of riding in the heat and freezing cold and the burning pain of exertion, cycling reminded me that I was more than my thoughts. Again and again, my body drawing me back to the present and allowing me to see the world which I'd relegated to mere simulacra with fresh eyes.

When forced to let go by the bicycle, a more basic truth emerged. The various processes taking place blended together, myself and the bicycle seamlessly interwoven – oxygen flowing to muscles, the beating of my heart melding with the hum of the tire on the road's surface, the chain passing over the cogs, and the spinning of bearings – a single thoughtless entity speeding along towards nothing in particular but an escape from myself. Here there was no news, no internet and no politics, no spirit of the times springing forth to color and inform reality – only the long and incommunicable silence of an unspeakable ultimate, lurking behind the everyday and banal, every pedal stroke whispering over and over again to those with ears to hear it, *you are, you are, you are.*

Chapter 1

On Purposes and Origins

In my beginning is my end.
—T.S. Eliot

I'm still not certain which of the three of us first had the idea to ride down the California coast. Now in our late thirties, we all had young children, and even though we'd all been professional road cyclists, there was certainly no one paying us to race our bicycles any longer. The basics of the ride were agreed to via text message: six weeks from now, we'd ride the three hundred or so miles from the San Francisco Bay Area to Southern California along the Pacific Coast Highway. We couldn't shirk our jobs and family life for more than about three days, so to cover the distance, we'd need to ride at least a hundred miles each day. For a *real* cyclist this would be challenging but far from insurmountable, but as I contemplated what I'd agreed to, it was clear that I could no longer place myself in this category.

I'd ridden very little since I stopped racing a decade and a half ago – mentally burned out and inexplicably unable to recover from hard training. Still, motivated by some lingering bravado which I'd thought I had long ago outgrown, I humored myself that, with a little training, of course I could still do three hard days in a row. By the time Jackson, Zach, and I were planning to leave in early November, the stream of tourists who make their way down Highway 1 during the summer would have subsided and with any luck we'd still be just early enough to beat the impending first rains of the year. I tried suggesting something shorter – maybe just one or two long days – but seemingly always our de facto leader, Jackson assured us confidently that for us to even bother, the route needed to be difficult enough to ensure that it was memorable. Deep down I knew that he was right, and hoped that even though so much had changed in the intervening years, the three of us riding would still feel like it once had.

Zach still rode a little, as did Jackson who now worked as a *directeur sportif* – a team director for a top European cycling team – but in the years since I stopped racing, I'd never settled into riding on a regular basis. There had been fits and spurts, an exhibition race here or a group ride there, but I couldn't recall the last time I'd even ridden two consecutive days. Trying to move on with my life, I'd tucked away the few old team jerseys and medals I'd saved and sold nearly all the rest of my equipment barring my prized track bike – an Eddy Merckx which had been hand-made for me at the now-shuttered factory in Flanders. As I looked down at my pale, hairy legs, the only remaining evidence of my having ever been a cyclist were the scars from long-ago crashes which ran across my hips and kneecaps, and as I thought about riding again, the person who'd once wanted nothing more in life than to be good at cycling felt incredibly remote. Why had I invested so much in this sport?

Φ

Through a certain lens, nearly every sport can be seen as not merely superfluous, but even entirely pointless. Much like art, when someone sees the world through the lens of concepts like utility and progress, no clear value is added from athletics. The hitting or chasing of balls, swimming, running, or in the case of this book, the nuances of cycling, can appear indulgent in the face of so many other existentially pressing social and cultural concerns. This begs the question – why care about riding bicycles? Such an answer can only be personal and, in some ways, *artistic*. For those fortunate enough to have had their basic needs of safety, food, and shelter met, other questions appear – questions of fortitude, perseverance, character, and meaning which for millennia have been answered through either religion or the elective hardships imposed by organized competition. This isn't because sports are intrinsically meaningful – quite the opposite. Rather, the value of any athletic pursuit is derived precisely from the fact that they aren't necessary for survival. Like the deepest meaning in any walk of life, the value of sports lies beyond practical considerations – its magnitude and scope proportionate to the investment and temperament of the participant. Each sport can be thought of as a personal answer of sorts, and much like an artistic medium, needs to be in keeping not just with the age and culture, but to fit with the particular personality of the athlete. In my case, the fit was cycling.

The epitome of the forbidden sort of freedom I craved, I vividly remember being in middle school, walking to the periphery of the schoolyard and watching through the chain-linked fence, transfixed as a cycling team made its way down the wide boulevard in the slipstream of their team car.

This would be my way out; my way to free myself from a future of sitting in traffic and of jobs that no adult seemed to like – my way out of the pain and stupidity that seemed to infect everything and everyone. I imagined hour after hour on open roads, and of being good enough to be exempt from the pointless and arbitrary rules imposed on children.

It was only a few months later that I saw my first race at the local velodrome, Hellyer Park. There, on the banked concrete surface illuminated by the cinematic glow of the yellow lights that dotted the perimeter of the track, I saw tall riders and short ones, thin and stocky ones – all seemingly capable of competing successfully. There were races which went on lap after lap and others which only consisted of a frenetic sprint to the finish line. Perhaps most appealing to me, it seemed contained enough that it was possible to learn from and correct your mistakes. One lap identical to the next, the finish line was always in the same place, the bike straightforward, and the distances and rules codified each event in a way which made it feel more possible to control. I'd seen the Tour de France on television and, where road cycling seemed chaotic with wind and rain, flat tires, and courses that the riders would often ever only ride once a season, track cycling on a velodrome was precise – its variables limited in number. It melded the speed and mechanical precision of cars and airplanes (two things which I, like many other teenage boys, had an affinity for) with a psychological element which seemed the most fascinating of all – the ability to endure the physical suffering necessary to win.

While I don't recall the particulars of who won or lost any of the events that first night, I have a distinct memory of watching a cyclist come off the track and ride to the grassy infield at the center of the velodrome only to collapse – the agony of exertion and oxygen debt spread across his face as he heaved deep breaths. While the rest of life seemed ossified – polite, decent, and constrained by decorum, schoolwork, and good manners, the outcasts who I saw that night seemed to relish the collective disenfranchisement that drew them together. In the suburban world I knew, hurting, not only oneself, but exacting physical pain upon one's competitors, felt primal. The velodrome was an outlet where much of what was repressed beneath a thin veneer of civility in other walks of life was not merely permissible, but rewarded – a stage upon which my furtive ambitions and hidden drives were made manifest. Years later, when I was at my strongest, I recall lining up for a race, surveying my competitors and thinking sadistically, *tonight, I'm going to make all of you hurt worse than you've ever hurt before.* Cycling wasn't merely about enduring pain, but also taking pleasure in your ability to *inflict* it.

I'd already begun riding on the road, and shortly after seeing that first race, my parents bought me my first track bike, a used Pinarello Amatore painted in a distinctive azure blue with the Olympic rings on the head tube; like so many others before me, years before I could drive, the bike became my escape. My parents' marriage was far from good, and in the midst of screaming and fists through drywall, I would escape on my bike for long enough to ensure that I returned to a calm, darkened house with the telltale sign of shut bedroom doors indicating that, for now at least, the storm had passed.

That first summer of 1995 I raced on both the track and

the road, often setting out with my father before sunrise for far-flung road races and distant velodromes, and it was near the end of that season that I competed in my first junior state championships. Against a laughably small group of competitors, I won every event. Insignificant as it was in the grand scheme of the sport, this was all the validation I needed, and it was then that I decided that I was going to do whatever was necessary to become a successful bike racer.

Obsessed with improving, I started working with my first real coach, Christopher Campbell. Hour after hour, through the cold winter and into the long, hot days of summer, he would watch my workouts from the infield of the velodrome. In his booming, baritone voice from beneath a sun hat and dark glasses, Christopher would shout not just times, but criticism as to how I sat or moved on the bike – 'straighten your arms,' 'sit back,' or 'look through the rider in front of you' – and it was from him that I started to learn what real training was like – not just going hard, but through endless repetition, baking into your nervous system how to ride a bicycle both naturally and efficiently.

When I first began, the sport had appeared straightforward and my calculus simple: to excel I had to train, prepare my equipment well, and make sound tactical decisions about when to use my energy. However, the more I improved, the more complex cycling became. Was it the physical or the mental which was more important? Exertion or rest? Power or aerodynamics? It wasn't merely that when you break any seemingly simple activity into its constituent components that it grows more complex, rather, at each plateau of competency – just when I thought I was close to mastering some element or other – I discovered that the very thing I thought I was near mastering was so enigmatic as to be self-contradictory. To improve it was necessary to stop *wanting* to improve: although training was necessary, it was of no use without rest and recovery and, perhaps strangest of all, I found that it was when I stopped trying to win that I seemed to perform the best.

Φ

With a little more than two months to train, I began to prepare for our ride down the coast. I'd kept some clothing, a few helmets, and a pair of shoes – but most importantly, I still had the road bike which had been sent to me by my last bike sponsor. Matte black, its set-up identical to my old racing position, the saddle height correct to the millimeter, and as they'd been for as long as I could remember, my handlebars exactly 61 centimeters from the tip of my preferred saddle.

I fill my water bottles, change – or as we always called it, *kit up*: a plain black jersey and shorts, an old team helmet, and tighten the ratcheting buckles on my slightly scuffed cycling shoes – before giving my bike one last check, and rolling out of the garage and into the bright, midday light.

Within seconds, I realize that the once smooth pedal stroke which I'd prided myself on feels choppy, and I stop repeatedly to measure and remeasure my saddle height – convinced that something is amiss with my bike. As I make my way down the circuitous series of sweeping switchbacks, I discover that somehow, I still know just when to brake and precisely how much speed to carry through the apex. Delivered to the valley below, I turn off the main road and, along with the late-afternoon joggers and dog walkers, meander through a tract of vaguely French-style houses with trim lawns and clean concrete driveways – each one nearly like the next – replete with pastiche and ready-made meaning.

Having only recently moved back to the town of Morgan Hill where I grew up, I discover that while the roads themselves have mostly remained the same, the landscape has changed. As far as I can see, tracts of houses have gradually come to replace the orchards and fields of the Southern Santa Clara Valley. In the distance I can hear the busy highway that, like the railroad before it, bisects the town. A light breeze swirls, buffeting my bike and as I make my way past one of the few remaining farms, the sweet, sulfur odor of apricots being dried in the sun hangs heavy in the air.

Past the barren, earthen face of a dam carved into a hillside, I turn back, heading south into a stiff headwind along a long straight section of road. In the distance, another cyclist gradually comes into view from the opposite direction – a lanky man in his forties with dark hair aboard a titanium Serotta – its front triangle painted the same shade of orange as Eddy Merckx's famous Molteni team bikes. Having seen him before, I offer a smile and wave before turning around and starting back towards the hill I've just descended.

As I start up the final steep climb which leads home, my legs burn, and my breathing grows deep and labored beneath my pounding heart. To my right, the road falls away steeply into an erosion-carved culvert and I remember that there'd once been a rusting Chevrolet hundreds of feet below, nested in the grass like a carcass – but now all I discern is the tall, late-summer grass and poison oak. Unable to keep the pedals turning over, I shift before standing up out of the saddle – one cog then another and another in quick succession as the pitch steepens, until the shifter will click no more. I glance back at the rear cluster – incredulous that I'm already in my smallest gear ratio. Just ahead of me, a crow lands in the road defiantly, only taking flight as my front wheel nears it. Without a heart rate monitor, I take my hand from the handlebar and feel my pulse: at least 175 beats a minute. It's apparent that there's a great deal of work to do in a relatively short amount of time if I'm ever going to manage three hard days on the bike.

Φ

As Alan Watts, the philosopher of Eastern religions, described in his lecture 'The Nature of Consciousness,' there are two fundamental types of people: the *prickly* and the *gooey*. Prickly people are essentially analytical, wanting to dissect the elements of a problem, while those who are gooey tend to see the world as an irreducible entirety which is inexorably linked to a greater whole. However, his categorization goes beyond a simple distinction between the analytic and artistic temperament. It's not merely that there are two basic ways of confronting the world, it's that each in fact demands the other, seemingly opposed outlook, for its own conception of the world to make sense. And while we all have our inclinations, we also embody these tensions and contradictions within ourselves, and if ever there was a sport which demands both prickles *and* goo, it's cycling.

To the casual observer the sport often appears to be all prickles – rail-thin gram-counting fanatics talking about drag coefficients and carbon fiber components – and admittedly this is an element of the sport. However, it is far from all of it, and the cyclists who have always struck me as most worthy of emulation were not those who were analytical and data-driven, but rather those who used the sport as a medium upon which to impose their own style and character – in Nietzsche's terms, those who used cycling to 'become what they already are.'

Throughout his life, Nietzsche returns again and again to the idea of style as a means of self-creation and it's important to understand that for him 'style' isn't superficial or mere ornamentation as we may think of it now, but something far more fundamental. As he wrote: '"Giving style" to one's character – a great and rare art! It is exercised by those who see all the strengths and weaknesses of their own natures and then comprehend them in an artistic plan until everything appears as art and reason and even weakness delights the eye.' And it was in this Nietzschean vein that I came to assess my own strengths and weaknesses – both mental and physical – and to admire riders who seemingly had done the same; riders like Frank Vandenbroucke, who continued on in a rain soaked World Championship road race after breaking both collarbones in a crash, Viatcheslav Ekimov who, against all odds of success would attack the raging field alone in the closing kilometers, or the World Champion and World Hour Record holder Graeme Obree, an outsider to the cycling establishment who not only constructed his own bicycle, but also developed an entirely new, aerodynamically superior riding position. Such riders were rare – and only grew rarer as sports science progressed and races grew more controlled – but the beauty of cycling seemed to be in using the sport as a means of self-expression, of appraising your particular strengths and weaknesses, imposing your will and personality, and then, through the rigors and challenges of competition, elevating your very existence into a work of art.

Counting grams and measuring your lactate threshold undoubtedly has a place in modern sport, but without the romantic gooeyness of chance, fate, and bravery, it seemed that you might as well just conduct races in the laboratory and compare power profiles in order to find the winner.

Φ

By the time I started in the mid-1990s, cycling in both Great Britain and the United States hadn't been truly thriving for decades. Like a once grand family in decline, stories of cycling's golden age abounded – tales of stands which had once been overflowing with spectators and Jazz Age cyclists being welcomed at the White House along with boxers and baseball players – of how Ernest Hemingway himself had attested to the beauty and grace of both the road and track racing which he'd witnessed during his years in France. From my earliest days of racing, I felt as if I was being brought into a withering tradition, the former glories of which were retained by the collective memory of nearly everyone involved in the sport. I heard stories of glamorous European riders – of Merckx and Gimondi, Simpson, and Hinault. Told on group rides and in cluttered bicycle shops like Shaw's Lightweight Cycles, with faded posters of riders on the walls, the tales of cycling's bygone era engendered a genuine reverence for the history of the sport. Maintained not just by the commonalities of equipment and events, but by way of a sympathetic understanding of the suffering and humanity involved in the achievements of the greats. And among the young and the bold, the hope of emulation and a belief – no matter how implausible – that, '*If they could do it, then so can I.*'

Φ

With each successive ride, the physical sensations on the bike began to slowly improve and, for the first time in years, I experienced the calm complacency which descends upon body and mind in the hours after a hard training ride. The bike began to feel familiar once again, and when I pedaled or reached for the brake lever, somehow everything was exactly where it was *supposed* to be. Not yet wanting to ride with anyone else, I traversed the same familiar roads I'd ridden when I'd been a racer – roads that by their very names reveal that they're lonely and remote – leading only to mountain cabins inhabited by people who don't want to be found.

On the cracked, pockmarked pavement of Rodeo Gulch, Redwood Retreat, and Old Mt. Madonna, I smelled the same distinctive scent of oak and scrub pine carried upon the morning fog. The great German philosopher Martin Heidegger often spoke of the best sort of philosophical thinking as wandering – as traversing paths and roads – and even the English verb to 'learn,' when traced back through the dense thicket of its Germanic origins to the Indo-European, means nothing less than 'to follow a path.' On a bike, the road was always *becoming* – always suggesting some once-and-for-all destination but never conclusive or final – and it seemed that if there was anything great and redeemable in the mythos of what it was to be American, it was the idea of being alone on the open road; of cowboys on horseback traversing desert paths, and Cadillacs being driven down desolate, sun-drenched highways. American to its core is the idea of the landscape somehow becoming inscribed upon the very marrow of your being as it flashes by. And, as I began to ride again, I realized that these old roads, in their tree-lined darkness – circuitous and leading nowhere – had remained with me wherever I went.

As pleasant as the hours spent riding were, it wasn't just the actual time on the bike which consumed my days, but also an ever-increasing list of tasks related to cycling which I'd somehow forgotten the full extent of: stretching, washing and maintaining the bike, and laundering my riding kit. More time-consuming than anything else, though, was my ravenous hunger as my body again became accustomed to expending, and then replenishing, thousands of calories a day. I'd thought that riding would break up my day and perhaps help my work as a writer, but instead it merely monopolized my energy. Ever tolerant, my wife Denika asked why I'd agreed to this ride, while my five-year-old son Graeme, not used to seeing me in my cycling clothes, asked if I was trying to be a bike racer again and I assured him that no, I most certainly wasn't. With a job and a family, training even this much felt indulgent although it was a mere shadow – not ever a quarter of what I'd once done on a weekly basis.

As I sat stretching after a ride, I recalled something Zach had told me some years after we'd both stopped racing and had lost nearly all of our hard-won fitness: 'Think about how strange it is that we spent years and years working at something and now it's pretty much all gone. We're no better on a bike now than someone who never did it.' It was impossible not to wonder who or what we might have been had we given ourselves to something more permanent – to some skill or ability less transitory than cycling. Ever so slowly, I was feeling like a cyclist again, but there was no doubt that I would never feel the same strength on a bike that I once had.

Φ

At first, my trips to the Olympic Training Center had been sporadic: a short regional team camp, or what at the time they'd termed a 'talent identification camp.' Slowly but surely however, the camps grew longer and more intense and I still vividly recall my mother picking me up from school and telling me that the national team coach had phoned earlier with the news that I'd been chosen to be part of the team.

Located high in the Rocky Mountains on a decommissioned Air Force base in Colorado Springs, the dormitory-style rooms of the Olympic Training Center had cinder block walls covered in numerous coats of thick white paint. We slept four to a room and each floor had its own central bathroom. All of our meals were provided, and in addition to mechanics and massage therapists, the velodrome was only blocks away. Wearing our national team jerseys, we would ride two-by-two as the team car followed our rides – each of us keenly aware that our every pedal stroke took place under the watchful eye of coaches who had the power to decide our future. But more than any other space at the Training Center, it's the roller room where we did our indoor training that I still recall most clearly.

Long before stationary trainers for indoor riding were hooked to the internet for virtual races, cyclists – in particular track cyclists – rode what are called rollers. Made of three drums, a frame to hold them in place, and a belt to turn the front drum, rollers require a rider to balance and apply power evenly throughout their pedal stroke so as to not fall off. It takes practice to even ride them, and while an amateur with a choppy pedal stroke will make a sound like a revving motor when riding them, a skilled rider with an even pedal stroke produces only a consistent monotone whirr. When the weather was too bad to train outside, we'd line up facing the wall and ride rollers for three or four hours at a time – just as we'd been told the Soviets and East Germans had – not only to become physically fit, but just as much to become mentally tough.

With nothing to do but pedal, I'd fixate on the cinder block wall that filled my field of vision, spurred on by thoughts of the great East German track riders – of Michael Hübner, Lutz Heßlich and Olaf Ludwig, and the Soviet pursuit rider Viatcheslav Ekimov. We'd all heard what Eastern Bloc sports programs were like, and however hard the American system was, they'd undoubtedly had it harder than we did, and succeeded not in spite of the harsh conditions, but because of them. However accurate or hyperbolic, we heard about how they'd had to live under velodromes; and about workouts where the front forks of their track bikes had been mounted to the bumper of a Lada or Trabant and how with the riders unable to coast or stop pedaling, the coaches had mercilessly enforced the speed and duration of their efforts with the very real prospect of tendons being ripped from the legs of those who failed to keep up. These stories of success which were the result of hardship were often weaponized against us – *how dare we complain about equipment or rest* – *by the standard which had produced so many champions, we had it good.*

We all internalized this – that having it too easy, having fallbacks, could be ruinous, and that we would be tempered by not just physical suffering, but just as much by monotony and boredom. Hour after hour, there was nothing but the sound of our tires on the aluminum drums of the rollers and our legs moving in concentric circles. Like meditating, I focused on what it was to pedal: innumerable muscles firing and tendons pulling, I learned as if for the first time exactly when in the stroke to start and stop applying power, and how to unweight my leg on the recovery stroke until finally, one day, something which had once been simple, at last became so again.

Our lifestyle was monastic and cloistered, revolving around eating, sleeping, and training. While some of the riders left their local high schools and attended Palmer High which was right next to the Training Center, I stayed enrolled in my hometown school, stuffing my completed work into a manila envelope and sending it home every week. Although we weren't officially permitted to leave the campus of the Training Center, we'd often hop the black wrought iron fence and walk to a convenience store across the street. It was nothing but a simple 7-Eleven, but somehow after weeks of training it always felt miraculous. There were real people there – people who knew and cared nothing about bicycle racing – and the simple fact of a world existing outside of cycling held an inexplicable mystery which only grew more pronounced the longer I spent at the Training Center. That people did things besides fixate on cycling came to feel strange and surreal, and as I watched teenagers buying beer or a woman purchasing a loaf of bread, I wasn't sure if I should envy their apparent freedom or pity what I imagined to be a lack of purpose which as far as I knew then, could only be filled by cycling. It's impossible for me to not think of the first lines of Tim Krabbé's beautiful book on cycling, *The Rider*. As he prepares for a race, the bicycle racer protagonist observes with a degree of detachment characteristic of Jean-Paul Sartre or Albert Camus, 'I take my gear out of the car and put my bike together. Tourists and locals are watching from sidewalk cafes. *Non-racers. The emptiness of those lives shocks me.*'

Having grown up in a house that wasn't at all religious, cycling provided not just praise, but the ready-made meaning and sense of purpose I deeply craved. And even though the life of an athlete was rigid – the polar opposite of the sort of freedom I held as my ideal – on the other side of some imagined success was a new sort of freedom, which in spite of being superficially similar, was as different as the acorn is from the oak.

Of course I wouldn't have put this in terms like this then, but similarly to how I would come to relate to philosophy some years later, the way towards what I wanted seemed to be through following that very thing's antithesis until it failed under the weight of its own logic and delivered me to my imagined ideal. The sort of freedom I craved wouldn't come from doing what I wanted or from simple hedonism, but from what superficially appears like *unfreedom*. Having intuitively absorbed our culture's lessons of hard work and delayed gratification, I felt that any sort of meaningful escape would have to be earned. My choices – which perhaps looked masochistic – were compelled by projecting myself into the future and imagining that I was embarking on something great – something that would free me from my small town with its boring jobs, and identical rows of houses, and that cycling's physical pain and psychological rigorousness would perhaps one day elevate me to a realm of the heroic.

Regardless of our backgrounds, each and every one of the young riders who had been selected by the cycling federation saw the sport as a way out of something – a dysfunctional family life, poverty, or simply a way to feel as if we belonged somewhere. Both culturally and geographically, the pool of riders was a cross section of America itself, hailing from the Louisiana Bayou, South Florida, Texas, Pennsylvania's Lehigh Valley, or nurtured on the languishing concrete velodromes which lie on the periphery of northern, rust-belt cities like Chicago, Kenosha, and Indianapolis. From our Stars and Stripes bikes and clothing, to the Training Center itself, we all sensed that we had been chosen and that, like our heroes, we too could achieve something lasting for ourselves through the sport.

While I rode and experienced life away from home for the first time, the true purpose was to identify who among us possessed the physical traits and psychological grit necessary to be world-class athletes. We underwent VO_2 max testing (which measured how efficiently our bodies carried oxygen to working muscles), body fat testing, as well as a test called a Wingate which involved sprinting for thirty seconds as hard as we could in order to determine our potential in shorter, more power-based track events.

Like SAT scores or IQ tests, the results of testing were shared and whispered about. Most of us had heard about the VO_2 tests of Lemond and Armstrong and how their exceptional results as young national team riders had foreshadowed their future successes and wondered if any among us might have the ability to follow in their path. But alongside this youthful hope was always the idea of 'squandered talent' – those now nameless riders who'd had one-in-a-million physical potential in the lab but who'd left the sport and faded into obscurity, never having been able to translate their physical ability into actually winning races. About those who washed out we heard rumors of working in coffee shops or food service – the implication being that *this* was our shot and that not just ruin, but far worse, *anonymity* awaited those who failed to work as hard as they possibly could to succeed.

It was surprising who the best in the laboratory were – and how little this seemed to correlate to real-world success. The riders who carved out real careers all seemed to possess something which escaped measurement. Being tactically astute and able to read a race certainly played a role, but beyond this, the best were also endowed with an inexplicable ability to push themselves just that bit further when they were already hurting. There were a thousand terms for it, but we all knew when we were going 'into the red' and surpassing what we were physically capable of. What varied was just what this yielded – and how often a particular person could do it without getting sick or becoming overtrained – and I quickly learned that while my physical ability was only average, several times a month I was able to push myself exceptionally hard and, on occasion, even ride at the same rarified level as the truly gifted genetic outliers.

While one of the national team coaches was a retired

rider from Trinidad, the other was an imposing former track sprinter from Poland with a baritone voice and a crater-like indentation in his skull which was the result of a horrific crash in which his partner had died while racing the tandem sprint event at the World Championships. The training they prescribed was far harder than anything I'd done before and I quickly came to learn just what I was capable of physically. Our days typically began with an early morning session on the rollers, followed by a long road ride, or weight training, and then another training session – either the velodrome or on ergometers – lasting into the early evening. The older juniors frequently rode with seasoned European pros in their twenties and thirties and I'd often return from long, cold rides to far-flung Colorado mining towns so tired and hungry that I'd collapse in the shower, struggling to even stand as the warm water ran over my body and unsure of how I would possibly complete the next day's scheduled training.

As I had in California, I came to learn this landscape by bike: its streams and grasses, its proud groves of spruces, firs, and pines, rising from the rocky earth, and its unremitting drags that led towards towering mountains shrouded by dark clouds beyond which trees no longer grew.

Owing to my sheer exhaustion, life took on a strange lassitude and things as simple as deciding when to eat my banana on a ride were not simply important, but seemed to fully consume my fatigue-diminished mental capacity. During these hard blocks of training, I read, thought, and worried less, and the memories that remain are suffused with a strange, hazy quality – as if suddenly I'd glimpsed a sea of untouched reality that was all around me. I remember the surreal feeling of sitting in the cafeteria in the dying days of December, gazing blankly past a tall, tinsel-covered Christmas tree as a gymnast whom I'd seen on television ate alone in the shadows on the other side of the expansive space. *Whose life was I inhabiting,* I wondered?

Like the film *Groundhog Day*, each day was eerily similar to the last. Without our own cars, few of us ever left the Training Center except to ride, and after returning, we showered, ate, and retreated to our rooms where, having been told that elevating our legs would drain the toxins and metabolic waste, we would lie on our beds with our legs resting high on the wall above us listening to the drone of MTV on the television in the background. The passage of time was demarcated by little more than the bike, meals, and sleep and I'd return home from training camps with a transcendent feeling of newfound possibility bordering on elation – but little idea of what to do with it other than to continue training.

In hindsight, the volume of training we undertook was undoubtedly far too much for athletes so young, but the philosophy was simple and followed the Eastern Bloc model in its attrition-based approach: after identifying talented juniors at the regional level, impose a training regimen which is so difficult that the majority of young riders wash out. Those who can handle the training load won't merely be talented, but also possess the physical constitution required to handle the workload of one hundred plus days of racing which is typical of professional cycling. In such a system, one thousand juniors, so it was thought, would almost certainly yield one world champion.

Having experienced this, when I now hear about retired

riders who had much longer and more successful careers than I did, I often imagine how difficult returning to the 'real world' must be for them – what it must be like to wake up from the insular trance that is professional cycling at thirty-five or forty years old, and not just have your identity stripped from you, but on a simple psychological level to have spent the better part of one's life in the stupor of fatigue that's so intrinsic to being an elite cyclist.

Φ

Not wanting to disrupt my training, my parents hadn't told me that my father had moved out of the family home while I'd been away. When I returned to California to start university, I found that his things were gone and his closet bare. Somehow none of this sank in – none of it seemed really real. In the face of this, cycling felt at once unimportant *and* like the lone constant in my life. Trading the cinder block walls of the Training Center for a dorm in Santa Cruz which overlooked the Pacific, I found solace on the bike. And, while I trained as seriously as ever, I also threw myself into studying philosophy with the same single-minded fervor I'd brought to cycling.

I already had enough insight to know I needed something more than being an athlete, and seeing normal people – typical college students – after the vacuum of life at the Training Center was eye-opening. Cycling had rewarded my obsessiveness – my ability to put aside everything and everyone which was not in the service of my singular goal. The house could be burning, and my only reaction would have been that this is something which is getting in the way of my training. But now, alone with my thoughts at night, I bristled at all the lives I wasn't living – everything that had been blotted out by the bike. As I recalled my late-night talks with my father under the stars about the nature of reality, philosophy remained a path that I knew I had to see to its conclusion; a way – perhaps the only one – which would lead me back to myself.

Chapter 2

The Promise of Thought

Man has achieved his present position by being the most aggressive and enterprising creature on earth. And now that he has created a comfortable civilization, he faces an unexpected problem ... The comfortable life lowers man's resistance, so that he sinks into an unheroic sloth ... The comfortable life causes spiritual decay ...

—Colin Wilson

For someone possessing the right combination of emotional and intellectual sensibilities, an initial encounter with Western philosophy can be nothing short of electrifying. Unlike other fields, philosophy isn't concerned with understanding or investigating this or that particular aspect of the world, but instead with knowledge of existence *in general*, and in my late teens and early twenties, philosophy's basic questions: things like *'How can we know we really exist?'* and *'Is there a world independent of the human mind?'* seemed both personally relevant and vitally important, speaking to my growing sense that just beneath my everyday socially constituted experience of reality was something simultaneously transcendent and terrifying.

The basic way in which I experienced the world seemed contingent – as if it all might have been otherwise – and I came to wonder by whom and through what means I'd been indoctrinated into a reality which was clearly anything but a given and experienced moments of insight in which workaday reality felt unmoored. In flashes and bursts – when I was gazing at the night sky, listening to music, or riding alone on a mountain road – and stretching deep into the recesses of my memory there's always been a persistent, nagging feeling of wonder at the mere fact of existence – that inexplicably *I was*. In the words of one of my early intellectual heroes, Colin Wilson, philosophy was a way to 'throw off the trivialities of everydayness.' Everything petty and crass seemed all the more contemptible and, as adolescence stretched towards adulthood, increasingly I'd pine after some contact with the eternal – for that which Hermann Hesse in his beautiful shorthand simply called 'Mozart and the Stars.'

It was a growing desire to bring words to my experience of the ultimate which attracted me to philosophy with a fervor which outstripped even my desire to succeed as a cyclist. These moments of insight somehow felt *truer* than anything I'd experienced – so profound that to my mind they demanded not simply to be lived but to be *justified rationally*. And, it was precisely this sense of wanting to articulate wonder in some coherent way which made philosophy so appealing.

The basic questions at the heart of philosophy were not only the polar opposite of the sort of tangible, data-driven questions I encountered everywhere else, but by their very nature they also pushed against the blinkered conformity I saw all around me which seemed to ignore (or even forcibly repress) ultimate, existential questions in favor of the superficial, technically minded busyness which characterizes so much of Silicon Valley culture.

Philosophy felt limitless in its potential to capture the entirety of existence under its conceptual net. With enough understanding, I imagined that existence would finally *make sense*, and this held not just an abstract intellectual appeal to me, but a deep emotional one. I projected myself into a calm, unshakable future built on immutable foundations. The secrets of the world understood, life's pain would once and for all dissolve in the clear light of understanding – intelligibility blunting the sting of uncertainty and the pain of loss.

As I looked around, it seemed that a great number of people went through life avoiding ecstasy and joy just as much as pain – expending tremendous amounts of energy to avert their gaze from deeper questions of meaning and purpose. With ideas of reality dictated by the prevailing pedagogical, social, and theological wisdom, success meant little more than a 'good job' which closed the cycle and defined those traits and tasks which are 'valuable' – namely those things that can be cashed out under the ever-calculating logic of capitalism. All of this to have the small consolation of hobbies which distract and the opportunity to beget and provide for children who learn more of the same. It was in the light of this assessment that, like many romantically minded teenagers before me, a vague notion began to form of how I might perhaps live differently or more authentically – how through a combination of rigorous thinking and the self-discipline of being an athlete, I might give 'style to my life' and in the process avoid the sort of spiritual death that seems to befall so many long before their biological one.

Among the philosophers I began to read, I found kindred spirits who reached out to me through the ages and shared a sort of terrible, ecstatic wonder at the basic situation of existence that I too found myself unable to look away from. But, just what is this '*basic situation*'?

If, as I had, you remove the answers provided by religious faith from the equation, you find that you enter the world from an incomprehensible realm of non-being – a void which no one understands in any meaningful way, only to be indoctrinated into a socially constructed idea of objective reality which takes place within the confines of an unfathomably vast and indifferent universe. Within this context it's necessary to believe that you possess a stable personality and set of beliefs which allow you to act and change a reality which exists 'out there,' independent of the human mind or sensory apparatus. Finally, you must go on in the face of the knowledge that you and everyone you love will one day die and once again disappear into an impenetrable oblivion.

With this basic appraisal, life's situation appears decidedly grim. And yet, in confronting these facts head-on, I found that there was the hazy outline of something inexpressible which was both terrifying *and* wonderful – something which was worth pursuing to its logical end; in the words of Oscar Wilde, 'We are all in the gutter but some of us are looking at the stars.' It seemed that dangerous ideas had the power to change the way I existed in the world and it was precisely because of my bleak assessment of the situation that I found the glimmer of the possibility that someday, I too might have the ability to face the bare facts of life and still say 'yes' to existence in all of its pain and ecstasy.

This idea of saying yes, of 'yeah-saying,' as Nietzsche terms it, is central to Nietzsche's thinking, and is related to what I'd later learn Martin Heidegger terms *Being-towards-death* – namely that existence is meaningful and significant not in spite of the fact that it is so impermanent – but precisely *because* of it.

Like living perpetually in the transcendent ecstasy of affirmation which comes with listening to the final strains of Beethoven's 'Ode to Joy' or reading the most spiritually potent lines of *The Waste Land*, I imagined an end point when thinking would turn on itself and become pure emotion.

This hope for resolution just at the point where rationality crumbles under the weight of its own internal contradictions is expressed poignantly by the cerebral Ivan in *The Brothers Karamazov*:

I believe like a child that suffering will be healed and made up for, that all the humiliating absurdity of human contradictions will vanish like a pitiful mirage, like the despicable fabrication of the impotent and infinitely small Euclidean mind of man, that in the world's finale, at the moment of eternal harmony, something so precious will come to pass that it will suffice for all hearts, for the comforting of all resentments, for the atonement of all the crimes of humanity, for all the blood that they've shed; that it will make it not only possible to forgive but to justify all that has happened.

I had many examples of those who'd pursued this course only to find themselves shipwrecked, but with the naivety and audacity of youth, I thought that somehow I would be immune from the perils and pitfalls that had befallen others – that perhaps I'd learn to turn my life into art and permanently inhabit the transcendent moments I'd experienced not only as a result of great film, literature, and music, but also just as often on the bike. Simply put, I wanted to live in a way that didn't make me feel dead but had no idea of just what that might look like.

I want to be unequivocal, however, that on a personal level, none of these predilections were easy. I thought long and hard about things in a way which isolated me from other people and did little to improve my performance on the bike. Even though I was attracted to it, I understood that philosophy was a siren song and in no way did I think that it was something that could improve or better me in any typical sense. In the words of the philosopher Slavoj Žižek, it seemed that the 'first duty of philosophy is making you understand what deep shit you are in!' and on the face of it, there's something comically neurotic about an athlete with existential anxiety. And, not surprisingly, when I tried to describe philosophy to teammates I was typically met with blank stares or questions about what I imagined all of this thinking would accomplish.

I have little doubt that much of the isolation I experienced was of my own making – I internalized the tensions and contradictions of being young and attempting to inhabit two worlds at once. Yet, compelled by my own demons and already trying to both outride and outthink the depression which would later catch up with me, I got to work, doggedly determined to pursue both thinking and the sport of cycling to their logical conclusions.

Φ

Aware that the success or failure of the ride hinged not just on fitness, but also logistics, as the ride approached, the three of us began to plan the details of our route. Hotels were booked, and each of us sent a box of spare tubes, fresh cycling kit, and ride food ahead to the places we'd be staying each of the three nights. Being a sports director for a World Tour team, Jackson approached the ride as he would Paris–Roubaix or the Giro d'Italia, methodically going over equipment selection, and laying out the total distance, elevation gain, and major climbs of each of our 'stages.'

Owing to its symbolic importance, it was decided that we'd begin the San Francisco leg from what is perhaps the most iconic landmark in Northern California, the Golden Gate Bridge. Not only had my maternal grandmother been born in San Francisco, she'd recounted how from the vantage point of her college dorm room across the Bay in Berkeley, she'd watched as the Golden Gate Bridge was built – piers, towers, and a roadbed gradually taking shape and spanning the dark stretch of water which separates San Francisco from Marin. Tied to my family and past, the bridge was far more than just a landmark to me.

It wasn't just San Francisco or the Golden Gate though; from beginning to end this stretch of coastal Highway 1 is dotted with personal reminders of life and death. Near the ride's terminal point, just north of Santa Barbara, was where my mother, father, sister and I had scattered the ashes of my grandmother into the Pacific. And, although it had scarcely been spoken of growing up, as I thought about the rugged coast, I also knew that somewhere along it was the nondescript cliff where my aunt and – some twenty-five years later – her daughter had both jumped to their deaths.

Although I couldn't bring myself to tell even my closest friends, there couldn't be a more personally significant stretch of road for me than this one. There's a Native American saying, *Your land is where you bury your dead,* and whatever it might mean to say you're 'from' a place, it was clear that I was forever bound to this stretch of California coast.

Φ

Like many other children of baby boom parents, my exposure to philosophy began with 'existentialism' – a term which at this point has been so abused that it demands further explanation.

Though its roots run far deeper, existentialism as a movement coalesced in the wake of the Second World War. Initially a decidedly Continental European phenomenon, existentialism wasn't exclusively a philosophical movement; also included were novelists, playwrights, artists, filmmakers, and psychologists – all of whom were united in their preoccupation with questions of meaning, alienation, absurdity, and the possibility of becoming a fully realized human being in an industrialized and increasingly secular society which had demonstrated itself capable of unspeakable moral horrors. Associated with figures as diverse as Samuel Beckett, Simone Weil, Ingmar Bergman, Hannah Arendt, Franz Fanon, and Hermann Hesse, those who were labeled as 'existentialists' shared not so much a fixed philosophical doctrine, as they did a certain emotional and moral temperament.

On a strictly philosophical level, Jean-Paul Sartre (one of the few thinkers to embrace the label 'existentialist') understood existentialism as an inversion of two and a half millennia of philosophical (and Christian) thought which, since Plato, had placed the conceptual realm of the essential over and above the ephemeral experiences of the sensory world.

In the view of the existentialists, this privileging of the abstract over lived experience had been nothing short of a travesty. Ideas existed to serve life, not the other way around – as Sartre famously states, '*l'existence précède l'essence*,' ('existence precedes essence'). However clear he was in his formulation, Sartre was intellectually indebted to both his contemporaries (familiar names including Albert Camus, Hannah Arendt, and Martin Heidegger) as well as the key nineteenth-century proto-existentialists, Friedrich Nietzsche and Søren Kierkegaard.

In the English-speaking world, two key popularizers of existentialism were the American academic William Barrett, whose *Irrational Man* was published in 1958, and Colin Wilson, whose 1956 book, *The Outsider* brought the then twenty-four-year-old, working-class Englishman an unprecedented degree of international literary acclaim. Excellent commentators who wrote about complex ideas in clear, lucid prose, both Barrett and Wilson brought what had hitherto been a primarily German and French movement to the attention of the general educated public on both sides of the Atlantic, and it was owing to my father (who had studied philosophy at Stanford University under a former student of Heidegger's named Kurt Reinhardt) that I first started to read the existentialists.

From how Sartre thought about the radical act of responsibility and self-creation, to Heidegger's raising anew the 'question of Being,' the existentialists shared a conception of the embodied and relational nature of human existence which placed the subject as an active shaper of reality. This made existentialism the ideal philosophical match for an athlete – and no individual thinker more so than Friedrich Nietzsche. However, before turning to Nietzsche, it's first necessary to give the briefest of overviews of the history of Western philosophy and sketch the intellectual landscape as he encountered it in the mid-nineteenth century.

Φ

The pre-Socratic Greek philosophers of the Ionian Peninsula, Greece, and Italy who lived about a half century before Christ were the first people to undertake the sort of critical reasoning and rigorous questioning of the world that we would recognize as 'philosophical.' They grappled with the basic nature of reality: Heraclitus with the divine law or *logos*, Zeno of Elea with motion and change, and Parmenides with the basic nature of change and the apparent fact that one can only have knowledge of what *is* and that nothing whatsoever can be stated or even thought about what *is not*.

Though their assumptions and conclusions varied widely, the pre-Socratics sought *first principles* – modes of understanding (and hence controlling) the uncertainties of the world they found themselves in without recourse to gods or the divine. And it is from this mode of thought that Western philosophy itself, as well as the three best-known ancient Greek philosophers of the classical age, emerge: Socrates, Plato, and Aristotle – their combined thinking laying the groundwork for much of modern science, rhetoric, theology, and politics.

Central to Plato's thinking – and key to understanding the whole of Western philosophy – is a concept which is so radical and fundamental to the trajectory of philosophy that a more robust explanation is called for: the theory of the forms. In Plato's account, the forms are the non-material, conceptual 'essence' of any object or even concept (such as goodness) which for Plato are far more 'real' than the transitory, imperfect copies which populate the empirical world of sense and perception. Any entity we encounter through the senses is merely a pale imitation of an immutable, perfect ideal and the role of philosophy is to bring the mind closer to the true and everlasting goodness of these forms. As Plato describes famously in the *Allegory of the Cave*, the role of philosophy is to help humanity escape from the chains which keep us facing a wall of mere shadows, and to turn and gaze upon the forms – the light and source of truth. All that is true, good, and beautiful resides beyond this world, unseen and unknown except by those who possess the rational powers to understand and access the unsullied treasures of the purely conceptual.

Tellingly, in *The Republic* – Plato's description of how a philosopher king might rule a just city state – Plato suggests that the epic poets would have no place. Even worse than the non-philosopher, the poets, engaged as they are with accounts of deeds and things in the world, are 'twice removed' from the ultimate truth of the forms, concerning themselves with the mere shadows of shadows and dangerously leading their fellow citizens even further from the clarity and goodness of philosophical truth.

I want to let the utter strangeness of Platonism sink in: *that which is most real is unseen and can only be understood conceptually*. In the history of thought there is no more revolutionary and counterintuitive a claim. From Platonism it is possible to trace a direct line to much of Christian philosophy whereby God's perfection is separate from (and yet far more real) than the visible world. While human endeavors in the material world are fraught with decay and corruption, heaven is perfect in its fixed, unchanging nature. Recall the famous verse from Matthew 6:19–20:

> Lay not up for yourselves treasures upon earth, where moth and rust doth corrupt, and where thieves break through and steal:

> But lay up for yourselves treasures in heaven, where neither moth nor rust doth corrupt, and where thieves do not break through nor steal.

Under different guises, this same division between the physical world of the senses and an invisible, metaphysical world of the purely conceptual manifests itself centuries later among Enlightenment thinkers (key among them being René Descartes and Immanuel Kant) who not only attempt to provide a sound basis for moral laws, but also seek to ensure the veracity of scientific discovery and safeguard the very possibility of knowledge. And, lest this all seem remote, impractical, and pedantic, think of the innumerable abstractions with which so many of us concern ourselves on a daily basis: everything from stocks to mortgage rates, to the law of thermodynamics, to the virtual world of the internet, all demonstrate just how salient the Platonic drive towards abstract ideals remains.

It's not hyperbolic to say that it was Plato who cleaved the world in two and it is in the context of the bifurcated, metaphysical world beginning to falter under its own weight some two and a half millennia later that the son of a Lutheran pastor from Saxony named Friedrich Nietzsche enters onto the stage.

Φ

Owing to his influence on the novelist Hermann Hesse (whose *Steppenwolf* I'd read and reread in high school), as well as Colin Wilson, I'd first heard about Nietzsche several years before reading him seriously. In Nietzsche, I found a thinker who was unlike anything I'd ever encountered – and one who further cemented my sense that philosophy was at least as important to me as cycling. Writing in aphoristic, literary prose, Nietzsche didn't attempt to construct an elaborate system like his predecessors Kant and G. W. F. Hegel, instead providing glimpses of insight like a bolt of lightning momentarily illuminating a dark expanse of landscape. In the history of Western philosophy, Nietzsche is undoubtedly an inflection point after whom nothing could ever be the same; for Nietzsche, privileging an unseen world – Platonic, Christian, or scientific – was a life-denying travesty and a sign of a culture in decline.

The son of Carl Ludwig and Franziska Nietzsche, Friedrich Wilhelm Nietzsche was born in Röcken, Saxony in 1844. While he held academic appointments early in his career, Nietzsche found the life of a professor deadening and by his mid-thirties set out to think and write, wandering the Alps and Southern Europe in search of health and solitude. A thinker who lauded the high mountains, and extolled the virtues of bravery, fresh air, and physical effort, there is simply no thinker better suited to the sport of cycling than Friedrich Nietzsche.

Trained in classical philology, when Nietzsche compared modern European culture to the world of ancient Greeks and Romans, he saw a Europe which had descended into decadence, arguing in *Beyond Good and Evil* that Christian morality itself was an inversion of all that had been strong and noble (that is, 'good') in other, more vital and life-affirming, historical epochs.

In his *Parable of the Madman* Nietzsche seeks to herald in the true spiritual consequences of the modern era. Upon entering a crowded market, the madman proclaims, 'God is dead,' but even more significant – if less quoted – is the consequential next clause which speaks to the drive for truth which has extinguished the possibility of the sort of faith which has sustained humanity for millennia, 'and it is you and I who have killed him.' For Nietzsche, questions of epistemology – that is humanity's ability to recognize and act upon the truth – are inexorably connected to matters of faith, morality, art, and metaphysics, and he saw the prevailing scientific drive for facts about the state of the 'real world' hopeless and misguided, writing in *Daybreak*, 'The habits of our senses have woven us into lies and deception of sensation: these again are the basis of all of our judgments and "knowledge" – there is absolutely no escape no backway or bypath into the *real world*!' Given the nineteenth-century climate of rationalism and positivism which sought to uncover lasting truths about the nature of the physical world (and had been doing so with unprecedented success), it's difficult to overstate just how revolutionary Nietzsche's perspectival stance towards the possibility of knowledge was. Just as there was no fleeing the decay of the world for a perfect and immutable God, there was also no domain of perfect facts which probing scientific inquiry would one day explicate once and for all. Claims about truth and the so-called 'laws of nature' are necessarily also claims about the human senses and there's simply no way of escaping our own subjectivity in order to fully grasp the world of *things-in-themselves*.

However, it's far from the case that Nietzsche is simply an atheistic materialist and, when attempting to understand him, it's critical to point out just how little Nietzsche shares with the current 'New Atheists' – Richard Dawkins, Sam Harris, and the late Christopher Hitchens. Unlike the New Atheists – and I would argue, modern culture as a whole – Nietzsche senses a great tragedy at the loss of the divine, and while a new sort of self-creating individual is his ideal, he also warns against allowing technical and scientific materialism to fill the spiritual vacuum left by the death of God, writing in *Beyond Good and Evil*:

It is perhaps just dawning on five or six minds that physics too is only an interpretation and arrangement of the world [. . .] and *not* an explanation of the world: but insofar as it is founded on belief in the senses it passes for more than that and must continue to do so for a long time to come. . . . 'Where man has nothing more to see or grasp he has nothing more to do' – that is certainly a different imperative from the Platonic, but for an uncouth industrious race of machinists and bridge-builders of the future, which has nothing but *coarse* work to get through, it may well be the right one.

Reading this section, with its description of an 'industrious race of machinists and bridge-builders,' it's impossible not to recognize the pervasive drive for technical and material progress which is the hallmark of our own cultural moment. In the wake of God's death, we're now left in a lifeless world populated by things and incidents of which all we can say, with an indifferent or ironic shrug, is that 'they happened.'

Throughout his writing, Nietzsche uses the metaphor of humanity having been 'unmoored' or 'set adrift' upon the open ocean. In the face of this absolute abandonment, individuals must *themselves* become like God, creating their own – always preliminary – values without recourse to any ultimate ideal. But, rather than simply disenchanting the world with the death of God and the overturning of Christian values, Nietzsche wishes to reimbue the here and now with meaning, but is astute enough to realize the demand – the sheer psychic stress – that this monumental task places on the individual.

The process of self-creation Nietzsche envisions is intimately linked to his other well-known idea, that of 'will-to-power' (*Wille zur Macht*). For Nietzsche, joy itself is power (*Macht*), but this sort of power is nothing like the dumb, brute force of the tyrant. Rather the sort of power which interests Nietzsche comes from overcoming one's self without recourse to ultimate values; it requires no leap of imagination to think of a well-trained cyclist at the peak of his or her physical powers, moving confidently through the peloton – responding instinctually to the ebb and flow of the race – as an example that would have pleased Nietzsche himself had he lived to see it. Through the self-imposed rigors of becoming proficient at any arduous or physically difficult skill, Nietzsche thought that one was on the path towards the ever-retreating horizon of becoming who they were supposed to be.

For Nietzsche, *style* – an artistic approach to not just one's work but one's life as a whole – is critical to the reclaiming of life. An aesthetic approach which makes no claim to ultimate truth is the path towards the always preliminary sort of redemption that Nietzsche thought would sustain his higher individual, his famed *Übermensch*. Best translated not as 'superman' but rather as 'over-man,' the *Übermensch* has freed themself from the gnawing self-loathing that is intrinsic to Christian morality and a belief in an unseen, ideal world. Independent and self-sufficient, the *Übermensch* is motivated not by guilt or fear, but by a self-surmounting will-to-power. As he writes in the foreword to one of his final works, *Ecce Homo*, which is worth quoting at length:

He who knows how to breathe the air knows that it is an air of heights, a *robust* air. One has to be made for it otherwise there is no small danger that one will catch cold. The ice is near, the solitude is terrible – but how peacefully all things lie in the light! how freely one breathes! how much one feels beneath one! – Philosophy, as I have hitherto understood and lived it, is a voluntary living in ice and high mountains – a seeking after everything strong and questionable in existence, all that has hitherto been excommunicated by morality. [. . .] – How much truth can a spirit *bear*, how much truth can a spirit dare? That became for me more and more the real measure of value. Error (– belief in the ideal –) is not blindness, error is *cowardice* . . .

> Every acquisition, every step forward in knowledge, is
> the *result* of courage, of severity towards oneself, of
> cleanliness with respect to oneself . . .

To fully grasp just how different Nietzsche's account is from that of the Platonic, Christian or, Enlightenment rationalist, it's useful to recall Plato's call to banish the poets in *The Republic*. In sharp distinction to Plato, Nietzsche believed that it was art – poetics, music, and aesthetic phenomena – which made life bearable. However, in a way which prefigures much of modern art and is diametrically opposed to Plato's understanding of the poets, Nietzsche is only critical of art which continues to 'pull on the metaphysical heart strings' – Gothic cathedrals, Dante, the paintings of Raphael, and the music of Bach – and he says that it is in these moments of religious and metaphysical rapture when a thinker's 'intellectual probity is put to the test.' Nietzsche thus lauded precisely the kind of poetry and art which Plato regarded as the mere shadows of a shadow; art which depicts the here and now of lived life, subjectivity, and the transitory nature of existence.

Nietzsche's account is not an easy one to stomach. Not only does he offer no solid foundations to live by, he does away with their very possibility. Like life itself, values and ideals are ever-changing and can never be anything other than subjective and contingent. To cling to abstractions or to posit an immutable realm populated by the conceptually perfect is to deny the beauty of lived life as we find it. To face up to this world without recourse to another metaphysical realm brings not just the pain of loss, but also the poignant beauty of a true encounter with all that is evanescent. Nietzsche self-consciously saw himself as a 'philosopher of the future' – as intellectual 'dynamite' after whom nothing could ever be the same, and his influence on existentialism and modern thought have borne out the veracity of his grandiose self-assessment. On the one hand Nietzsche's prescience seems nothing short of astonishing, but on the other, it seems he failed to anticipate the full extent to which the spiritual crisis he anticipated could be glossed over by our collective drive for physical comfort and mental numbness.

For those who still have ears to hear it, Nietzsche's bold challenge is to muster the bravery required and live up to this task and to say 'yes' to existence not with stiff upper lip stoicism, but with playful joy – and what is any sport but essentially play?

Φ

As the ride down the coast approached, I continued to train entirely by feel and intuition – without a power meter or even a heart rate monitor. If I had time and felt recovered enough, I rode. If not, I didn't. After all these years, I discovered that I was still able to read the thousand nuanced sensations that told me if it was more work or more rest that my body needed and I realized just how much I'd overcomplicated it all when I'd been racing. Then, rather than adapting to how I felt, I imagined that my training program itself was sacrosanct, and that if I didn't complete precisely what was prescribed for a given day I was failing and I'd inevitably feel guilty and worry that other riders were working harder.

The idea that success depends simply on doing the most work is naïve, but nonetheless remains pervasive. On the wall of the room where we rode our rollers at the Training Center was a poster in plain black font which read, 'Right now there's someone training harder than you,' and this ethos fueled a sort of paranoid arms race of training and exhaustion – a nagging belief that no matter what you were doing it wasn't enough. And, as the weeks of hard training in the thin, high-altitude air of Colorado stretched on, I remember being so exhausted that I began to have trouble sleeping – a telltale sign of overtraining. As my roommates slept, I'd turn towards the cinder block wall next to my bed and listen to my German language tape – *Ich bin, Du bist, Er, Sie, Es ist* – in my semiconscious stupor, trying to absorb not just the only other language my father – who'd lived in Berlin – spoke, but what was also the language of so much philosophy – the language of Kant and Hegel; of Nietzsche and Heidegger. Day and night – on the bike and off – exhaustion and German began to bleed together in the haze of my fatigue, disconnected phrases coming to me while on the ergometer and drafting behind the team car, and I wondered who I'd be and how I'd think if English had not been my mother tongue – how reality itself would perhaps be altogether different.

Knowing that each day on the bike with Jackson and Zach would likely be more than five hours, with each passing week I steadily extended the duration of my rides. Three hours grew to four, four to five. Climbs that only weeks before had forced me out of the saddle and into my largest 28-tooth cog now disappeared beneath me with relative ease, my fitness seeming to change the very topography of the world. Riding felt nothing short of physically addictive and I'd return home wanting to ride more for the sheer physical pleasure. My body felt lighter and stronger and it seemed that just maybe, I was even thinking better and more clearly – as if a layer of filth had been wiped from my perceptual windshield and for the first time in years, I was seeing the world as it truly was. I imagined what awaited me – what awaited *us* – riding next to the ocean, free from all of life's obligations and distractions, and I found that I was starting to look forward to what had initially felt like a chore.

Φ

As I worked to not merely understand, but even perhaps live the ideas I found in Nietzsche and the other existentialists, I distinctly remember trying to reconcile them with cycling and wondering if perhaps I was asking too much of my sport – too much of any sport. If you subscribe to Nietzsche's narrative of how one should live – what should you do on a practical level to live up to his challenge? Clearly neither productivity nor financial success would be enough, and in a very tentative way, I already sensed that more philosophy would just be so many more words on top of words. Maybe once I'd gotten the proverbial message I ought to hang up the phone, and what Nietzsche had to impart had come through to me loud and clear.

The question became how to live this insight in some meaningful way – how to resist the call of comfort and normalcy which everywhere seemed to deny the recognition of life's utter strangeness which I had adopted as the defining (and perhaps only) feature of who I was.

My first year of university, I trained like I never had before. I'd finished in the top five at the Olympic trials on the velodrome but hadn't made the team, so armed with a training program from my personal coach Harvey Nitz, I sought to turn my finishing speed on the track into success as a road sprinter. Every day, after morning classes, I'd eat and set out for five- and six-hour rides, deep into the Santa Cruz Mountains. At the Training Center I'd grown used to being watched from the velodrome infield or the team car which drove behind us on the road and now, finally alone and unobserved, I found that I relished the long days on the bike, the foggy air in my lungs and against the exposed flesh of my face. Unlike the roads of Colorado and the Santa Clara Valley – open to the sky and cutting across the landscape – the Santa Cruz mountain roads were narrow and intimate, many little more than hastily paved logging tracks following the topography of least resistance. Shrouded by lofty, old-growth redwoods and bounded only by the occasional moss-covered cabin, the world was drawn near and revealed itself only gradually, with each successive bend in the road. Populated by reclusive owls peering through the dark wood and salamanders with bright orange bellies that inched along the soft forest floor, I was porous to the subtleties of smells and the currents of the gentle breezes that moved through the trees and, in the most profound sense, alone without being lonely, I drifted ever deeper into solitude.

On these dark mountain roads, spurred-on by dreams of future success and listening to PJ Harvey, Radiohead, or The Smashing Pumpkins, it often seemed as if cycling perhaps *would* be enough, and that maybe all of my hopes and feelings could be channeled through the bike. At other times though, when I was tired or changing a flat with shivering hands by the side of the road in far-flung towns – in Ben

Lomond, Freedom, or Boulder Creek – I was sure that cycling was too pedestrian, too crass, to ever possibly help me live up to not just Nietzsche's ideals, but even my own. I sought out examples of people who validated my physical path with even greater certainty than Nietzsche had. I found just the assurance I needed in the figure of the Russian dancer, Vaslav Nijinsky.

I first read about Nijinsky in Colin Wilson's book on existentialism, *The Outsider*. In keeping with Nietzsche, Wilson frames existentialism not just as an abstract crisis of meaning, but as a lived problem to be overcome. In order to understand the true contours of the problem, Wilson presents case studies in *The Outsider*, dividing past outsiders (who Wilson defines as those who 'sees too much and too deep') into four different types: the intellectual, the spiritual, the emotional, and most interesting to me, the *physical outsider* – the exemplar of whom was Nijinsky.

The most famous male ballet dancer of the early twentieth century, Nijinsky performed to acclaim throughout Europe, his fame reaching its peak in the years just before the First World War. In 1917, while living in Switzerland, Nijinsky began to keep a journal. Rather than dance or personal matters however, it's the horror of the war and the works of Nietzsche, Tolstoy, and Dostoevsky which haunt Nijinsky. Throughout the painful pages of his diary (which he kept until a mental breakdown at just twenty-nine years old) there are flashes of insight unlike few other documents, and it's possible to trace a path in which the physical takes precedence over the intellectual – where questions of meaning are transfigured into the pure emotion of the body. 'I am a man of motion,' Nijinsky writes. And later, even more pointedly, '*I am feeling through flesh and not through the intellect.*' With this radical rupture, Nijinsky hadn't merely moved beyond the detached, philosophical intellectualism he so detested, but even the rational language of a figure like Nietzsche.

It seemed that cycling could likewise serve this purpose – could be this immediate, bodily, and aesthetic – and the photos of top European professionals I saw in the pages of magazines like *Cycling Weekly* and *Cycle Sport* possessed a strange allure – if only I could decipher it, somehow holding the secret to becoming a great rider. Forever ingrained in my memory is a photo of the Belgian star, Frank Vandenbroucke during his years on the French Cofidis team. Helmet-less, with his bleached blond hair slicked back, he's lightly grasping his Campagnolo brake hoods in his gloved hands – seemingly floating above his machine as he applies power out of the saddle. From the angle of his ankle to the position of his saddle, I had a visceral understanding born from the thousands of hours I'd spent on a bike myself of just how great Vandenbroucke was.

Just as I understood (or perhaps more accurately *felt*) in the case of Nijinsky, there existed not just intellectual genius, but also a sort of kinesthetic genius. This didn't consist simply of a rider's strength or endurance, but his or her style on the bike – an ability to turn the physical and embodied into art – and for me Vandenbroucke was the epitome of this ideal, using the sport as his stage to win with otherworldly grace which made it look as if the bicycle was an extension of his own body. Climbing high mountains in the thin air and not merely enduring, but relishing the pain and physical danger of bike racing,

Vandenbroucke seemed nothing less than Nietzsche's will-to-power personified.

Himself a capable athlete who studied philosophy, the American novelist David Foster Wallace also makes this connection between athletic beauty and embodiment, in his essay 'Both Flesh and Not':

> Beauty is not the goal of competitive sports, but high-level sports are a prime venue for the expression of human beauty. The human beauty we're talking about here is beauty of a particular type; it might be called kinetic beauty. Its power and appeal are universal. It has nothing to do with sex or cultural norms. What it seems to have to do with, really, is human beings' reconciliation with the fact of having a body.

With the insight afforded by sports, it seemed possible to think *through* thinking. As tempting to me as it was, philosophical thought held the world at a distance, and I didn't want to live my life as a disengaged spectator. When I gave myself over to riding, the words and concepts which had plagued me would fade into the background and, like Nijinsky giving himself over to ballet, or Vandenbroucke flawlessly pedaling his machine, the thoughts would recede and there would only be me and the bike. Cycling could indeed be enough – perhaps not forever – but at least for now.

Chapter 3

The Materials

*The bikes – I think of them as creatures, not crea-
tions – they feel like my sons; like my biological
children.*

—Ernesto Colnago

In spite of its numerous moving parts, there are only three points where a cyclist is in direct physical contact with a bicycle when it's being ridden: the handlebars, saddle, and pedals, and it's through these points of contact alone that the rider subconsciously processes, and acts on, the constant flow of information being communicated by his or her machine. Just as the skilled musician becomes aware of aspects of their instrument which would be impercep- tible to anyone else, the cyclist comes to understand on a preconscious, neuromuscular level, the sensations particular to their bike as they navigate a technical descent or thread their way through a field of riders.

Every component influences the type and quality of feedback the rider receives: a stiff frame with narrow tires chattering through a rough corner and forcing you from your line while a more compliant frame, paired with wider, more supple tires will allow you to track uninterrupted through the very same corner at higher speed. The ideal is to be aware of what is taking place at every instant such that you can understand and respond without ever bringing the inputs to the field of your conscious attention.

While some riders (even very good ones) are indifferent to anything other than the most basic elements of fit, others – myself included – are obsessive when it comes to the fit of their bike and selection of equipment and tasks, like the wrapping of handlebars or gluing of tubular tires, take on the hallowed character of religious ritual. While obsessing over this sort of minutia might sound petty, the aim isn't to fetishize the bike as a mere object, but instead to make it as transparent as possible; any creak, loose bolt, or missed shift – anything which announces the bike's presence – detracts from this. And, perhaps counterintuitively, this means that you must pay a great deal of attention to your equipment precisely because of the desire for it to disappear beneath you.

I'm far from unique in my meticulousness; Eddy Merckx was known to be fanatical about his equipment, testing frame after frame with only infinitesimal changes to their geometry, and often stopping multiple times while riding – or even racing – to adjust his saddle or cleats by mere millimeters. So too, Frank Vandenbroucke, who was said to have demanded no fewer than seventeen different versions of his road frameset prior to the 1999 season in order to perfect its geometry. More recent is the case of Rohan Dennis – the World Time Trial champion who left his team (and a reported million-dollar contract) over the quality of his sponsor-supplied time trial bike. Equally obsessive and innovative when it came to his equipment, my longtime coach and Olympic medalist Harvey Nitz always told me in a tone which implied the sort of first-hand wisdom which was the result of some long-ago mechanical failure, 'Equipment won't win a race, but it sure as hell can lose one.' There's also a strange flip side to this painstaking attention to detail, however, in as much as the rider who takes to the start line with a fast, well-tuned machine also forgoes a whole slew of excuses and rationalizations – if you lose on good equipment it's clear to you and everyone else that you have only yourself to blame.

It's striking that without ever seeing its rider, you can discern from how a bicycle is set up not just how tall or short the owner is, but even their skill; from the angle of the brake hoods, to the tilt of the saddle, and placement of the bars – in an instant, it's possible to see a bike and immediately know if it's the machine of a skilled cyclist or a neophyte. Cycling is undoubtedly an equipment-heavy sport, and at any point in time I typically had at least four different bikes that I competed on: a road bike, a mass-start track bike (sometimes just called a points bike), a pursuit bike which was optimized for timed events on the track, as well as a road time trial bike – each with two or perhaps even three wheel sets. Often, when a young rider would complain about having to deal with his or her equipment, a more seasoned rider would quip, 'If you don't like dealing with bikes then you should have just been a runner.' Caring about – and for – the physical bicycle is intrinsic to the sport.

Stretching back to Fausto Coppi aboard his *celeste*-green Bianchis in the 1940s, many stars of the sport become inexorably linked to their bicycle suppliers – at first small artisan shops, and later larger, international brands; in the 1960s and '70s (before founding his own brand) Eddy Merckx raced on bikes made in the shop of Ugo De Rosa and Ernesto Colnago; the American Greg Lemond was tied to a small builder from Reno, Nevada – Roland Della Santa; and more recently the Italian brand Pinarello has become known for supplying a slew of Tour de France winners including Miguel Indurain, Jan Ullrich, Chris Froome, Sir Bradley Wiggins, and Geraint Thomas, while the prodigious Dutch champion Marianne Vos has spent nearly all of her career aboard bikes made by Taiwan's Giant Bicycles.

From cycling's inception in the late nineteenth century through the 1990s, frames which were intended for racing were typically the product of a single skilled builder who'd honed his or her craft over the course of a lifetime. Racers would seek out a builder based on skill and reputation and work closely with them to design a bike specifically to suit not only their morphology and flexibility, but also their style. A powerful rider requires a stiffer frame constructed from more robust tubing than a wispy high-cadence climber who'd want a very different machine – lightweight and with more relaxed geometry suited to climbing rather than the high speeds of sprinting. With tiny shops, builders like this had the ability to select each tube and tailor the geometry of every frame.

Since the 1990s however, the frame builder as artisan has given way to teams of engineers, industrial designers, and aerodynamicists who model the forces which go into a bike with strain gauges, sophisticated software, and wind tunnels. The cost and design of modern carbon fiber frames have made it next to impossible to tailor the geometry and ride characteristics to a particular rider, and even top-of-the-line bicycles have become a mass-produced commodity which is updated on an annual basis with sales figures in mind. Here, it's worth pointing out that while this desire for the newest and best might be described as a symptom of our culture's 'materialism,' such an approach, as Oscar Wilde famously wrote, 'knows the price of everything and the value of nothing.' Viewing the objects we use as disposable commodities is in no way materialist, in as much as true materialism would involve a genuine love of things. Say what you will for its merits, true materialism involves caring for material objects – not an eager rush to replace them – and I was perhaps the last generation to have spent any part of my career racing aboard artisan-crafted frames. And, while today's mass-produced carbon frames are undoubtedly stunning in their objective performance, I still vividly recall the hand-made bikes I received during my first season on a small American professional team called Shaklee.

Although the frame was badged as a 'Marin,' it had actually been made outside of Milan by Billato Bicycles – a small family-owned company who had been hand-building racing frames since the early 1950s. The geometry of this bike was nothing unusual – my 58-centimeter top tube and seat tube lengths were paired with a slightly steeper than typical head and seat angles owing to my track background. The bike was long, low, and undeniably well-proportioned with a straight-bladed fork with chromed dropouts which made it look somewhat like a Colnago. The Italian theme continued with our Campagnolo components and Cinelli handlebars and stems, and, only months after signing with the team, I appeared in a magazine advertisement for Marin Bicycles with the tagline '*Andiamo Shaklee*,' which had been shot on a cold January day on a ribbon of a road overlooking the Golden Gate Bridge. Although the ergonomics of the Campagnolo shifters weren't ideal for the quick downshifts of a sprint, with cranks and hubs polished to a reflective sheen more reminiscent of jewelry than bicycle parts, there was still an undeniable romance to the storied Italian brand which had supplied so many of the sport's champions.

Compared to other bikes I'd raced, this one had something which was ineffable. Not only did it fit me perfectly, but it was stiff when I sprinted while still somehow smoothing even the roughest chipseal roads. Both tool and art object, I remember coming back home from the training camp where I'd received the bike and putting it at the footboard of my bed so that it was the last thing I saw as I fell asleep and the first thing when I opened my eyes in the morning.

Before I was capable of discrimination, there had been a series of less than ideal bikes as a junior: a Cannondale track bike which had been so stiff as to feel what riders call 'dead,'; an early Specialized Epic which, with its carbon tubes epoxied into aluminum lugs, had been so flexible that when I was sprinting hard, the bike would deform enough that the crank arm would hit the chain stay as it passed; and, as an older junior I'd briefly had a custom stainless-steel bike which had had a bottom bracket so high that its center of gravity made it feel frighteningly unstable through fast corners. One had to become obsessive to figure out what worked and what didn't, and unlike today, there were still bikes on the market which were, by any definition, simply bad.

While it would be easy to survey today's professional peloton and assume that the only possible material for a top-flight racing bike is carbon fiber, from the late 1980s through the early 2000s frame materials were in a state of flux with riders competing on frames made from no fewer than four materials: steel, aluminum, titanium, as well as early carbon fiber frames. With each of these materials, engineers and frame builders were attempting to create a bike that struck the ideal balance between light weight and stiffness – just stiff enough for the rider's energy to not be wasted, but not so stiff that the rider becomes fatigued owing to every imperfection of the road surface being transmitted up through the bars and saddle. In order to achieve this, a well-built frame has a certain resonance to it. Rather than being immovable – something that you merely push against – as you apply force to the pedals, ideally a frame should deflect ever so slightly, storing energy like a loaded spring and releasing it in time with the sway of the bike as you sprint. Striking this balance is subjective and difficult to quantify, which is why certain frames by certain makers still remain sought after, years after going out of production: titanium Litespeed Ultimates, steel Merckx MX-Leaders, aluminum Cyfacs and Merckx Team SCs, and the carbon Colnago C-40s which carried the legendary Mapei and Rabobank teams to numerous professional victories throughout the late 1990s and early 2000s. Much like the rider who on paper should be nothing of note – endowed with only a good VO_2 max and passable power-to-weight ratio – there are bikes which somehow transcend their weight or lab-measured stiffness;

bikes that seem to float over cracked pavement and surge forward when you accelerate.

The ride quality – essentially the resonance of the bike – is highly variable, and akin to describing the tone of a stringed instrument, the taste of wine, or the driving qualities of a sports car. Influenced not just by material or geometry, there are innumerable other factors – from the wall thicknesses of the tubes, to how they were joined – which also dictate the feel of a particular frame, and this is what makes the relationship between bike and rider as uniquely intimate as it is and which distinguishes the bicycle from other objects in the world.

Φ

Most cyclists – even those who are poor climbers – have a climb near their home or training base which has been ridden so many times that they know every corner and pitch – every crack and hole in the pavement. When you're going well – able to glance down and look on as your legs turn over a small cog effortlessly, you relish the climb, while in a patch of poor form, you inevitably find yourself out of the saddle, muscling the bike with brute force and inelegantly struggling over the same stretch of road.

However, climbs like these don't simply demarcate fitness, but also the cyclical passage of time. No matter how your life might change, that particular climb – *your climb* – remains a touchstone. As people are born and others die, you ride past the same features of the landscape – bearing witness to its changes just as much as yours: in early spring, leaves emerge from well-known trees only to wither in the gutter in the fall. While, during the last throes of winter, the brown hillsides gradually return to green – silently announcing that life has renewed itself and the worst of the cold and darkness has passed.

From dense oak groves to grassy, flower-filled meadows, to mountains which rise heavenward, the landscape of one's youth isn't incidental, but births the metaphors by which we come to make sense of our own, internal topography – in a word, the landscape of certain stretches of road become *sacred*.

About three miles from my childhood home is a desolate single-lane road which dead-ends at the entrance to a sprawling state park called Henry Coe. Over a series of switchbacks that resists even the best rider's attempts to settle into a rhythm, the road climbs nearly three thousand feet in just over eleven miles and with less than a week to go until Jackson, Zach, and I set off for our ride, I decide that the time has arrived to test myself on my old climb.

Even though it's already late October, the warm summer has persisted deep enough into autumn that I need neither leg warmers nor a jacket. After what I've done earlier in the day, this final climb will push my total ride to over five hours, so as I near the base of the ascent, I quickly eat an energy bar – the last food I have. In the first mile or so, the road meanders by dirt pull-outs which overlook Anderson Reservoir, making its way past ancient oaks and through groves of manzanita – a few rises but nothing more – until you cross the rusty bridge which spans a narrow finger of the lake. It's here – on the other side of the lake – that the climb begins in earnest.

It now feels like the events of another lifetime, but when I was sixteen or seventeen, my father had once followed me up the climb in his car on a dark summer night. Fresh from a training camp, I was fitter than I'd ever been. As he followed me, his headlights cut through the darkness, illuminating the swathe of road directly in front of me as mosquitoes and gnats danced in the shafts of light. My father had been a cross-country runner – once finishing second at the state championships – and wanting to show him not just that I'd been training hard but that I was like him – that I too could suffer – I climbed rapidly in the cool night air, cresting the summit minutes faster than I ever had before. At the top he'd handed me my jacket for the descent, before telling me just what I'd wanted to hear more than anything else, that he was proud of me.

Now as I reach the first steep switchback of the climb, even all these years later, it's him that I find myself thinking about. He's only met my son once, and I'm not sure how long it's been since I last spoke to my father. I miss him, but I don't have any answers as to what to do differently – how to make everything that's happened any less painful. As the road steepens, I'm forced to stand to maintain my cadence and as my legs flood with lactic acid, I realize that I've gone too hard.

As the road flattens, I remain in the saddle, spinning a gear and resting my hands lightly on the handlebar tops. I've never been able to climb well, but found through trial and error that the best way to at least mitigate my inevitable losses was to remain seated and climb at a consistent pace with a high cadence reminiscent of the track. As a dust-covered station wagon passes in the opposite direction, I downshift, increase my cadence, and turn up the volume of the music on my headphones. The canopy of oaks which had been shading the road ceases, and for the first time I'm able to feel the full intensity of the sun on my arms and the tops of my legs. My line of sight now unobstructed, I glance to my right. The lake has already grown small below me, and over the ridge I can see the sprawl of the Santa Clara Valley. In my jersey pocket, I have an ancient iPod but no smart phone. At least for the duration of this ride, there will be no distractions – no phone calls, texts or notifications.

If my years of studying philosophy had instilled anything, they'd helped to immunize me against the belief that the contemporary is somehow of greater value than all that's come before. In many ways, I've come to feel like a stranger to my own culture and don't want any part of the collective fever dream of distraction – of memes and viral videos and YouTube stars. I'm no *Übermensch*, but I've at least followed Nietzsche's lead and managed to continue to flee from the herd. The older I've become though, the more I've grown ambivalent about what this has ultimately achieved. Perhaps I'm better for it, but just as likely I'm only more alone.

After crossing the rusty cattle guard which spans the width of the road, I have to stand and stomp hard on the pedals to maintain my momentum over the final steep pitch, and by the time I arrive at the ranger station, salty perspiration has begun to run into my eyes. I pull up next to a bench, lean my bike against it, and sit down. As far as I can see is undeveloped land. In the wide expanse of windswept silence, resolute oaks and bay trees dot the steep slopes blanketed in golden brown grass. A sharp ridge rises in the distance and sitting atop it is a moss-covered oak starkly backlit by the bright sky. I want to take a photo and send it to Denika, but without a camera phone, I can't. I tell myself that I need to just really be here – to notice it myself. Starting to get cold, I survey the vista one last time, get back on my bike and begin to ride home.

The descent back down is fast and technical and here there's no option but to be fully present. Totally absorbed in what I'm doing, the past and the future retreat as mere abstraction. Diving from one corner to the next, I pilot the bike down the narrow road. On the long straight descent, I assume an aerodynamic tuck – reaching 80 kilometers an hour, maybe more. Tucking like this – my hands on the bar tops and sitting crouched low on the top tube – is three or four kilometers an hour faster than holding the bar drops, but it also means that the bike is far harder to control. I scan the road for any stray branch – any pothole – which could spell catastrophe. As the sharp right-hand hairpin at the end of the straight approaches, I wait a split second longer than my intuition tells me, before sitting up, moving my hands to the handlebar drops and firmly squeezing the smooth carbon surface of the brake levers. Having scrubbed just enough speed, I lean the bike, sweep across the entirety of the road, stand out of the saddle, and sprint out of the corner.

At home, when Denika asked with a smile how the ride went, 'Pretty well,' was all I'd told her. Perhaps the real horror of life wasn't being misled about the nature of reality or even not finding meaning, it was being trapped in your own mind. The true horror was being alone.

Φ

Popularized by the feminist thinker Gloria Steinem, the adage 'A woman needs a man like a fish needs a bicycle,' says something critical not just about gender relations, but also about how by their very nature, bicycles are fundamentally different from nearly any other object. As a simple thought experiment, imagine showing an intelligent alien species who was totally ignorant of any of our physical features, *a bicycle*. At first it would be simply absurd to this creature, but you can also imagine the very form of the bicycle – bilaterally symmetrical with handlebars and two pedals – allowing this intelligent life form that's never seen a human being to deduce some rough idea of our morphology. As an object, the bicycle only makes any sense in relation to the peculiarities of the human body. Tools, buildings, books – there's perhaps no other object as reflective of the form and kinetics of the human body as the bicycle, and this can tell us something critical about how we relate to the world and conceive of ourselves as thinking subjects in a world of objects. But, before turning to the ways in which the bicycle (and tools more generally) unseat the idea we have of ourselves as mere 'thinking subjects' attempting to control an uncertain and chaotic world, it's worth stepping back and examining just how this modern conception of the self came to be.

Φ

Stretching back to the French philosopher René Descartes with his famous *Cogito, ergo sum* ('I think, therefore I am') in the seventeenth century, Western philosophy provides a very particular understanding of the human being as a thinking subject who encounters the world with a cool, rational detachment. While this view of what it is to be a human being has been undermined by thinkers ranging from Nietzsche, to Sigmund Freud, to Martin Heidegger, to the 2013 Nobel Prize-winning economist Robert Schiller, this Cartesian idea of a rational self is at the heart of much of how we understand what it is to be human and remains bound up with how we conceive of progress, utility, and even free will.

Born in 1596 near Tours, France, Descartes had a Jesuit education and wrote widely across a broad array of burgeoning fields, including philosophy, the natural sciences, and mathematics. Often called the 'father of modern philosophy,' Descartes sought to place the empirical observations of natural science on equal footing with the certainties he found in mathematics.

With fallible senses and error-prone judgments, Descartes wonders how it's possible to obtain accurate knowledge about the state of the world. Dreams, hallucinations, and optical illusions all undermine our ability to trust the information of our senses and seem far from sufficiently trustworthy to ground the empirical observations of scientific investigation. Sunsets might appear one color from one vantage point and another from somewhere else, dreams might seem real enough that it's possible to confuse them with waking reality, and from a distance it's easy to confuse one object for another. While radically skeptical, Descartes' aim isn't the simple dismantling of his previously held beliefs. Instead, he hopes to wipe away the haze of unexamined belief and inherited convention in order to rebuild anew and secure a solid conceptual basis for what it's possible to know with absolute certainty.

With the immutable certainty of mathematics as his standard, Descartes begins his investigation from a position of radical doubt about our ability to know anything whatsoever. In direct, lucid prose which epitomizes the best of the probing, philosophical mind, Descartes writes:

> I kept uprooting from my mind any errors that might previously have slipped into it. In doing this I was not copying the sceptics, who doubt only for the sake of doubting and pretend to be always undecided; on the contrary, my whole aim was to reach certainty – to cast aside the loose earth and sand so as to come upon rock or clay.

While still very much within the horizon of the sort of metaphysical thinking which Nietzsche will seek to free himself from some three hundred years later, Descartes' willingness to question everything represents a conceptual break from the centuries of scholasticism which had attempted to reconcile Greek philosophical thinking and Christian dogma and heralds in what we now think of as modern philosophy. Seeking some bedrock of certainty, in his *Meditations*, Descartes entertains the possibility of his own madness, that the world is merely a dream, and even that rather than a perfect, omnipotent, God, there instead exists an 'evil deceiver' who has maliciously misled him as to the nature of reality. However, it's from this seemingly hopeless impasse for knowledge that Descartes begins to formulate his way out, often simply referred to as the *cogito:* 'I think, therefore I am.'

Even in the absolute worst case – that of a malicious evil deceiver – the self-reflective awareness of the thinking subject is the Archimedean lever by which Descartes is able to draw himself out of his radical doubt. No matter how error-prone your perceptions and judgments might be, there remains a thinker who is the *subject* of the deception. 'So after considering everything very thoroughly,' Descartes writes, 'I must finally conclude that this proposition, *I am, I exist*, is necessarily true whenever it is put forward by me or conceived in my mind.'

Armed with certainty about his own existence as a thinking, rational entity, Descartes is able to build a bridge back to the world and redeem not just himself, but humanity, from an initial position of radical doubt. The world of the senses – of taste, smell, and touch – may indeed deceive, but the *rational*, abstracted mathematical properties about things in the world can be understood 'clearly and distinctly' through reason alone, and provide the requisite certainty that's necessary to ground and grow scientific understanding. For the rationalist Descartes, the 'reality' of thought – including mathematics and our ability to make quantitative claims about things in the world – is far more 'real' than our error-prone sense perceptions.

In this privileging of the rational and abstracted, Descartes establishes the basic terms of both modern metaphysics *and* the modern individual. We are thinking subjects in a dubious relationship with not only the external world, but even our own bodies. Cut off from direct contact with the sensory world, and unknowable to ourselves except as thinking things, at every turn the modern, Cartesian subject is constantly haunted by solipsism – that is, by the lingering possibility that all of the world is merely in his or her head (which in many ways it objectively *is*).

While this line of reasoning has the easy-to-parody elements of an introductory philosophy class (*man, is this table even really real?*), facing the problem of how to obtain trustworthy knowledge was vital for the trajectory of the Enlightenment and the development of modern science. It is not a stretch to claim that this Cartesian idea of the self remains the unexamined basis for how many modern people conceive of what it is to be a human, and it has remained potent not just because of what it professes to solve philosophically, but also because of the scientific and material successes which have been a direct result of understanding the world in rational terms. Metaphysical through and through, the Cartesian subject places the entirety of the external world at arm's length – in so doing, gaining the calculating control of the conceptual and abstract which has yielded the modern, technological world as we know it. From the Cartesian armchair of reflective doubt, the world passes by like so many phantoms which one can never fully trust or grasp the full reality of. Even Descartes himself admitted in his *Meditations* the enigmatic character of the 'I,' the self who for all of its thinking, can never rationally grasp *itself*. That which is nearest and most proximate remains forever remote. The emotional consequences of this idea of self are far reaching; not only are mere appearances not to be trusted, the very person doing the thinking will as a matter of logical necessity remain blind to him or herself.

It would be easy to think that this understanding of our-selves has faded with the passing of the centuries, but, owing to the influence of modern technology, the idea that we are all essentially rational, detached thinkers and evaluators of the material world is in many ways stronger than ever. Confronting the world technically – as a series of problems to be overcome – is a Faustian bargain which has demanded that we set ourselves apart from the world of appearances. And, although it has been the basis for unprecedented technological innovation and insight, it would likewise be naïve to believe that it hasn't come at some cost.

In all of its alienation, doubt, and detachment from the world and its own body, the Cartesian self not only sets the stage for the existentialist revolt, but also begins to explain the way in which the bicycle is unlike so many other things in the world and how it can dislodge us from the endless stream of technical distraction which has come to characterize modern life.

Φ

The day before our departure, I wake up early, fill my bottles, pump my tires, and head out for one final training ride. By this time tomorrow, Jackson, Zach, and I will be setting out from the Golden Gate Bridge. As I ride south into a steady headwind, I feel strong and fresh. The muscles in my legs are loose and my heart rate rises easily in response to my effort. A storm is coming, and I can feel the humid air rhythmically move in and out of my lungs. Over the course of the ride, low dark clouds blow south into the valley and just as I start to make my way back home, it begins to lightly drizzle. I'd always liked riding in the rain – I'd raced well in the cold and wet – and today it's just warm enough that I can smell the distinctive odor of water evaporating from wet pavement; I recall the beautiful German phrase which still haunts me whenever it rains, '*Es regnete ununterbrochen*,' *It rains uninterruptedly* – the famous agentless *it*, both everywhere and nowhere invoking something basic and primordially beautiful.

Even though it's only a light rain, it's steady and consistent, blanketing the landscape, and I ride tentatively. The first rain of the year is always the most dangerous, bringing to the surface the long summer of spilled oil and gasoline which had been dormant in the porous tarmac. As it drifts away from the crown of the road, a prismatic pool of red, blue, green, and yellow suddenly appears beneath your tires, and in an instant you're sliding across the pavement, hips and elbows and knees bloodied. From experience, I knew to ride cautiously, and ever so slowly I make my way around the final steep corners as I head home.

I'm about to hang the bike up when I notice just how dirty it is; there's no avoiding it – it simply has to be washed before the ride. So, still in my wet clothes, I fill a bucket with dish soap, wheel it back to the driveway, and like so many times before, begin to wash the bike. Although it's made of carbon fiber and mass produced, I've always liked this bike – I understand and trust it. Rather than appearing carved or chiseled, the shapes of the tubes are fluid and organic. The top tube gently flows into the seat stays, and rather than a hard, angular transition, the head tube smoothly gives way to the down tube with a gentle radius. Dripping with soap suds and streaked with degreaser, I rinse the bike off with the hose and watch as the gleaming silver of clean chainrings and cogs reveals itself.

I replace the wheels, tighten the quick-release skewers, and carefully dry the bike. When I'm riding, I don't conceive of it in a detached theoretical sense, but in a practical, relational one. For a cyclist, a bicycle is always more than what it can be reduced to abstractly – more than its carbon fiber and aluminum components – more than its weight or geometry.

Entering into a relationship with the bike, I don't just regard it with the disinterested detachment of an observer, I *use* it. And in return it takes me out of my head – re-enchanting life and putting me squarely back into the world of lived experience.

Φ

Implicit in conceptualizing the self as a Cartesian, thinking subject is the belief that all of the things we encounter in the world are essentially similar. Regardless of what something is or how it's used, for Descartes any object is real and useful only in as much as it possesses intangible rational properties. The sun and the moon, houses, hammers, and vehicles are all thought of as things which we might make errors about when it comes to their color, size, or other qualities, but which we're able to conceptualize accurately as a result of our abstract knowledge of them.

In sharp distinction to Descartes' conception of how human beings relate to objects, Martin Heidegger is adamant that although this way of thinking is undoubtedly useful, it's not how we actually inhabit and experience the world. Certain objects – primary tools and equipment – are what Heidegger terms, 'ready-to-hand' (in German, *Zuhandenheit*). Things which are *ready-to-hand* aren't best understood through the analysis of their rational, intangible properties, but rather through the attitude of care and concern that we bring to these things as we use them – the way a cyclist relates to his or her bike, a musician to her instrument, or a woodworker to his tools.

My relationship with my silver Marin road bike so long ago had nothing to do with any of its abstract, essential qualities; instead it was one of care and embodiment – an exemplar of Heidegger's *ready-to-hand*, and the way I related to it was predicated on the way that particular bicycle communicated information to me as I rode it, and as Martin Heidegger writes in 1927's *Being and Time*:

> The kind of Being which equipment possesses – in which it manifests itself in its own right – we call '*readiness to hand*.' [. . .] No matter how sharply we just *look* at the 'outward appearance' of Things in whatever form this takes, we cannot discover anything *ready-to-hand*. If we look at Things just 'theoretically', we can get along without understanding readiness-to-hand. But when we deal with them by using and manipulating them, this activity is not a blind one; it has its own kind of sight. [. . .] Dealings with equipment subordinate themselves to the manifold assignments of the 'in-order-to'.

Through their use, the *ready-to-hand* object draws the Cartesian subject out of his or her abstract, theoretical comportment and reinserts him or her into a world which is thoroughly suffused with human purposes and concerns, in the process undermining the limited, Cartesian idea of self which is divorced from the sensory world.

For Heidegger, we're not mere subjects confronting a world of objects locked in what he terms the 'cabinet of consciousness.' We're part of the world – transfixed and fully absorbed by it. In its immediate, visceral utility – unmediated by either abstraction or interface – the *ready-to-hand* bicycle undercuts the strictly theoretical view of the world and ourselves. Unlike the experience of driving a car or being a passenger in a plane or a train, the cyclist is exposed to the elements – to rain and cold, to heat, scent, and the play of light across the landscape. A rider's speed is dictated only by their skill and physical effort; the cyclist is brought into direct contact with not just distance, but even the landscape's topography – the exertion of every hill and the respite of every descent written into lungs and muscles.

A telling and idiosyncratic example of how bicycle racers intuitively recoil from anything which diminishes their immediate sensory contact with the world, is the type of tire which is largely still preferred by professional riders: the tubular or sew-up. Unlike a clincher tire which is easy to change and mounts on the rim with a hooked bead, a tubular tire is mounted directly to the rim with glue. Like a clincher tire, a tubular has an inner tube, but its inner tube is literally 'sewn-up' into its casing. Mounting a tubular is an arduous process involving the stretching of the tire and the application and curing of multiple coats of specialty glue. Worse, with the difficulty of replacing the encased inner tube, if you puncture a costly tubular tire it is likely not worth repairing. On top of these practical difficulties, lab testing in recent years has shown that the storied tubular tire is often not even the tire type with the least rolling resistance. So, with all of this in mind, why do the vast majority of pros still race on tubulars?

The answer has a great deal to do with a rider's desire for the most direct source of information as to what the bicycle is doing at any given point in time. While there are three points where a rider's body touches the bike, at any time the contact patch of a road bike tire is only around two square centimeters – making the sensations from the tires critically important for the rider's understanding of what is happening with the bicycle. While the profile of a clincher tire is similar to a tucked 'U' – with the ends of the 'U' hooking onto the rim – a tubular retains its round profile owing to it being glued directly to the surface of the rim. This means that when a rider has leaned the bike over in a corner, rather than a shape which slopes away (as with the U-shaped cross section of a clincher) there is a constant, round profile that the rider knows will remain consistent even as the bike is leaned over; the tubular tire simply does a far better job of 'communicating' what it is doing to the rider than the clincher tire.

On some level, the governing body of cycling – the UCI – understands that it's the relationship between rider and bicycle which makes the sport what it is, and although it never uses the term, from the byzantine rules governing the design of bicycle frames, to the long-held resistance to disc brakes on road bikes, there has been a considerable effort to limit technology and keep bicycles recognizable as bicycles – that is, as 'unmediated.' While the UCI has often been bumbling and ham-fisted, the overarching aim has been to ensure that cycling remains visceral and athletic – a contest between human beings and not just technology.

Φ

As our world has become abstracted, it has also grown increasingly *intangible*, making our belief in, and contact with, sensory reality ever more distant. In what is perhaps the ultimate expression of Descartes' rationalism, large percentages of the population – particularly in California's Silicon Valley – deal not with the creation or care of things or people, but with so-called 'knowledge work' and a great many spend days swimming in a sea of unreality. From finance, to technology, and engineering, this type of work almost exclusively concerns itself not with this or that particular thing, but instead with some abstract element or detached concept – all under the pretense of 'innovation.'

Suffused deep with class connotations, the idea of being an 'innovator' has come to be valued far more than becoming highly skilled at a trade or craft or working to care for another person. Under this paradigm of value, the only worthwhile task for the brightest of my generation has been to uncover hidden truths: facts about the world (or more often, facts of commerce) which had hitherto remained unexploited. Under the logic of Silicon Valley innovation, understanding and engaging fully with the existent, known quantities of this world is of little significance and likely the hallmark of a less than first-rate mind. Here we see plainly that the metaphysical draw of the abstract and rational (though greatly reduced in its ambition and scope) remains as strong as ever. Information is the only currency, and work which was once tangible – its outcome and utility evident – has grown ever more remote and for the most part, alienating.

Even what were once reality-bound, tactile tasks like driving, using a tool, or speaking to another person now often rely on an interface which mediates your contact with the experience. Rather than engaging in face-to-face conversation, you see a screen with the image of your interlocutor; walking down the street in any major city, you see throngs of people less than fully present as they stare down at their phones, each occupying their own sliver of virtual space. Even in the case of the software I'm using to write this, I find that it often attempts to introduce bullets or tabs – formatting the words on the page automatically in a misguided attempt to anticipate my intentions, drawing me out of the preconscious process of my fingers striking the keyboard. Where once skill was valued and the user trusted, with the intention of maximizing safety and convenience for the greatest number, an additional layer has been inserted which isolates you from confronting the sloppy uncertainty of reality directly.

There is a real danger that this version of reality will become the way a sizable portion of the population understand what it is to be alive. If your only litmus test is ease and comfort, one might perhaps not see a problem with the state of affairs I've just described. However, if you take the lead of the existentialists, it becomes impossible not to see the alienation – the less than fully realized lives – as the obvious price we pay, and the question as to the ultimate endgame of this technical progress quickly appears: *Ease, comfort, and material convenience in order to do or feel what?* As Colin Wilson states the problem in *Religion and the Rebel*:

> The more one has to fight against, the more alive one can be. That was why, for me, the problem of living resolved itself into the question of choosing obstacles to stimulate my will. Instantly, I came to recognize that our civilization is flowing in the opposite direction; all our culture and science is directed towards enabling us to exercise as little will as possible.

With cycling as my standard, I found this diminished idea of what it was to be alive – a life informed by what Wilson calls 'meaningless repetition' and 'human futilities' – was frightening beyond measure. Like living in a dream from which you never wake up, these sort of anesthetizing comforts don't just distance you from the world, but impinge on your ability to see other people as anything more than objects who need to behave in a fashion which doesn't result in your being inconvenienced in your rush to flee from yourself. Reality no longer holding sway, everything becomes a mere simulacrum – a parody of a parody – until, dreamlike, everything seems possible because nothing is. Truth matters little, and the terms of what is real are dictated by those who serve to benefit from whatever definition the distracted masses will flock to. Within this horizon of understanding, I have little sympathy for people who simply desire progress for its own sake. Rather than progress or material comfort I've always craved meaning – even as I've grown aware that on a long enough timeline, those who crave such meaning almost invariably turn out to be dangerous.

Here I want to be clear that I don't see cycling as any sort of self-help tool – as something that will free people or solve philosophical, spiritual, or psychological problems in any definitive way. What cycling can do, if only for a moment, is to disabuse you of the idea that you're a Cartesian mind trapped in a decaying body with limited knowledge of not just the world, but even of other people. As ephemeral as it may be, cycling has served to draw me out of my head and bridge the gulf between me and the world. In the freezing cold and sweltering heat – in the tactile feel of the handlebars in my hands, and the pain of exertion – I'm no longer a thinking subject in a world of objects, instead I merely *am* and all the abstractions of intellect simply fall away as so much noise.

Chapter 4

On Bodies and Pain

*The body is not a thing, it is a situation: it is our
grasp on the world and our sketch of our project.*
                                    —Simone de Beauvoir

Even more than other sports, cycling has always fetishized
pain. Not just the suffering of physical exertion, but
also the pain of crashing and enduring scorching summer
heat and freezing rain. Etched into the collective memories
of the *tifosi* – the rabid fans of cycling – are not just
glorious wins, but also the more personal victories over
the elements or the misfortune of a crash: Tyler Hamilton
winning a stage of the Tour de France with a broken col-
larbone; Andy Hampsten's famous Giro d'Italia win on the
snowy Gavia pass; even the seemingly superhuman Eddy
Merckx collapsing after setting the world hour record and
swearing he'd never attempt it again owing to the sheer
physical pain of such an effort in the thin air of Mexico
City. From the stark images of dust-covered riders in the
showers of the Roubaix velodrome, to gaunt climbers with
sunken cheeks cresting freezing Alpine summits, and even
the British rider Tom Simpson's death from exhaustion on

the slopes of the famed Mont Ventoux, cycling aestheticizes suffering, transfiguring hollow faces and bloody bodies into something beautiful and ripe with meaning, making it possible to imagine that your struggles too are in the service of some greater, mythologizing purpose.

As a young rider, it was this sort of heroism I desperately wanted to emulate, and I projected myself into the world of cycling I saw on grainy VHS tapes. All of the English-language tapes came from one source: World Cycling Productions, and the commentators, Phil Liggett and Paul Sherwen presented a world filled with heroic attacks, brave descending, and chivalrous sacrifice for a team leader in difficulty. Riders didn't simply climb, 'they danced on the pedals,' as they ascended moonscape mountain roads far above the tree line; in this world, riders didn't merely hurt, they 'dug into their suitcase of courage.' And so, with this as my touchstone, hard training rides in the rain, or remounting after a crash just to hopelessly chase the field for hours, were suffused with this same sense of bravery and heroism. In bike racing I'd finally found a domain in which pain *meant* something.

With the grand stage of cycling as my standard, most people's idea of fun struck me as little more than a distraction, and as a teenager, the hardships of cycling came to be the most pleasurable thing I knew. I'd often go to the velodrome, warm up, and do three or four one-kilometer efforts so hard that I'd have to recover for an hour or more before mustering the will to undertake the next effort. Concerned as it was with pain, tribulation, and overcoming, my version of the sport had little to do with the hobbyist ideas of riding for self-betterment or physical fitness. Suffering of this magnitude seemed destructive and, in all likelihood, *bad* for one's health. I repeatedly forced my body beyond its limits, and at least once a year could count on falling heavily in a race. Day in and day out, I hurt so badly that I simply assumed it had to be taking, not adding, years to my life.

A near daily companion, I studied the pain of the bike, slowly coming to learn its infinite gradations and subtle variations; the creeping gnaw of fatigue over the span of five or six hours of hard riding as opposed to the acute staccato agony of a short, frenetic one-kilometer time trial on the velodrome which seared my lungs and flooded my bloodstream with lactic acid. There's a telling term used by riders to describe going over your physical limit: *turning yourself inside out*. As strange as it may sound, this turn of phrase captures something fundamental about suffering on the bike; you're not simply exerting yourself as you would digging a hole, chopping wood, or slogging through a physical chore. When you're suffering on the bike, you're bringing to bear the full depths of all you are and have ever felt.

Making little differentiation between physical and emotional pain, I thought surely that those who felt more and deeper should be able to hurt more. It seemed that there was but one currency of suffering, and that I should be able to translate all of my emotional pain into the physical realm. Like the artists and writers of existentialism, I imagined externalizing my feelings through the bike – somehow validating all I felt but had no words for. The suffering of racing and hard training not only brought me into the present, but also deadened the emotional pain which I could never seem to make sense of, and at its most fundamental, the sport seemed little more than a contest of who could endure the most.

It seemed that the pain was only in my head – that I should be able to *will* myself to overcome whatever protective mechanism exists so as to prevent a human being from harming him or herself through exertion. I wondered just what combination of my mind and body was stopping me – why it was that no matter how hard I tried, I was inexplicably prevented from exerting myself past a certain point. Giving up seemed like a *choice* – a matter of volition and will – and it became possible to pinpoint the very moment a rider relented. Shoulders slump, cadence slows, and almost inevitably the cyclist's gaze grows vacant before turning downward towards the chainrings of the bike; what seems to be a *conscious decision* is written across the face and manifested in a posture of defeat. Even as I recall it now, the image of a rider relenting still elicits a contempt for weakness that feels out of character – a visceral mixture of shame and disgust – directed not merely at the weakness of others, but in equal measure at myself, for all the times when I too found that no matter how hard I tried or how much I wanted it, I could simply ride no harder.

It's not difficult to comprehend how this understanding of suffering as a function of one's will quickly takes on a moral dimension: *I didn't just win, I won because I was able to hurt more than you.* Like the Christian mortification of the flesh through self-flagellation or the wearing of a horsehair shirt, being able to endure pain on the bike brings with it a sense of not just physical but *moral* superiority and it becomes easy to look upon those who don't know the hardships of the bike with a degree of disdain. You hear phrases like, '*he just wanted it more*,' which cast winning and losing in terms of character – a reflection of grit and tenacity – rather than more prosaic things like physiology, preparation, or genetic endowment, which no reasonable person would judge in a moral light. This character-based outlook to suffering and achievement, which values ostensible choice over genetic circumstance, also goes some way in explaining why far more top-flight professional athletes have a streak of political conservatism than one might imagine.

In cycling, as in all walks of the life, it seems that the successful tend to overvalue the role played by their will while minimizing the fortuitous structural factors which have underpinned so much of their success.

Φ

When I wake, it's still dark outside. In bed next to me, Denika is asleep, her body forming a gentle crescent under the duvet. I listen for our son Graeme, but from the direction of his room, there is only silence. I make my way up the dark staircase and see that Jackson and Zach have already been texting me last-minute details about spare inner tubes and which one of us is bringing the frame pump.

As I make coffee, I settle into the comfort of what had once been a well-worn routine on the mornings of races and big training days and wonder how many hundreds of other mornings there have been like this one. Afraid of bonking – of running out of glycogen, your fuel source when exercising – I force down eggs, bacon, hash browns, and a protein shake. In the other room, I can hear Denika and Graeme awake and beginning to get ready. I'm not really hungry and, rather than pleasant, food is a necessity – insurance against what I know will be a long, exhausting day.

Today is the first leg and perhaps the hardest. We'll set out from the Golden Gate and ride a little under a hundred miles, from San Francisco to Soquel – a sleepy beach town just south of Santa Cruz. The route is rolling, with some steep pitches within San Francisco proper and numerous thirty- and forty-second drags once we're out of the city and onto Highway 1.

The night before, I'd packed my bike into the car and laid out my cycling kit. Wanting to ride unencumbered, all of us have already sent fresh clothes and food ahead to where we'll be staying each night. I check the weather and I debate the necessity of a jacket before deciding to just wear a base layer. It'll be warm enough that the jacket will undoubtedly have to be shed by midday, and I decide that I'd rather use the limited space in my jersey pockets for food.

Not just me, but Denika too, had been part of countless early mornings like this with worries about food, the packing of bikes, and the pumping of tires. For years before we were married, she'd traveled with me to local races, sitting on velodrome infields and by the side of desolate wind-swept roads waiting for hours to hand me a musette bag full of food or a fresh water bottle. Looking back, it feels shamefully selfish. It had all been about me – about my goals and what I wanted to achieve. I hope that at least in some small way I'm now a better person than the one who'd once been so narcissistic – who'd once thought almost exclusively about winning bike races.

Denika walks into the kitchen, looks at me and smiles unexpectedly. Surveying the pile of gels and bars I've collected on the counter she asks if I want another bottle of electrolyte mix. 'No, it's okay,' I reply. She glances up at the clock and asks if everything is in the car. I tell her it is. She brushes her brown hair back behind her ear, shuts off the lights, and we gather Graeme and pile into the car as a family. As I buckle Graeme's seatbelt, I move my head close to his, look him in the eyes and smile.

'What, Dada?' he asks.

'Nothing buddy,' is all I can reply before kissing him on the forehead. Time has always felt both inexplicable and sad: I'd gotten married and seen Graeme born, but somehow at these moments, when other people proclaim that they're the happiest they've ever been, I felt like a mere spectator, unable or unwilling to fully register what was happening for fear that if I did, I'd crumble under the poignant gravity of the event.

More than cycling – and certainly more than thinking – having a child ties you once and for all to this world. Through his existence my fate is externalized. Spirit is made flesh, and the questions and anxieties that had once felt pressing suddenly recede into the darkness of irrelevance.

'Come on – let's go,' Graeme says.

And, so we do.

Φ

It always seemed that there were essentially two options when it came to what I knew was going to be a painful effort; the first was to flee from it: to simply tell myself that it wasn't happening and to put my mind elsewhere. The other approach was to face it head-on: to study the sensations and try to understand exactly what it was about them that I so wanted to flee from. Of these two, I learned that going into the pain was by far the better option. Fleeing – imagining that I was on a sunny beach or tucked into the clean white sheets of a warm bed – only made the pain more acute. So, rather than attempting to avoid the inevitable pain, I'd resolve myself to confront it directly.

When I was a child, I remember that as some sort of a philosophical thought experiment, my father had asked me, 'Where do you live in your body?' and the matter of how to deal with pain brings this unanswerable question to the fore. Who or whatever I really was seemed separate from the sensations, and during time trials or VO_2 max testing in the lab, I learned to look on like a curious spectator at the growing gnaw of exertion. 'I' was a master located in my head, telling my body what to do and how – relentlessly spurring it on through the sheer force of my will. Almost fundamentally incommunicable in all of its varied forms, there's a poverty of language when trying to describe the experience of pain. From within the bounds of my sub-jectivity – my Cartesian self, locked in a bag of skin – it's impossible to ever know how like or unlike my pain is from yours. From one moment to the next, the pain seemed different in its texture and intensity, and I would settle into the effort and examine exactly what these sensations were as they arose. What it was and how badly it hurt varied – depending not only on how long the effort was, but also from day to day – an endless litany of unknowable factors influencing how my body performed. I thought of anaerobic thresholds, blood lactic levels and how working muscles are using fuel and spinning off metabolic waste. Riders usually talk about being *blocked* – about dead legs that won't *open up* – and thinking of it like this, fuel going in to produce energy and waste out through my body's delicate biological plumbing, helped me to frame the sensations and endure the inevitable discomfort for as long as it lasted. After exceptionally hard, intense efforts on the track, I'd writhe in the grassy infield and gasp for air, often throwing up as all of the blood in my body was drawn from my gut to the muscles in my legs. The periphery of my vision would grow black and, unable to even remain balanced on my bike, I'd have to be intercepted by a coach or handler who would help me from my bike and keep me from falling over.

Strangely though, while this binary of flight on the one hand, and examination on the other, almost always applied when I was alone, there were other instances when none of what I've just described was applicable. When I was racing and fully absorbed in the tactics of other riders, or navigating my way through the peloton, the physical pain which had seemed almost unbearable often retreated to the background. Engaged with the task at hand, the discomfort of the effort fled to the margins of consciousness in something like the 'peak experience' described by humanistic psychology when your skill level aligns perfectly with the demands of the task. Here I wasn't a dictatorial sovereign willing on my body from my head, instead I was both *in* and *of* my body – fully present in where I was and what I was doing.

Regardless of whether you're confronting or fleeing from pain, there's always the assumption that there is some essential *you* in your brain who is able to look upon the events of the body with either disinterest *or* engagement. But, fully absorbed in racing, I wasn't escaping to either some place more pleasant or trying in any conscious way to face the discomfort – as a matter of necessity I simply had to apply my full attention to what I was doing and, when I did, it seemed as if the long shadow of pain which I'd tried to negotiate some way around or through had been cast by a figure so diminutive I never should have feared it in the first place.

Φ

While philosophers since the ancient Greeks have been acutely aware of spiritual and emotional suffering, for the most part they've devoted very little attention to physical suffering.

This changed in the nineteenth century however, first with Arthur Schopenhauer, and a generation later – much influenced by Schopenhauer's thinking – with Nietzsche who, as we've seen, explicitly links physical and intellectual hardship. Considered seriously, the physical pain which suffuses cycling provides a window of insight into the existentialist revolt against Western metaphysics and gives voice to the sort of alienation experienced by the disembodied Cartesian thinker. For Schopenhauer, Nietzsche, as well as many later existentialists, what's at stake in matters of pain and physical embodiment is acknowledging that 'we're all in the ditch,' and turning that awareness into not merely stoic, stiff-upper lip acceptance, but into something beautiful – into, 'looking at the stars' from our excruciatingly limited vantage point.

Born in the port city of Danzig in 1788, Schopenhauer's philosophy was one of the central influences on the young Nietzsche who, while still a student, famously chanced upon Schopenhauer's best-known work, *The World as Will and Representation*, in a bookshop in Leipzig. Although Nietzsche would later renounce Schopenhauer's philosophy for what he saw as its life-denying pessimism, the way that Schopenhauer conceives of the human body and the nature of suffering is key to understanding later existentialist thinkers and provides one of the best descriptions of the bizarre, twofold way that the athlete relates to his or her body as both subject *and* object.

Beginning from an initial position of near nihilistic skepticism, Schopenhauer sees suffering of all sorts as the result of human beings' insatiable desiring and vain striving. For Schopenhauer, life is little more than endless oscillation between the poles of boredom and pain, spurred on by an ever-retreating horizon of desires which can never be fully satisfied. With this seemingly hopeless state of affairs in mind, Schopenhauer suggests that the path towards happiness – or at least to the minimization of suffering – is the wholesale cessation of the endless, insatiable desires which beget our suffering. The question quickly becomes: how is this renunciation of desire possible?

For Schopenhauer, the answer largely lies in relinquishing your individual ego and embracing an ineffable, mystical state of universal empathy which delivers the individual from suffering by freeing him or her from the toxic fiction of Cartesian subjectivity. In order not to suffer, one must first relinquish the idea that you are an isolated, striving subject who endlessly desires, seeks, and wants. Here it may perhaps seem that Schopenhauer is highly derivative – merely recasting, in Western terms, the ancient wisdom of the Upanishads, Lao-Tzu, and the Buddha. However, similar in outcome as he may be to Eastern philosophy, Schopenhauer arrived at his conclusions from squarely within the tradition of Western metaphysics, and in his treatment of the body as at once subjective *and* objective (in his terms as both *Will* and *Representation*) the true originality of Schopenhauer's thinking reveals itself.

Take the example of your hand. Tangible rather than conceptual, it exists in space and time and is governed by natural laws. This means that in one sense you can observe your fingers, tendons, and nail beds and regard your hand – or any other part of your body – as you would a mountain, a car, a chair, or the body of another human being. However, we of course don't relate to our own bodies in only this detached fashion – we're also subjects who feel, move, and inhabit them with our will. And for Schopenhauer, it's this twofold nature of our bodies which make them distinct from all other things.

With the insight that our bodies are the one thing that may be understood simultaneously as both subjective will, and as objective representation – Schopenhauer's thinking takes its final and perhaps most novel step: the world of things that we encounter and have been trained to think of objectively – as mere representation – like us, also possess an interiority – a universal will which we're also a part of. In an act of radical empathy, Schopenhauer grounds his mystical transcendence in moral logic: *If I have a will – an interiority, as well as an objective representation – than perhaps the rest of the world does as well.* Schopenhauer's thinking locates the root of suffering in the feeling that you're an individual locked in a bag of skin – in Heidegger's 'cabinet of consciousness.' The clue out of this impasse lies in the double-aspected nature of our body, and the fact that with an unusual act of empathy, it is possible to project your own interiority onto a world which otherwise would appear foreign and comprised of little more than dead matter.

As any cyclist who has been pricked with needles and tested in a lab can attest to, the body of an athlete is both objective and subjective in precisely the way Schopenhauer describes – producing watts and lactic acid and kilojoules of energy and feeling good or bad when you call on it to perform. This was how I or indeed any other athlete related to his or her body and Schopenhauer provided an elegant, rational accounting for the Buddhist points of view I'd read about in books by the likes of Alan Watts and D.T. Suzuki but could never reconcile within the compelling but tragic logic of Western philosophy.

In his later writing, Nietzsche would go on to be critical of Schopenhauer's cleaving of the world between 'will' and 'representation' as just another life-denying instance of metaphysics, but unlike many other philosophers, Schopenhauer provides something more than a mere escape into an idealized world of ideas or abstractions – he provides a path to escape from yourself. It's easy enough to believe that solipsism – thinking that only you are really real and the entirety of the rest of the world is your dream – is merely a pseudo-intellectual problem, but in practice, having empathy and knowing that other people are really as real as you is far from easy. As I thought about Jackson and Zach – friends with whom I'd laughed and cried and seen get married – I knew that on the bike they hurt just as I did. I'd seen in their struggles and suffering, in exhaustion and contorted faces, pain like my own. 'Love,' Iris Murdoch wrote, 'is the extremely difficult realization that something other than oneself is real,' and, in Schopenhauer's leap from *your* interiority to the interiority which suffuses and enchants the whole of existence, he justifies what the rest of the world outside of philosophy simply calls *love*.

Φ

Although it had been what I'd wanted more than anything else, when my depression had been most severe, a ride like the one I was about to undertake down the coast would have been both physically and psychologically inconceivable.

The very word *depression* has been so overused and degraded that it has now come to mean little more than a down mood, but as weeks stretched to months, it became apparent that what I was experiencing was profoundly different from anything I'd ever felt before and it wasn't abating.

It had come on slowly and, with the wisdom of hindsight, it was clear that although it was the most severe episode, it wasn't the first. Frightening in its intensity, the first had been when I was a university freshman. I'd told myself that it was just overtraining, and after a few months of rest and with the help of medicine it had gradually lifted. This time – ten years later – it was far worse.

Already retired from cycling, I'd recently left graduate school and begun to work in marketing for a bicycle company. It wasn't just my mood which was affected, but the entirety of my mind and body. My thoughts were garbled and distant, as if a hazy glass window had been erected between me and reality. I couldn't concentrate to read, my vision was inexplicably blurry, and I began to fear that my very identity would irrevocably be blotted out. Exhausted all the time, paradoxically I was also too agitated to sleep, and for perhaps the first time in my life, I prayed for oblivion, pleading – if not exactly to God, at least to the space that God should occupy – for the unremitting, incomprehensible pain to stop.

With symptoms that were just as much physical as they were mental, I went to doctor after doctor, certain that there had to be some underlying organic cause. Early on, I tried to ride but found that rather than make me feel better, exercise only made me worse. With no appetite, my weight fell until my clothes hung from my six-foot, 120-pound body like oversized sacks. Set adrift upon an ocean of meaninglessness, all of my previous ways of making sense of the world were blotted out by the fog of the despair. Divorced from life as they seemed, the swirling of disparate signs and symbols – of information seemingly devoid of meaning or context – haunted me. The speed of sound and the Suez Canal, Heisenberg's Uncertainty Principle and the beheading of Louis XVI were somehow all essentially equivalent: fact upon fact meaning both everything and nothing, when set against the terrifying silent indifference of the universe.

The dizzying vastness of existence and the sublime transcendence of art and philosophy which had always meant so much to me were transfigured – not merely uninteresting, but like the two faces of Janus, suddenly infused with an uncanny sort of terror which threatened to annihilate what little of me that still remained. I craved the familiar, and struggled through work each day, weepy and anxiety-ridden, only to return home and watch television until falling into a fitful, unrefreshing sleep.

I thought often of my family's history of suicide and depression – of the aunt and cousin who'd taken their lives – and found that rather than seeking philosophical ways of understanding what was happening to me, I was inclined to make sense of things in medical terms which before I would have thought too materialistic and reductionist. I read about hormones, neurotransmitters, and vitamins, and spurred on by this research paper or that, tried drugs, acupuncture, freezing showers, and meditation – anything to make it better.

Finding little solace in the books, music, and art which I thought would carry me through, I dreamed about the world coming back into intelligible focus – about the pain stopping and recovering enough to ride, and I'd try to recall the sensation of my bike beneath me – the warmth of the sun on my skin – as I piloted it through a sweeping corner on a warm summer afternoon. Like the child who wakes up at night and finds his once familiar home transformed by the darkness with ghosts and monsters lurking in every shadow, from the vantage point of depression, philosophy itself felt as if it had failed. Nothing felt real, and the entire net of concepts and ideas which I'd struggled to internalize were suddenly reduced to meaningless vanity.

In a cruel parody of Schopenhauer's idea of the world being suffused with will and interiority which had once seemed so appealing, pain which meant nothing and tragedy too great to ever be grasped or reconciled spoke to me from every tree and blade of grass – the pain of loss in every sunset and written across the faces of every person I passed on the street. The unrelenting competition of existence – one thing digesting another only to turn it into shit, blood, and viscera – seemed too horrible to be real – the stuff of science fiction. In the most basic sense, my own existence felt alien, as if something foreign had inexplicably taken hold of my body and mind. And what was perhaps the most frightening was that through it all, some small part of me was still present, observing the experience and recognizing the full extent of the horror, but powerless to change it one iota.

As David Foster Wallace pointed out several years before taking his own life, it's not incidental that so many people who are suffering from depression shoot themselves in the head. It's not just that the brain is the locus of the unremitting pain, it's that when you're most depressed, the thoughts go on and on until one feels that the only thing to do is to once and for all stop what the poet Emily Dickinson called the 'funeral in your brain' at its source.

Normally a voracious reader, the only book I read when I was at my worst was the novelist William Styron's book *Darkness Visible* which chronicled his hospitalization and slow recovery from major depressive disorder. An admirer of Styron's fiction, I'd read *Darkness Visible* before, but hadn't understood or fully sympathized with his description of depression, which at the time had seemed excessively clinical. Now though, it was as if the book had been written explicitly to give me a glimmer of hope when I most needed it. Styron seemed to be reporting back from the same alien land I was traversing – a place of such desperation that is, 'so mysteriously painful and elusive in the way it becomes known to the self – to the mediating intellect – as to verge close to being beyond description.'

I thought often of how Styron described his depression, and like someone lost at sea and cut adrift from the rest of humanity, his writing was the only thing that made any sense and placed the experience of depression in its proper context. Never a good sleeper, there had been a period when

I was ten or eleven years old when nearly every night I'd fallen asleep to a cassette tape of Dante's *Inferno* and it's the final line of the epic poem – as Dante emerges from the depths of hell, that Styron evokes at the conclusion of *Darkness Visible* – so poignant in the context of recovering from depression that it still brings tears to my eyes; 'And so we came forth, and once again beheld the stars.'

Φ

When we pull up in front of Zach's childhood home, Jackson – having ridden there – is already outside waiting with Zach. Located in a quiet neighborhood in Los Gatos at the base of the Santa Cruz Mountains, the two-story house is bounded by a wrap-around porch and a picket fence. For years this house had been where we'd started our rides and set out for far-flung races. On long summer days, the three of us would head north along the peninsula towards Palo Alto or Los Altos or over to Saratoga, past the hillside vineyards which line Highway 9, and into the Santa Cruz Mountains. After spending the better part of the day on our bikes, we'd return to Zach's parents' house, where we'd eat, shower, and watch old bike races, only to repeat it all again the next day.

Zach's father had raced during college – his vintage Cinelli road bike still hung in the basement – so a group of teenage cyclists taking over his house was never cause for consternation and for years, Jackson and I came and went without so much as knocking, bathing and taking food from the refrigerator, as if Zach's house was our own.

Jackson coasts towards us and dismounts, embracing Denika and smiling to Graeme as I take my bike and helmet from the back of the car. Jackson's light-brown hair is short-cropped and, having just returned from working a stage race in China, he tells us that he's been running, but since the staff aren't allowed to ride when they're working races, he hasn't been on the bike much. Slightly shorter than Zach and me, Jackson has a warm, mischievous smile, and the classic barrel-chested physique of a *rouleur* – a powerful rider who can get over climbs and still sprint. Jackson and Zach are both in unusually high spirits and suddenly mine are lifted too.

'All right, you guys,' Jackson says, 'I have this whole thing figured out. We roll out by nine thirty, stop in Pescadero for lunch – that puts us into Soquel by sixteen hundred at the latest.' Having worked in Europe for years, Jackson steadfastly refuses to use twelve-hour time and I have to quickly count forward from twelve. The math complete, I nod in agreement as I wheel my bike towards the house.

'Sounds like a plan,' Zach says in a flat tone that I've heard him use with Jackson a thousand times before, but that nonetheless still brings a smile to my face. Jackson casts a quick grin at Zach before starting to calibrate his power meter. My things unloaded, I kiss Denika and Graeme goodbye.

'I love you so,' I tell her.

'Be safe. Have a good time.'

'I will. I'll miss you,' I reply, as I take my phone from my jersey pocket and hand it to her through the car window. 'I don't want anyone to be able to find me but you. If we need to text, we can use Jackson or Zach's phone.' I kiss Denika one last time and watch as the car disappears down the tree-lined street, before joining Jackson and Zach in packing our bikes into the back of his SUV. Once they're securely stacked inside, we pile in and with Zach's father Gary at the wheel, head north up 101 towards the Golden Gate.

Φ

Be it of the spiritual, emotional, or physical sort, it's easy to fall into the trap of believing that all pain has a purpose. Armed with a strong enough *why*, nearly anything can be endured, so it demands no great leap to comprehend the desire to ascribe meaning to suffering. For me, the true difficulty wasn't in the pain itself, but in being astute enough to know the difference between pain which indeed meant something – the sort which tempers you and forces you to change your life for the better – and the other sort: suffering which in the end changes nothing.

The thought that the pain of the bike means something – that it reveals someone's basic character and somehow prepares you for life after the bike – is at minimum overstated, if not outright wrong. Certainly, being an athlete can instill discipline and an ability to prioritize, but the aspirational bourgeois myth of successful athletes slipping seamlessly into careers in banking and finance owing to their grit and work ethic leaves countless former athletes adrift. After knowing no other life for years, many of the riders I know and respected – cyclists far better than me, with Olympic medals and World Championship titles to their name – have struggled to adjust to life after retiring, ending up homeless, sleeping in their cars, or with depression so severe they take their own lives. The work ethic and ability to endure on the bike rarely map as easily onto other pursuits as young athletes are made to believe, and often the demons that you were trying to exorcise through the sport catch up with you after you're no longer racing.

Make no mistake, cycling is a business and an athlete never really owns their body. A rolling billboard for this or that brand of bicycles, wheels or pedals – vitamins or health insurance – you're conceived of in terms of your marketing utility. Every day, you ask things from a body which grows ever more remote from yourself. Taking the form of race results and power files, your body's outputs are reviewed by coaches and trainers, your muscles are rubbed and tendons stretched by masseuses, and your blood and urine taken for analysis by doctors and anti-doping officials.

When I was living in Santa Cruz, I had a friend and training partner who, several years older than me, had followed the same trajectory in the sport that I had – moving through the same systems and progressing from regional camps, through the national team program, to top-ranked domestic professional teams before fulfilling his dream of a contract with a professional European team. Upon returning home for the off season after his first year of living in Europe where he'd been racing for Lance Armstrong's U.S. Postal Team, we did a long winter of base miles together and slowly, as our rides grew longer week after week, he revealed the realities of the sport to me like a reluctant older brother. 'Don't ever be confused,' he said, 'we're all replaceable – no better than racehorses, and one doped donkey can easily be substituted for another.'

At once malady and cure, cycling taught me to not only hurt myself, but also how to exchange psychological for physical suffering. If I was anxious or depressed, I trained. When my parents fought, I trained. As questions of death and purpose and the limits of knowledge swirled in my head, I rode until all the doubt had been beaten into submission.

Every lung-searing interval or sprint session externalized everything I felt but knew could never truly be resolved. The suffering of cycling brought all of my questions and doubts into razor-sharp focus – transfiguring them into something productive – right up until the point when it no longer was.

It wasn't just a matter of avoidance or repression, but of seeking out internal contradictions and carrying them to their breaking point. In cycling and life, I sought reconciliation and understanding from the very things and people who'd broken me in the first place. Pain to once and for all end pain – thinking to end thought. Not wanting to ever relent, my inclination was always to force that which I wanted to extract myself from to its logical conclusion with the hope of breaking it from within. I imagined philosophy without thinking and the dogged suffering of the bike transformed into effortless beauty. Everything of beauty and grace had suffering as its common root, and with every painful interval – every session on the ergometer so intense I vomited – I was inserted into a narrative of progress, compelled by an inveterate gambler's hope that *this will be enough* to at long last bridge the gulf between who I was and who I wanted to be.

Φ

When we arrive at the Golden Gate Bridge, the parking lot is crowded with tourists, and parked tour buses line the narrow band of sidewalk. As a child, San Francisco had simply been called The City – a dense metropolis with buildings taller than I'd ever seen, car horns echoing through glass and steel canyons and well-dressed men and women in the Financial District rushing towards something that had seemed incomprehensibly important and glamorous.

We unpack our bikes quickly, deftly slipping wheels into dropouts, tightening skewers, and closing brakes. A small group of friends has come to see us off and ride the first few hours with us, and amid the nervous tics of idle cyclists – sips of water and the pulling-up of arm warmers – bikes and equipment are discussed and admired. The wind picks up and for a moment the sun is unobstructed before again passing behind a dense layer of fog. Glancing across the expanse of the parking lot, I see the rust-orange bridge spanning the dark water of the Bay, before making contact with Marin County on the other side.

After the steep climbs through the neighborhoods of San Francisco, we'll climb Highway 92 to Half Moon Bay before settling into what's certain to be a windswept Highway 1. As if simultaneously prompted by the darkening sky, Zach, Jackson, and I look at each other in silent agreement that we've been standing around long enough and motion that we should set off. Behind us, cleats click into pedals and we lead the small procession of riders out of the parking lot.

As we start up the first rise, I realize that we're already going harder than I'd imagined. The next three days may be uncomfortable, but as I think back on the depths of my depression, I'm certain that they won't hurt – at least not like that. This sort of pain – the burn of oxygen-starved legs and the searing of lungs – feels like nothing less than the warm embrace of an old friend.

Chapter 5

On Winning

You need not see what someone is doing
to know if it is his vocation,

you have only to watch his eyes:
a cook mixing a sauce, a surgeon

making a primary incision,
a clerk completing a bill of lading,

wear that same rapt expression,
forgetting themselves in a function.

How beautiful it is,
that eye-on-the-object look.

—W.H. Auden

Deeply embedded in the American psyche is the idea that the world is divided between winners and losers. Steeped in the logic of social Darwinism, life itself is little more than a merciless and unremitting competition in which the rich and successful are in a fundamental way *deserving* of what they have. The United States is a land fraught with contradiction: simultaneously kind and unspeakably cruel, cocksure and diffident – but the idea of merit stands singular, and to question this logic of meritocracy almost instantly casts someone as not just jealous or lazy, but deserving of what is perhaps the single most disparaging label in the American vernacular, a *loser*.

Even in the ostensibly liberal San Francisco Bay Area, the heroes are often 'self-made' entrepreneurs – Steve Jobs of Apple, Larry Page and Sergey Brin of Google, and Mark Zuckerberg of Facebook – and explanations of success which highlight the role played by matters of circumstance or luck rather than individual greatness are often seen only as so many excuses and rationalizations. It's exceptionally telling that few people in America see themselves as poor, only *not yet rich*, and the working masses drive themselves on with the simple credo, '*If they can do it so can I.*' Predicated on the idea of the autonomous, rational subject we see throughout Western thought, the prevailing sense is that individuals make their own success and, conversely, those who fail ought to be left to wallow in the misfortune of their choices unaided by those who have somehow 'chosen better.'

Elegant in its simplicity, the idea of becoming a 'winner' framed how I saw the world, and in spite of my outsider tendencies which ought to have made me more distrustful of the value judgments of the herd, I knew which side I had to end up on. Mediocrity held a strange sort of terror, and long before I started racing, I remember wanting to be good at *something* and believing that it was far better to be interesting and successful than well-adjusted and average. Harkening back to the ancient Greek ideal which equates truth, beauty, and goodness, the idea of athletic success – particularly in endurance sports – was suffused with a *Chariots of Fire*-like purity which seemed an indicator not simply of hard work or athletic talent, but even virtue.

In the meritocratic world of elite cycling, things like support systems and development curves were rarely afforded the importance they deserved. The prevailing narrative – perhaps a necessary fiction for an athlete – was that those who rose through the ranks of the sport deserved it owing to their grit, tenacity, and hard work. As I projected myself into the future, it seemed as if becoming a winner would justify my very existence – repaying some inchoate debt which I felt I owed and earning a sense of peace, whereby who I felt I was deep down and how I was perceived, would finally be reconciled.

In the early years of my racing this worked flawlessly. I was just talented enough to be the proverbial big fish in the little pond of my hometown velodrome at Hellyer Park, and the wins came easily. As a fourteen-, fifteen-, sixteen-, and seventeen-year-old, I was unbeatable at the junior state championships, and by the time I was seventeen I was a category two – often competing against the professionals. I went to the junior track nationals where once again, I found I measured up, and over the course of several years, I steadily accumulated a drawer full of state and national championship medals.

At first it was intoxicating; I'd leave the velodrome after a night of being unbeaten and feel as if I could do or be anything. Having pushed aside the specter of mediocrity, from the vantage point of my success, it seemed that while the other riders merely rode in circles and hoped, I was capable of bending the world to my will. I hadn't just won, but with every victory I was on my way to something far more profound and lasting: once and for all becoming *a winner* – in a fixed sense which transcended any single race victory.

Slowly however, this sense of exhilaration and mastery transformed into anxiety such that anything other than winning felt like failure. If five events took place on a Friday night of track racing, success didn't just mean winning three of them, but winning each and every one. I'd dig deep into my physical reserves to make this a reality – riding a local scratch race as if it was the World Championships. Here, by way of context, it's worth keeping in mind something rather unique about winning in the sport of cycling – unlike team sports where, at least in theory, each side has a fifty-fifty chance of victory, the odds in cycling are far lower – during his single best season in 1972, the greatest rider of all time, Eddy Merckx, won 'only' 37 percent of the races he entered.

While many of my race days have bled together in my memory, when it comes to the matter of winning, one telling instance stands out. A springboard to the national championships, the state championships usually took place over the course of an entire day – a title and jersey awarded to the winner of each of the five or so events. On this particular day, I'd won every event, while another rider with dark hair and melancholic brown eyes whom I'd often seen at races had placed second to me each time. I'd heard his father screaming at him to beat me – to 'try harder', but regardless of his tactical approach or how hard he tried, I'd still easily won.

As we lined up for the final race, he turned to me and asked, imploringly and in hushed tones his father was sure not to overhear, to please let him just win one race – just one. 'You'd always know I let you so what would be the point?' I responded – baffled that he would be desperate enough to ask – and without saying a word, he looked down and nodded in agreement. I won that scratch race just as I'd won the others that day, and even though I looked for him the next season, I never saw him or his father at a bicycle race again.

Losing – much less giving a race away – was something to be avoided at all costs. It would have empowered him – made him the one that beat me – which at the time seemed utterly unacceptable. I wanted only to be the best, and had to ensure that my trajectory was incontrovertible. However, as with many pursuits, success coming too easily or too soon in the sport of cycling can be a curse.

Φ

Riding two-by-two in a tight paceline, we weave through San Francisco's narrow streets. Skirting the ocean only to cut inland again, we make our way through the outer Richmond District and past the decaying concrete footprint of the once elegant pools of the Sutro Baths which are slowly being reclaimed by the Pacific.

As we pass the verdant, tree-lined edge of Golden Gate Park, the hustle and grime of the city's core gives way to residential neighborhoods: at first mansions with manicured yards visible from behind stacked stone walls and ornate wrought iron fences, and then the three-story walk-ups of the Sunset District, until finally we reach Lake Merced where low-slung ranch houses from the late 1950s – each one nearly identical to the next – run up and down the treeless hills in tidy rows.

Not fully confident in the skill of the other riders, I gravitate to Zach's steady wheel as we crest one of the small rises. Up ahead, Jackson stands and sprints out of the saddle – several powerful strokes opening a gap between him and the next rider. Comfortably ahead of the group, he takes his hands from his handlebars, removes his thin black wind jacket and deftly stuffs it in his jersey pocket. The broad residential thoroughfare lined with parked cars suddenly narrows, and after a steep, fast descent we thread our way around a sharp right, pass a cemetery, and are dumped out on a frontage road which parallels the busy highway. After only a matter of minutes, we turn again – right onto an elevated overpass that overlooks a reservoir – and I realize that we've already reached the base of the day's first real climb.

Our friend Matt Dubberley – another former domestic pro – is one of those who's joined us for the first leg, and as the pace increases on the climb, I see that it's Matt who's on the front of the group and driving it. Conversations cease – now there's only the sound of breathing, and the definitive clunk of the occasional shift over the whooshing of the passing cars. Slightly annoyed at the pace, I look over to Zach who nods in agreement.

'Doable but harder than I want to go,' he says.

'Same here.'

Thinking of the long day still ahead, I take a gel from my jersey. Thick and viscous in my mouth, I wash it down with a sip of water just as a pickup truck passes uncomfortably close to us. In an attempt to maintain my speed, I move my hands from the tops of the handlebars to the brake hoods, shift to a smaller cog, and stand as I crest the top of the climb just off the rear of the group. Over the summit, jerseys are zipped back up and sunglasses repositioned for the descent. Falling back into a single file line of sun-darkened legs and crisp white cycling shoes, we traverse several high-speed sweeping corners until, around one of the bends, the unobstructed Pacific comes into view.

As the road gradually flattens, we begin to rotate in a paceline – twenty or thirty seconds at the front before pulling off and drifting to the back of the line of cyclists. Even though we're nearing the outskirts of the town, we've still yet to encounter any stoplights to slow our pace, and as the cars bunch up in the lane beside us, we easily outpace them. Next to the road is a brackish marsh with reeds and rushes, and then, jarringly, a strip mall anchored by a Burger King. On the sidewalk in front of it, a bag of food has been discarded and a murder of crows fight over the bits of fries that are strewn across the concrete. Up ahead, I spot an American flag – edges frayed and red stripes faded, it's stiff with the tailwind that's driving us, and after a few more hard pulls at the front, we're quickly delivered to the quaint downtown of Half Moon Bay.

One of the most pleasurable things about riding – and being friends – with Jackson and Zach is that we no longer have anything to prove to one another. Our literal and figurative race has been run, and the respect we have for one another transcends who was – and certainly who's now – the strongest on the bike. Tellingly, at one point or another we've all been sick and overtrained, and though I was a stand-out on the velodrome and Zach as a time trialist,

Jackson, having raced in events from Paris–Roubaix to the World Cyclocross Championships, emerged as undoubtedly the most talented and versatile among us.

Jackson rotates through the tight paceline, and with a flick of the elbow indicates he's pulling off. We still have the tailwind, but as the road begins to rise almost imperceptibly into a false flat, I have to ride harder to maintain my speed. As I had on the track, I creep onto the nose of the saddle and lower my head in an attempt to make my tall frame just that little bit more aerodynamic. After about thirty seconds on the front, I count ten more pedal strokes and pull off, slipping back to Jackson's wheel at the end of the paceline. Not only have we ridden thousands of kilometers together, but he's also been my partner for two-man time trials and madisons – a relay-like track race contested by teams of two in which the riders take turns hand-slinging one another into the race so that the other partner can rest. Year after year, kilometer after kilometer, I've come to learn his pedaling, and like identifying the make of a car from the sound of its engine alone, without even seeing his face, I can tell Jackson by the way he pedals a bike – the distinctly fluid way he drops his heels ever so slightly later than most riders and how his left ankle is just that little bit less inflected than his right as it moves through the recovery stroke.

Now on the front, the rider who'd been riding on my wheel surges. My heart rate increases, and I can feel the lactic acid in my legs. Wanting to maintain my cadence, I tap my shift lever and stand briefly once I feel that the chain has fallen onto a smaller cog. I've forgotten that while Jackson, Zach, and I no longer have anything to prove, for local amateurs – now frankly stronger than the three of us – as ex-pros we remain a measuring stick of sorts.

As we turn south, onto Highway 1, what had been a tailwind is now a stiff crosswind, cutting across the band of road which threads itself between the tall, eroding cliffs to our left and the sandy beach to our right. To shield ourselves from the wind we ride staggered in a tidy echelon which uses the entirety of the wide shoulder. As we approach a rise, the pace increases again and a small gap starts to open in front of me – one bike length becoming two and then three. Seeing I'm struggling to remain in contact, Jackson drops back beside me, wordlessly takes his hand from the bars and extends it towards me with a wry smile. I take the hand of my old madison partner and, as we ride only inches apart, he accelerates briefly before winding up his shoulder in the motion of an underhand pitch and slinging me ahead. Effortlessly my bike surges, and I close down the gap just as we crest the hill. I settle back into the slipstream of the rider in front of me and, just like that, I'm back with the group.

Φ

Much like the mile in athletics, cycling's hour record – the distance a lone rider can pedal a bicycle in one hour on a velodrome – has always been a benchmark of performance. The distance achieved by the Italian cyclist Francesco Moser in the winter of 1984 was a clear inflection point which irrevocably altered not just the record books, but the very nature of what it meant to be a professional cyclist.

Led by a small army of experts which had been assembled by his energy drink sponsor, the plans for Moser's hour record attempt were first conceived in the summer of 1983. From heart rate-based training, to computer timing, to aerodynamic optimization, no aspect of Moser's performance was left to chance by him and his team in their quest to break Eddy Merckx's long-standing record. Just as Merckx had some twelve years earlier, the Italian rider and his team elected to attempt the record at the high-altitude concrete velodrome in Mexico City. However, any similarities between the two attempts ended with the venue. While it had been designed and constructed specifically for the hour record, Merckx's bike had been almost identical to a standard track bicycle. Hand-made in Ernesto Colnago's shop, the frame was constructed with lightweight round tubing and equipped with standard drop handlebars and traditional spoked wheels. In stark contrast to Merckx's machine, Moser's hour record bike made use of every possible aerodynamic feature. From the design of his frame and his solid disc wheels, to his specially designed shoes and skinsuit, Moser's team of engineers understood that the enemy wasn't weight as Merckx had thought, but drag.

This radical new paradigm of the sport wasn't merely limited to equipment however, and perhaps even more influential for me and generations of athletes to come, was the role played by Moser's approach to training and physiology. Rather than racing into fitness as was then typical, Moser trained specifically for the hour record with the help of a team of doctors and physiologists led by Dr. Francesco Conconi at the University of Ferrara. Intervals with tightly controlled ratios of work and rest at specific heart rates were prescribed, and Moser's fitness was monitored with an unprecedented degree of rigor. Needing to quantify and measure Moser's maximum possible pace for the duration of the one-hour effort, Conconi monitored Moser's training with what was then a very new tool – a portable heart rate monitor – and it was from the daily use of this device that Conconi arrived at the key physiological insight which forever changed how endurance athletes understand training: 'lactic threshold.'

To understand what Conconi means by lactic threshold, it's useful to think of a cup with a small hole in the bottom. The more intense a cyclist's effort, the faster this cup is filled with lactic acid and other metabolic waste, until a certain point when the effort is so hard that the cup is being filled faster than the rate at which it's draining through the hole in the bottom. This point at which the cup overflows came to be known as the rider's 'lactic threshold,' and Conconi surmised that by knowing the precise heart rate at this point of maximum maintainable workload, training could be prescribed which would extend it – in theory allowing a cyclist to ride faster for longer, and informing not just training protocols, but also pacing strategy.

Conconi's insight was like understanding the workings of an automobile's engine for the first time, and on the cold morning of January 19th, 1984 in the thin air of Mexico City, Francesco Moser bested Eddy Merckx's seemingly unbeatable hour record by over one full kilometer.

Days after Moser's ride, the cycling magazine *Winning* interviewed a stunned and skeptical Eddy Merckx:

It surprised me so much because a man cannot perform above his natural capacity – no one can transform themself into an extra-terrestrial otherwise an old donkey could become a race-horse! . . . Of course, at the time, I didn't know the exact nature of the equipment being used. The only requirement is to have a large budget and to have the courage and merit to undertake a lengthy scientific preparation program. From now on, anything is possible.

To the surprise of many – including Merckx – the UCI allowed Moser's record to stand in spite of his disc wheels and other rule-skirting equipment. This decision opened up a Pandora's box of technical innovations which would be allowed and barred seemingly at random over the next twenty-five years.

Moser's record attempt had cost upwards of a million dollars (almost three million dollars today), and though he would later be less than forthcoming on the topic, shortly after breaking the record, Moser told the media that prior to the attempt under Conconi's supervision, in addition to his cutting-edge equipment and training, he'd undertaken another novel procedure which at the time was still legal: he'd re-infused his own red blood cells in order to increase his aerobic capacity.

Rather suddenly, a sport which had largely been characterized by suffering and perseverance, was transformed into a series of technical problems to be overcome by skilled engineers and scientists: with Moser's hour record, the traditional sport of cycling became not merely technological, but calculative – with the choices made in laboratories and wind tunnels becoming critical aspects of a rider's success.

What had once been art had now entered the realm of science, and there was no going back. Cycling's arms race had begun.

Φ

When I was a child, Heidegger's 1927 opus *Being and Time* sat thick and foreboding on the family bookshelf, seeming to hold the answers to life's mysteries on its pages. Philosophy engendered an unusual sort of intellectualized intimacy between my father and me: like being in on the same joke, we both understood that reality wasn't at all like what nearly everyone else thought it to be. And when I was a teenager, I recall asking my father what *Being and Time* was about and simply being told that he wasn't sure that he really understood it, but that he thought it was about how in order to understand what existence is, you have to understand the true nature of what it means 'to be,' and that in all likelihood *Being and Time* was the single greatest philosophical work of the last century.

For me, the figure of Martin Heidegger has always loomed large – as an exemplar both of the moral shortcomings of philosophical thinking, and as a thinker who nurtured my supreme hope that one day there would be some future moment of resolution in which thought would become transfigured into something akin to the universal understanding of music – into the language of pure emotion.

Though forever tainted by his support for National Socialism in the 1930s, when it comes to insight into matters of technology and modernity, there's perhaps no more original twentieth-century thinker than Heidegger. Neither reactionary Luddite nor an advocate for material progress, Heidegger places technological thinking within the framework of his larger concern for the history of Being – a question which he believes Western philosophy to have discounted in its rush towards knowledge of this or that particular thing, and which in his words needs to be 'raised anew,' namely, *what does it mean to exist?*

In Heidegger's retelling of Western philosophy, stretching back to Socrates and Plato, Being has been 'covered over' – understood as either a separate metaphysical entity akin to Plato's realm of forms, or in more materially minded approaches, conflated with the existence of this or that particular entity. The 'forgetfulness' of that which is nearest to each and every one of us – namely Being itself – has led the modern individual to feel 'homeless' and cut off from the very basis of his or her existence. Throughout his long academic career, Heidegger pursues the question of how we might recover a largely pre-Socratic way of thinking which regarded existence not as a mere property of things which exist in the world, but as a near mystical opening. For Heidegger, thinking which takes Being into account allows for a sort of *clearing* – for the space and freedom to once again allow human beings to feel at home and part of (rather than separated from) the natural order. With Being brought to the forefront, Heidegger envisions reclaiming a way of experiencing our existence which is enchanted, poetic, and suffused with meaning.

In his treatment of the so called *ready-to-hand* object, Heidegger extols the virtues of the pre-conceptual way in which the craftsperson relates to his or her tools, and this understanding also helps to explain why late in his life – in the 1950s and '60s – he began to explicitly focus on the 'question of technology,' and the extent to which technical thinking had come to eclipse all other modes of thought.

Here, by technical thinking (which he carefully distinguishes from technology itself), Heidegger doesn't mean any particular technology or level of advancement achieved by a given field, but rather the way in which, almost as a matter of course, technologically minded thinking forces you into a limited view of the world which understands existence itself as little more than resources to be exploited. In the light of calculative, technological thinking, the world is understood as a 'standing reserve' which is 'on tap' for humankind to exploit. 'The earth reveals itself as a coal mining district, the soil as a mineral deposit,' the dammed Rhine, little more than a 'water power supplier' or tourist attraction. The sole aim is 'maximum yield at minimum expense,' but no one knows what the ultimate purpose of this yield is other than profit, so that 'man stumbles aimlessly about' in a world which he or she is incapable of understanding.

As Heidegger stated pointedly in his 1955 Memorial Address:

> In all areas of his existence, man will be encircled ever more tightly by the forces of technology. These forces, which everywhere and every minute claim, enchain, drag along, press and impose upon man under the form of some technical contrivance or other – these forces, since man has not made them, have moved long since beyond his will and have outgrown his capacity for decision.

It is not simply that technology has outstripped our ability to control it, but that it has reduced human existence to matters of will, control, and self-assertion as we race to extract resources and value, thereby reducing both ourselves and the things we use and produce into mere objects to be exploited and 'used up.'

Prescient in his anticipation of the disposability of consumer goods like mobile phones, computers, and bicycles with their annual product cycles and 'planned obsolescence,' Heidegger writes, 'The more quickly they are used up, the greater becomes the necessity to replace them ever more quickly and more readily.'

Following Nietzsche, Heidegger recognizes not only the death of God, but even more radically, the death of the human impulse for meaning which created God in the first place. 'Not only have the gods and the god fled,' Heidegger writes, 'but the divine radiance has become extinguished in the world's history.' To what does he attribute our modern homelessness – this 'flight of the gods'? To technical, metaphysical thinking, which necessarily occludes the mystery of Being – the mystery and divinity of existence itself.

It is with this decisive, final coda that Being – and with it the very idea of 'the holy' – becomes once and for all obscured, completing our abject alienation and utter homelessness. And yet, even in this darkest hour which he terms 'the world's night,' Heidegger proposes a path forward, believing that poetic, philosophical thought can work to recall Being and draw us back into contact with what he calls 'the fugitive gods,' the divinity and wonder which has fled. Invoking Nietzsche's 'death of God,' Heidegger writes:

The time remains destitute not only because God is dead, but because mortals are hardly aware and capable even of their own mortality. Mortals have not yet come into ownership of their own nature. Death withdraws into the enigmatic. The mystery of pain remains veiled. Love has not been learned. But the mortals *are*. They are, in that there is language. Song still lingers over their destitute land. The singer's word still keeps to the trace of the holy.

Rather than the rational philosopher, it is the 'singer' – the poet – who is able to maintain our increasingly tenuous link 'to the trace of the holy.' Instead of casting the world in technical, calculative terms, poetic thought – in its unique ability to recall Being – provides 'releasement to the mystery' of existence.

Fundamentally, it isn't Heidegger's philosophical reasoning, but his *story* which is so enticing to me: a fall from the grace of our original unity with Being into a destitute, technical world which has been stripped of its mystery and purged of its primordial wonder. In Heidegger's account, the entire trajectory of the West is a tragic arc which begins with Plato and concludes with Nietzsche and the death of God, and the way back from the 'homelessness' of modernity is to 'renew the question of Being,' – of 'presence,' or 'the holy,' and in so doing, re-enchant the world of everyday experience with ecstatic wonder at the simple and yet inexplicable fact that there is *something* rather than nothing at all.

Φ

As an athlete, I'd always wanted to be someone for whom things came effortlessly, but as I progressed, I came to suspect that the very fact of my so wanting betrayed the fact that I wasn't among the chosen. Though I possessed an unusually good power-to-weight ratio which allowed me to accelerate to sprint speed far more rapidly than other riders, in almost all other regards, I was physically unexceptional and the opportunities for me to shine were mostly limited to punchy uphill sprints and standing starts on the velodrome. As the limits of my physical talent began to reveal themselves, each new season washed away the failures of the last and brought a sense of renewed hope: a change to my position on the bike, or a new approach to training; more time spent training at altitude or perhaps less. And, like a gambler of sorts, it always seemed that I was only one step away from manifesting my full potential and so, with my coach Harvey as my guide, I worked with fitters, doctors, and physiologists to do all I could to improve.

Success in international cycling tends to come in discrete generational waves – groups of riders from the same country pushing one another towards success – and for the most part it was members of the storied 1984 U.S. Olympic team who guided the American cyclists of my generation. The Soviet-boycotted 1984 games had taken place in Los Angeles, and it was here that for the first time in the modern era, the U.S. cycling team shone on the international stage – ending its long medal drought and taking nine medals on both the road and track. Coached by a Polish émigré named Eddie Borysewicz, riders of this period had borne witness to the changes brought about by Moser's hour record and, depending on their age, raced into an era of wind-tunnel testing, aerodynamically optimized bikes, and pharmacological interventions.

A stand-in father figure, who I was desperate to please and eager to emulate, my coach Harvey Nitz had been a mainstay of the U.S.'s 1984 Olympic team, earning a silver medal in the team pursuit and a bronze in the individual pursuit. As Harvey had, I wanted to carve out a track-centered career across an array of events ranging from the kilometer to the points race. Innovative with his equipment, tactically astute, and able to suffer, and having garnered the near-universal respect of everyone I encountered in the sport, he was my ideal of what it meant to be a successful bike racer; as the pressure began to mount on me, it was Harvey, who'd been through it all, whom I trusted above anyone else.

Fresh out of the junior ranks, and with a professional contract with the track-focused Shaklee cycling team in hand was when the full scope of what elite sport truly entailed began to slowly reveal itself to me. With intensive media training which spelled out how to represent our sponsors to the press, to advertising photo shoots and jerseys like billboards, I understood that I was an easily replaceable marketing commodity and that every year or two, another stand-out junior – eager to carve out his place and with talent at least equal to my own – would be delivered to the elite ranks. Even though they no longer served as the stepping stones they once had, it was local races that became the most toxic. Often from the mouths of hangers-on who'd never so much as raced a bike, inane criticism as to who was deserving of what abounded, and even if I was simply using a particular race to cap off a hard block of training in preparation for a bigger event, being beaten at a local event invited judgment: *my rider beat this professional, ergo he should have his professional spot.*

On the one hand, I still wanted to win desperately – to be seen in a certain light of success – but on the other, I began to question my motivations for wanting this. Whose respect was it I craved? People I barely knew at the local velodrome? The parents of other riders? Teammates? Perhaps the 'cycling community?' – whatever that may have meant. It was easy enough to see that people's memories are short and that even successful riders were quickly forgotten. Athletes are essentially entertainers, and I saw how people's interests passed from one young hope to the next with astonishing speed as soon as a rider's trajectory showed the slightest hint of faltering. So, like any outsider, the question I asked myself was why I was so divided? Why was it that I so craved the adulation of people whom for the most part I didn't even respect? And, ever so slowly, I settled on the fact that the one person I really cared about pleasing was Harvey.

During long stretches of pre-season training, I'd stay at an apartment he owned near his home just outside of Sacramento establishing the necessary aerobic base for the season of racing to come, and I came to know Harvey's stories and adages. How he'd competed against (and sometimes bested) the feared – and very doped – East Germans and Russians, his horrific, face-first crash after federation mechanics failed to tighten the front wheel of his pursuit bike, and how much he'd suffered to earn his bronze medal in the pursuit at the L.A. Olympics. And even though the sport had already changed a great deal since Harvey's retirement, we did what we could in order for me to compete ethically against what were increasingly tough odds.

In the wake of Moser, there hadn't just been doping, but also ballooning budgets for both professional teams and national federations. Champion riders were increasingly the product of highly developed, well-funded systems, and the U.S. cycling team as I found it was frankly neither. I was at a training camp outside of Dallas, Texas with the junior national team when we all sat rapt in front of a television in the hotel watching Harvey's former teammate, Lance

Armstrong – who'd come through the U.S. cycling team program less than a decade before – win the 1999 Tour de France prologue. Little did any of us know then the full extent of the choices Armstrong and many others had made to achieve what they did.

And so, with other riders' performances improving rapidly (and often inexplicably) ahead of the 2000 Olympic team trials, Harvey and I invested energy into what seemed to offer the greatest advantage: legally increasing my hematocrit – the oxygen-carrying capacity of my blood – with an altitude chamber. Since the commercially available models were at the time both rare and prohibitively costly, we decided to build it ourselves. A three-quarter horsepower motor was obtained from Sears, along with a drainage pipe which was both thick enough not to implode from the pressure and just wide enough for my shoulders to fit into. In an attempt to monitor just how 'high' I was, we used an inexpensive car altimeter from RadioShack. And so, as the trials approached, after spending the morning training with the benefit of sea-level air, in an attempt to force my body to produce more red blood cells, I would spend the afternoon and evening at 9,000 feet in the homemade altitude chamber which we hoped would give me the performance advantage I needed.

I did well at the trials for an eighteen-year-old – placing fifth – but it wasn't enough to make the Olympic team, and as teammates flew to Sydney, I returned to California to start university. Several years later, my training partner leading up to the trials – who'd won his event – would garner the dubious distinction of becoming the first American athlete in any sport to be banned for using the synthetic red-blood cell booster EPO. I didn't realize it then, but my homemade chamber and I were simply no match for the technical and pharmacological arms race that cycling had become.

However, even as I began to question many things about the sport, Harvey remained a shining example of someone I wanted to emulate. I held out hope that even if the sport was different now, that if he'd been able to excel, then so could I. He was someone who'd been able to succeed through determination and ingenuity and without compromising himself in the process.

Φ

As the day goes on, our small group settles into a comfortable pace. The wind isn't as strong as I'd feared and, midway through the day, we jog inland and stop for sodas and food at a small market in the coastal farm town of Pescadero. Bounded by the ocean to the west, and the Coastal Range to the east, Pescadero and the tiny towns of the San Mateo County coast are only accessible from Silicon Valley by a winding two-lane highway. As a result of their isolation, they remain a backwater of farms, cabins, and century-old general stores. Mostly low-lying farmland, Pescadero is little more than a single main drag of utilitarian buildings from the town's heyday in the late nineteenth century: the market, along with a gas station, a taqueria, and an antique shop. On the worn benches next to the market, several tourists mill about along with a group of middle-aged men on well-appointed touring motorcycles.

Both Zach and Jackson look fresher than me as they dismount and lean their bikes against the building. I watch as Jackson – always talkative with Zach and me, but shy and circumspect around mere acquaintances – is pulled into a conversation with another rider who's set out with us. Intrinsic to his having been around cycling for all of his adult life, is not wanting to be goaded into explaining this or that team transfer, win or inter-team rivalry, to anyone who lacks the context to understand just what the true stakes are – what it means to be a top-flight professional and just how unbelievably difficult it is. For him, cycling isn't gossip, or armchair observation, it's people's lives and livelihood in a way that the uninitiated simply can't comprehend.

Inside the market, our cleats are loud on the hardwood planks and people glance at us curiously as we walk down the narrow aisles gathering soda, candy bars, and energy drinks. As I make my way to the cash register, I think of the hours still in front of me and at the last moment, grab a final candy bar and banana before paying and making my way back towards the concrete benches where the rest of the group is sitting.

As we clip into our pedals in anticipation of leaving I quickly gulp down a Coke and eat a candy bar. Before I know it, we're already back on our bikes and heading south towards Santa Cruz. Now more exposed and closer to sea level, Highway 1 stretches out like a dark ribbon; miles away from shore, a small fishing boat sits lonely on the dark water in a way that I'm tempted to ascribe more meaning to than it deserves. I remember being deeply depressed and fearing that who or whatever I was had been irrevocably lost – that the light of hope and the force of will that made me who I was had been extinguished by some incomprehensible force. But now, as the blood pulses through my body and the sun is warm on my bare skin it's as if I've been reborn.

After a fast descent, the road skirts a beach nestled in the embrace of a small sandy cove. Close enough to see the waves breaking against the shore, suddenly the whole world seems alive – blooming and buzzing with purpose. I think of my father and my son – of one generation following another and the seen world both coming into being and passing into oblivion. The wordless mystery of existence suddenly feels palpable, and for a fleeting moment that I know will soon retreat into the pale domain of memory, I'm certain that I'm meant for this world.

Φ

For the traditional cycling nations of Belgium, Spain, Italy, and France, the Anglo-American style of winning epitomized by Lance Armstrong's U.S. Postal Team and later by the British Sky and Ineos teams – wins which were the result of a sterile, soul-less sort of dominance dictated by power meters which helped riders to dose their efforts and race radios which allowed tactics to be prescribed by team directors in cars – rob the sport of its fundamental romance. Following the existentialist thread which is present in both Nietzsche and Heidegger, for many close to professional cycling, *how* a rider wins continues to be of the utmost importance – a brave loss often being judged superior to a victory born of cold calculation. And in professional cycling today, there has been no stauncher an advocate for approaching cycling in this light than the former winner of Paris–Roubaix, the Frenchman Marc Madiot who runs the long-standing Groupama–FDJ team.

Outspoken in his opposition not just to doping, but also the stifling effect power meters and race radios have had on the dynamics of professional racing, Madiot implored fans and the media to support his long-standing team leader, Thibaut Pinot on revealing grounds: 'because he's different,' Madiot said. 'He'll make you cry, sometimes you'll be sad, but he'll also lift you right up to the ceiling. His wins will taste different from the rest.' Madiot is not alone in his romantic approach to the sport, and the well-known Italian sports director Luca Scinto went as far as to prohibit his riders from racing with either power meters or heart rate monitors for the 2020 season, saying 'I don't want to lead robots, but riders who listen to their bodies and can control themselves.' It's clear that in cycling at least, a backlash of sorts has begun.

It's not difficult to draw a direct line between Heidegger's critique of technology and some of the worst aspects of professional sports today. Technical thinking reduces the athlete to little more than a data set. A prisoner to information, everything is measured and quantified, from blood lactic levels to sleep quality, to wattage and heart rate. This logic not only circumscribes a rider's performance and potential; in many ways the doping scandals which have plagued cycling for more than two decades are merely a symptom of this logic and the pervasive winner-take-all approach to life which is blind to anything other than the extraction of the 'standing reserve' of resources.

From corporate malfeasance, to pollution – owing to egregious abuses of all types – public trust in institutions has been undermined by the short-sightedness which necessarily follows from confronting the world technically. And over the span of the last seventy years, we've seen Heidegger's prophesy come to fruition as a certain sort of calculative view of the world has worked in tandem with hyper-capitalism to leave large swathes of the population confused, alienated, and angry as they've slowly come to realize that rather than make their lives easier, many modern modes of thinking have sucked the very horizon of meaning from their lives.

Φ

When winning is all you've been lauded for, a certain self-obsession almost inevitably follows. Being on your feet, chores, or a missed night of sleep can in a very real way impact your performance, and nearly every successful athlete learns to control these variables and put their training ahead of everything else. Energy is conceived of as a finite resource to be expended only in service of the bike and any task besides either breaking the body down through training or recovering from it is simply a waste. All of life is thus easily divided into two simple categories: those things and people that hinder your ability to win and those that further it. Egocentric, single-minded obsessiveness is rewarded, and as a matter of necessity everything else falls by the wayside – often becoming the burden of a rider's parents or partner. There's a common adage among riders and coaches: *don't stand when you can sit and don't sit when you can lie.* Walks in the park, much less household chores, are simply out of the question; alpha and omega, the bike is all that matters. I still vividly recall being home for a brief period around Christmas – no more than seventeen years old – and driving to a vista that overlooked the city with my high school girlfriend. Her head on my shoulder as the lights in the valley below shimmered in the cold, she asked me if forced to pick, if I would choose her or cycling? Without hesitation, I responded, 'Cycling.'

Like Salieri to Mozart, I became just good enough to see

truly great athletes from a close enough proximity to realize that in many cases those same traits which had allowed for their performance on the bike made them at best insufferable and at worst outright narcissists. Undoubtedly there were exceptions, generous, multifaceted people – people like Harvey and Jackson – who were able to excel in the sport while retaining their decency, but as I got older the question became not only what the ceiling of my physical talent was, but also what sort of person I was willing to become in order to succeed.

Looking back now, I find it almost incomprehensible why winning once felt so deeply important. Every explanation I'd venture seemed overly psychological – based on coming from a broken home, filling a void, or gaining the affection of my parents – but somehow none of these seem to fully account for the feeling of wanting something as badly as I did. In spite (or perhaps *because*) of my experience as an athlete, I'm skeptical of a certain sort of unreflective pursuit of excellence. At every juncture, the question seems to be who or what has a vested interest in your so-called 'betterment' – what institutions or economic systems your improvement serves to benefit.

One needs to be exceptionally careful what they wish for – success can deform just as much as it can improve and it's possible to see even a seemingly great achievement as at best essentially pyrrhic, and at worst, as incontrovertibly destructive. It's not merely a matter of 'opportunity costs' – of what someone might have given up in the process of accomplishing what they did, but also a matter of how success shapes how you conceive of yourself and relate to the world.

Chapter 6

On the World, Self, and Other

> The feelings that hurt most, the emotions that sting most, are those that are absurd: the longing for impossible things, precisely because they are impossible; nostalgia for what never was; the desire for what could have been; regret over not being someone else ...
>
> —Fernando Pessoa

There is perhaps no more pervasive and enticing an idea than that buried deep inside each of us exists a true, fully authentic 'self', and that if it were only possible to overcome the corrupting influence of society, we could once and for all resolve the tension between who we feel we are at the core of our being and the social masks which at every turn appear to be imposed upon us.

You see vestiges of this idea of there being a fixed, immutable self in Greek metaphysical philosophy with its near obsession with the defining traits which make something 'this and not that,' in Christian theology with the concept of the 'soul,' and in later eighteenth-century Romantic thinking beginning with Jean-Jacques Rousseau, with the idea of the 'noble savage,' whose original nature has been preserved by remaining outside the pale of corrupting society.

In America, this idea of not just self-sufficiency but outright self-creation is a crucial aspect of the national character. From 'going west' to seek one's fortune, to Henry David Thoreau's retreat to Walden Pond, there's the sense that not simply finding, but *creating* yourself is central to what it is to be an American. The American ideals of 'liberty' and the 'pursuit of happiness,' all take place within the context of having already been freed from the restrictive chains of geographical location, hereditary ties, and predetermined identity. Rather than interpreting this as a loss of meaning or tradition, in the United States this freedom has almost universally been celebrated. By being tied to and defined by nothing – so the myth went – one is free to be absolutely anything. Bob Dylan is only loosely tied to Robert Allen Zimmerman from Minnesota, the pop singer Elizabeth Woolridge Grant from upstate New York is somehow *more* Lana Del Rey than she is herself; in the American psyche, the most fully realized examples of what it is to be a person spring from neither social context nor one's own past, but *ex nihilo* – as singular acts of will and self-creation. *Don't like your life? Simply pack up and start over somewhere else – as someone else.*

Guided by our individualistic, Cartesian notion of selfhood, contemporary notions of authenticity almost always involve finding and then embracing 'who you really are,' and rather than the exception, self-creation – or at least the parody of it – has become the rule. The famed enjoinder, 'know thyself' inscribed above Apollo's temple at Delphi, has degenerated into the project of developing a version of yourself which appears inviting for others in its apparent sincerity. This has reduced the radical self-creation implicit in Nietzsche's idea of the *Übermensch* to little more than a well-cultivated, fictionalized self, strategically conceived for public consumption until the idea of one's 'brand' has entered common parlance. Tellingly, even the word *person* itself – derived from the Latin *persona* for the mask that an actor assumed in the theatre – reveals the possibility that the 'genuine person' in the most literal sense is little more than an 'authentic fake'.

With Andy Warhol's 'fifteen minutes of fame' now granted to everyone, even the once radical act of self-creation has become no more than another mask, and the question comes into stark relief: *is there even really a true self to find?*

Φ

The caffeine from the Coke I drank at the market back in Pescadero seems to have worked. Suddenly my legs are lighter and, like a well-oiled machine, we each take short pulls at the front of the group as the miles disappear beneath us. The wind again at our backs, we ride in a tight paceline and I find that the speed itself is pleasurable. Through my handlebars and saddle, I can feel the surface of the chipseal road – sharp bits of gravel imbedded in the asphalt beneath my tires. Having spent hours in a wind tunnel, I know how sitting up or leaving a jersey unzipped means I'll have to use more energy to go the same speed. So when I start to feel a tinge of fatigue, I flatten my back aerodynamically, lower my head, and reposition my hands in the gentle rubber cradle of the brake hoods.

Slowly the landscape changes as the rocky coastal cliffs of San Mateo County give way to the rolling hills and dark, freshly tilled soil of the fields of northern Santa Cruz County. By the side of the highway, the dusty cars of farm workers are interspersed with shiny SUVs carrying surfboards and mountain bikes. As the day wears on it grows warmer and, when I'm at the back of the group, I peel off my arm warmers and quickly stuff them into the pocket of my jersey. We're going hard enough that we talk only infrequently, and for long stretches, the distant melancholic cries of gulls are all that's audible over the sounds of breath and wind. Above us, the sun is high and bright, bathing the world in clean white light as it makes its slow arc towards the infinite blue horizon where the Pacific meets the sky.

As a child we'd often traveled to these same beaches to escape the stifling summer heat of the valley and, as I waded into the cold waves, my mother had warned of rip tides – of drowning and being dragged out to sea never to be found. The ocean came to feel different than any other sort of danger. It wasn't like car crashes, accidents, or illness. If the ocean swallowed you, it was as if you'd simply never been, and I remember sitting on one of these beaches – perhaps even the one that we were now riding by – staring out at the vastness, and for the first time understanding what it was to be terrified. Not the childhood fear of this or that *thing*, but true terror, which never takes an object: the terror of *nothingness* – of *not being*.

We crest a hill and start to coast down. A long row of cars are parked by the side of the road and instinctively we pull away from the shoulder to avoid the possibility of becoming the victim of an errant car door being flung open into our path. Next to me, Zach unclips from his pedal and shakes out his leg before resuming pedaling. On the horizon in front of us, the distinctive rusting silos of the abandoned cement plant in the tiny town of Davenport emerge among the trees – indicating that we're now in the final hour before we reach Santa Cruz.

Reflexively I start to think of food, of clean white sheets and a warm shower – of simple, tangible things. I find that when I'm rested and healthy and comfortable, I tell myself I want everything small and petty and stupid to dissolve. Yet to my dismay, I find that when I'm granted this wish I can only handle it in small doses. Whether it's the result of listening to music, reading, riding, or the few times I've taken psychedelic drugs, after a mere taste, my overriding desire is always to return to my small, everyday self, whose existence quickly comes to feel threatened in the face of trembling beauty which transcends the individual. Perhaps I was – and remain – something of a coward; perhaps, I'd truly seen Nietzsche's abyss staring back.

After rounding a bend and crossing a set of railroad tracks, we enter the town of Davenport. I can recall stopping here on training rides when the cement plant had still been operating, blanketing the town in a thin layer of cement dust – footprints crisscrossing the weathered concrete of the sidewalks. Where it had once emitted a low monotone roar, now I find that it's silent, and but for a few shops the town is practically deserted. As we ride past, I can see from the road that one after another, the sea-worn white and brown and blue paint of the old company houses is peeling. We start down a shallow descent, and what remains of Davenport comes to an abrupt end with an empty lot bounded by a chain-link fence, and we're returned back to mile after mile of uninterrupted road.

Φ

Often called 'an individual team sport' cycling is at once profoundly social, and intensely attractive to loners and outsiders. This sense of alienation – of feeling cut off not just from one's true self, but from society – pulses through the very veins of existentialism. In existentialist literary works ranging from Dostoevsky's *Notes from the Underground*, in which an unnamed civil servant extols the virtues of suffering and lambasts the deadening decadence of society; to Hesse's *Steppenwolf*, whose narrator is torn between the half-lived lives of middle-class comfort and the chaotic truth of his inner reality; to Kafka's *Metamorphosis*, whose narrator is famously nothing less than an insect, the common theme is the unremitting tension between the individual and the society which they've deemed both superficial and spiritually bankrupt.

The twentieth-century French existentialist Jean-Paul Sartre astutely diagnosed the problem: no matter how much you want to be a sovereign individual, at every turn your very sense of self depends on the Other. It's not just a matter of who or what you aspire to be, but more fundamentally, if there is even a self which exists in the first place. If you only know yourself through other people, how do you possibly resist their influence to become some more authentic version of the very thing which always escapes your grasp? In Colin Wilson's vocabulary, the unhappiness of these *outsiders* is owing to the fact that on some level they all want to resolve the tension of their alienation – namely to become 'insiders' – but in this quest, they remain forever divided against themselves. The rejection of the values of the herd has become intrinsic to their very identity, and even though the outsider craves it deeply, to become an insider to mainstream, bourgeois society owing to some sort of success or artistic recognition, would feel like a death of sorts.

Yet no athlete can improve without at least to some extent becoming part of an already established community. You may race and suffer alone, but you depend on coaches, bike fitters, mechanics, and most importantly, your fellow riders, to tell you who you are and how you're performing. Through and through, cycling is a social enterprise. Not only do individual riders play a specific role on a team, but even the most basic modes of self-understanding are in some ways relative and contingent upon others. Being a climber or sprinter, a *rouleur* or a time trialist, merely means that compared to other riders, you climb, sprint, or time-trial well.

In the peloton, respect is earned, and rather than the unmitigated aggression one might imagine, riding only centimeters from other riders at 50 or 60 kilometers an hour requires a great deal of trust in the skills and choices of other riders, and acts which endanger the group are dealt with harshly. Even winning and losing are relative rather than absolute, and without a large field of 'losers' there by definition could be no 'winner', and in a very real way the winner thus *needs* losers. With this in mind, the conception of competitors as mere 'problems to be overcome,' if not wrong, at least comes to feel exceptionally reductive. As Sartre formulates it, 'The Other holds a secret – the secret of what I am.'

Rising through the ranks of a sport is thus the epitome of an *outsider*, attempting to become an *insider* – to become seen and recognized as he or she hopes to be seen. In a very real way, you're forced to trust others to tell you who and what you are – something I was always suspicious and mistrustful of. Just what were the values of the mirror I was looking into for the recognition and understanding I craved? On the one hand, I wanted to remain an outsider, but on the other – irrationally and paradoxically – I wanted to be recognized for being one.

Φ

From a relational and psychological perspective, there's perhaps no more astute a guide to understanding the lived experience of existential philosophy than Jean-Paul Sartre. Sartre wasn't simply an academic, but a Left Bank public intellectual, novelist, playwright, and member of the avant-garde in a fashion conceivable only in France. With his signature pipe and thick, Coke-bottle glasses, for better or for worse, the media-savvy Sartre, along with his partner Simone de Beauvoir and erstwhile friend, Albert Camus became the standard bearers of post-war existentialism in the United States and Britain, exerting an influence which continues to this day.

Perhaps the most psychologically minded of the existentialists, in both his fiction and academic writing, Sartre is deeply concerned with what he describes as our 'radical freedom' which takes place against the backdrop of the 'nothingness' of a world which has largely been drained of its meaning. For Sartre, the process of self-creation is not only unremitting, but also highly social. There is no soul – no fixed self or identity to cling to – only the radical freedom which we are 'thrown' into, and he both describes in philosophical terms and dramatizes how with every glance, catty remark, or bit of praise we're desperately grasping for that which is nearest and yet most enigmatic – *Who am I really?*

In sharp distinction to the thoroughly 'academic' Heidegger, who seems to issue his profundities from the rarefied mountain air of his hut in the Black Forest, Sartre is both socially and politically *involved* and conceives of philosophy not as a strictly theoretical practice, but as inexorably linked to the practical choices and actions of embodied men and women when faced with the full magnitude of their own freedom.

Having read Heidegger's *Being and Time* while a German prisoner of war in 1940 and 1941, Sartre's major philosophical work – 1943's *Being and Nothingness* – maps Heidegger's thinking about the nature of existence (Being) onto the social and psychological plane. Although Heidegger himself famously referred to *Being and Nothingness* derisively as '*Dreck*,' in the sprawling, nearly 900-page work, Sartre seeks to provide a rigorous account of consciousness from a phenomenological perspective.

In *Being and Nothingness*, Sartre divides the world into objects whose mode of being is what he terms *being-in-itself*, and the human subject, a special mode of existence which he calls *being-for-itself*. While a thing, an inanimate, *being-in-itself*, is complete and fully realized, the identity of the conscious human subject – the *being-for-itself* – is never fully settled. For an individual to live what Sartre calls 'authentically,' they must confront the fact that unlike the type of being of a table or a chair, by virtue of our freedom as a *being-for-itself* we remain forever irreducible. As Sartre said, 'we are our choices.'

However, in spite of his emphasis on freedom, for Sartre,

the twenty-first-century ideal of the individual finding or creating him or herself in isolation would be grossly over-simplistic. It is not autonomously, but rather relationally – through our dealings with 'the Other' – that we establish the terms of our freedom and can come to live authentic lives which embrace our unique capacity to make choices and constitute ourselves.

As Sartre famously writes of the waiter in a café in his 1938 novel *Nausea*, 'When the café empties, his head empties too.' This 'head emptying' is true not just of the waiter, but just as much for the identities which we think we've chosen. Tinker, tailor, soldier, sailor, or even bicycle racer, rather than a fully realized human being who is capable of choice and able to exercise a negative freedom which resists the narrow definition of selfhood imposed by our social roles, Sartre identifies the fact that in an act of bad faith which rejects our freedom we all too often allow ourselves to be reduced to little more than an object – fully internalizing social masks and the way we see ourselves being seen by others.

In Sartre's relational, psychological account, it's a careful examination of the true stakes of romantic love which pushes his ideas about self and other – subject and object – to their most extreme. For Sartre, genuine love is invested in the Other without reducing them to a mere *thing-in-itself* which, like a tool or inanimate object merely performs a function or makes you feel a certain way about yourself. Here, think of phrases like *I love how you make me feel*, or even *I like who I am when I'm with you*, which, no matter how well intentioned, reduce the object of one's love to a mere tool such that you can regard yourself in the light of the identity you strive for. For Sartre, true romantic love and genuine friendship transcend this objectification, rescuing you from what Sartre calls 'the reef of solipsism,' by forcing you to recognize the Other not as a mere means but, like you, as another subject. Though Sartre is far less explicit about it than other thinkers we've considered, his largely psychological account also plays on a metaphysical level which relates back to the criticism of metaphysics which we've seen in both Nietzsche and Heidegger.

Recall Nietzsche's critique of Platonism and how at every turn it reduces lived life to a deadening abstraction. For Sartre, to reduce another person to a fixed ideal which serves a given purpose for you – no matter how flattering this ideal may be – imposes a certain thing-like fixed identity onto them which deprives the Other of their subjectivity and freedom. Though in many ways still a Cartesian dualist, when it comes to how we relate to other human subjects, Sartre is keenly aware of the pernicious effects of abstract, metaphysical thinking – a key trait of nearly every existentialist.

The language is often clunky in Sartre's philosophical writing as it strains under its own weight to convey the contours of experiences which lie at the periphery of what can be described philosophically. In his literary writing however, rather than an abstract accounting, Sartre attempts to illustrate how these different modes of being are actually experienced by the individual. In Sartre's fiction, the contours of the physical world and physiological states are described in agonizing detail in order to reveal the preconceptual strangeness which underlies existence. For Sartre the atheist, there is no metaphysical or divine standard to defer to – no 'purpose beyond,' just a frighteningly indifferent universe comprised of things whose very existence is so unbearably profound that, stripped of their typical meanings and ways of conceptualizing them, the pressing weight of their very *existence* becomes threatening. And, in what is one of his most memorable and revelatory passages in *Nausea*, Sartre's loosely autobiographical main character – a historian named Antoine Roquentin – sits on a park bench staring at the roots of a nearby chestnut tree:

All at once the veil is torn away, I have understood, I have *seen*. [. . .] The roots of the chestnut tree sank into the ground just beneath my bench. I couldn't remember it was a root anymore. Words had vanished and with them the meaning of things, the ways things are to be used, the feeble points of reference which men have traced on their surface. I was sitting, stooping over, head bowed, alone in front of this black, knotty lump, entirely raw, frightening me. [. . .] And then all at once, there it was, clear as day: existence had suddenly unveiled itself. It had lost the harmless look of an abstract category: it was the dough out of which things were made, this root was kneaded into existence. Or rather the root, the park gates, the bench, the patches of grass, all that had vanished: the diversity of things, their individuality, were only an appearance, a veneer. This veneer had melted, leaving soft, monstrous lumps, in disorder – naked, with a frightful and obscene nakedness.

The existence of things in the world – of tree roots, the sea, and even other people – is, in Sartre's words, 'frightful and obscene,' revealing the oppressive and overwhelming *nothingness* which appears when the conceptual edifice which contains and orders existence is stripped away.

In an attempt to maintain the collective fever dream of meaning, lives are filled with busyness – with meetings and prestigious job titles which imply importance – but just beneath an uncanny groundlessness lurks in the silent indifference of a universe which will, ultimately, devour each and every one of us. For Sartre, once life is stripped of the ways we've become habituated to make sense of it, you're not simply tasked with Nietzsche's herculean task of creating your own values and meaning from the rubble, but must also overcome the overriding sense that existence itself is *grotesque*. Devoid of God or transcendent meaning, what remains is the radical freedom of choice and the burden of self-creation in what Sartre's friend and fellow existentialist Albert Camus termed an 'absurd' situation.

While Nietzsche's and Heidegger's accounts both remain suffused with the mystical and poetic – in Heidegger's case still holding out the possibility of a redemptive return to the non-conceptual, poetic bosom of Being – Sartre holds no such hope. In Sartre's words, 'we are condemned to be free,' and must face up to this freedom clear-eyed, stoically, and without falling prey to the savior who promises redemption.

Φ

In the year 2000, when I was eighteen years old, I was selected for my first elite international event by USA Cycling – the Southern Games which took place in the small Caribbean island nation of Trinidad and Tobago. My large bike bag in tow, I flew alone from California to Miami, Florida where I was to spend the night, before meeting up with a coach and my Training Center roommate, a powerful track sprinter from Indianapolis named Josh Weir.

After landing in Miami, I took a cab to the hotel the federation had booked for my layover. Art deco with a marble entrance, it was unusually upscale relative to where we typically stayed. I unpacked and walked down from my room to a small secluded pool. A gentle, humid breeze blew through the palms and with a flash of surreal, doubling insight which rendered life cinematic, it seemed that I had finally become what I'd so desperately wanted to be. Both more me *and* less, I'd escaped the stifling boredom and tedium of my hometown and seemingly succeeded in becoming something of my own making.

The next morning I ate breakfast alone, packed my things, and met Josh and our coach at the airport. By the time the three of us had cleared customs in Port of Spain, night had fallen and at the curb we were met by someone from the Trinidadian Cycling Federation. Our equipment was loaded into the back of the pickup truck and we set out towards the house we'd be staying at for the next week. As we drove, the four of us talked in the professional shorthand of cyclists the world over – about velodromes, times, and the weeks of racing ahead but also about the proud history of Trinidadian cycling and their star rider of the era, Michael Phillips.

Once we were no longer on the maze of well-lit roads which encircled the airport, it grew darker than anywhere else I'd ever been. To my left and right were expansive fields – the blackness was cut only by the headlights of cars and somehow accentuated rather than lessened by the fires which dotted the landscape burning in old oil drums next to the roadside stands we sped by. The truck's windows were open, and the cool night air mixed with the reggae music on the radio. The two-lane highway was smooth and looked new – or nearly so – but was undivided, and even as cars and buses came at us head-on in order to pass, our driver remained nonplussed and simply continued to ask us about our racing and what, as Americans, we'd heard about Trinidad and its sister island, Tobago.

Here, it didn't seem clear if in this context I was less me or more of who I essentially am – and it's these two views of travel, one in which the individual has to be removed from their environment in order to find him or herself, and the other more contextual one, in which a person is *most* themselves as part of their community, which further illustrate the varied understandings of self commonly at work.

It was after midnight when we arrived at the house where we'd be staying. We unpacked, were shown to our bedrooms, and I quickly fell into a deep sleep. The next morning, we were awoken before dawn by the sound of lug nuts being removed with a pneumatic wrench at the auto garage next door. After breakfast, we assembled our bikes and went for an easy road ride before coming back, changing into our USA Cycling polo shirts, and setting out for the drive back to Port of Spain for an interview we were scheduled to do on a television talk show.

In the daylight the city was larger than I'd realized the night before. On one side of the city, towering apartment blocks were pushed up against a mountainside lush with vegetation, while on the other, a band of high-rises formed a gentle arc along the crescent of coastline which touched the deep-blue ocean water.

The television studio was small but well appointed. As Josh and I were mic'd up, we were told by the production assistant that the host – a woman in her forties with a broad, friendly smile – was the Trinidadian Oprah. We were the second guests to be interviewed. The first was a high-ranking traffic official who'd implored the public to drive safely on Trinidad's roads – validating my assessment of what I'd seen the previous night on the highway.

When it was our turn, we emerged from the relative darkness into the bright lights of the stage facing a small studio audience. In her thick Caribbean lilt, our interviewer was interested in both us and the event, but it was what she'd said when we'd first walked on the stage that had mattered to me: she'd proclaimed exactly who and what I was, an 'American cyclist.'

In some ways this was all I'd ever wanted, and for the rest of the day I rolled the phrase over in my mind – *American cyclist* – trying it on and feeling the limits and contours of the label, a nationality I'd mostly taken for granted conjoined with my sport. Nothing more, but also nothing less than an identity.

In many ways more intellectually far-reaching than her partner Sartre, near the end of her life Simone de Beauvoir wrote, 'If you live long enough, you'll see that every victory turns into a defeat,' and as the years passed, my victory of recognition and identity undoubtedly followed de Beauvoir's prescient trajectory. Who or what does one wish to be recognized as and, most importantly, *by whom*?

In Trinidad, the racing itself went well. Motivated by

hearing complaints that USA Cycling had insulted the event by sending riders who were just out of the junior ranks, both Josh and I medaled against the international field in front of the packed velodrome. For years I believed that there would be some point in the future when my internal tension would be resolved – when at long last the ideal of who I wanted to be would square with reality, and that point in time had a name: *happiness*. However, it never arrived. To fulfill any notion of 'becoming someone' invites an inexplicable hall of mirrors and reduces 'you' to a concept which reveals the baselessness at the essential core of ourselves.

With his typical humor and clarity, Alan Watts talks about the modern notion of 'finding yourself,' describing it as peeling layer after layer of an onion, only to find – either to your horror or delight – that it has no core. I'd become part of a system far bigger than myself and by so doing, become seen as I'd always wanted to be seen, but now that I had I wasn't sure what to make of it.

You remain forever blind to yourself, but at least there's a degree of solace and sense of agency in the fact that you can choose the circumstances – the people and systems – that you deem the most valuable to tell you those things about yourself that you could never know first-hand. If nothing else, at least, I was an American cyclist.

Φ

For the next hour Highway 1 is desolate. Rolling green hills on one side, the ocean on the other, and only the errant car or camper van making its way along the coast. As I scan the road in front of me for glass, nails, or anything else that would puncture my tires, my mind wanders. Suddenly, behind me, there's the telltale sound of rhythmic hissing and I look back to see that one of the riders with us has flatted. Jackson, Zach, and I double back to see if he needs help but by the time we reach him, he's already pulled his rear wheel from the dropout and begun to unseat the bead of the tire from the rim. His clean, white Trek rests in a soft patch of grass by the side of the road and he offers a contrite apology for the forced stop. 'It happens,' Zach says, unconcerned. The inner tube is swapped, the tire inflated, and we set off again. After the stop my legs feel heavy and it takes a while to find my rhythm again. Afraid of bonking, I eat a banana and finish what remains of the tepid energy drink in my water bottle. The shoulder widens and, rather than ride single file, we form a group several riders wide.

The first thing you notice about riding in the peloton is the uncanny silence. Enveloped in the slipstreams of other riders, the noise of the wind abates – replaced by the characteristic hum of the supple cotton casings of racing tires. Like a school of fish or a murmuration of starlings, a field of skilled cyclists is comprised of individuals – each with his or her own role – and yet moves and acts as one.

Not just within the same team, but even among riders from different teams, temporary strategic alliances form and pass organically. If a group of riders has broken away from the field, those teams that are not represented in the move will go to the front, raising the pace and expending more energy as they cooperate in a short-term alliance which will end as soon as the shared interest of catching the breakaway has been fulfilled. An astute rider isn't merely strong, but understands the motivations of the different teams and riders like chess pieces spread out across the tarmac or boards of a velodrome. A series of if-then statements transpire over the hours of the race, predicated not just on the rider's physical attributes but how and when they are likely to use their strength as they act and react to the ever-changing choices of others. Races unfold according to predictable patterns which come to be understood intuitively – or as riders and team managers say, a rider can learn to 'read' a race. Influenced not just by the riders and teams, but by wind and topography, a seasoned rider can often know from the opening kilometers how aggressive a race will be and who is motivated and fit enough to be a protagonist on the day. While it may appear as if riders are simply pedaling along, every rider on a team has a specific role to play.

Unlike the immediacy of catching a ball or scoring a goal, tactical decisions evolve gradually with a graceful elegance spanning minutes or even hours. For the brave rider who has gambled with a breakaway, their strength plays out against a backdrop of time, and it's difficult to know at the outset if their decision will pay off or if they will be engulfed by the raging peloton in the closing kilometers and rendered anonymous once again.

This sort of gut-level intuition for who will do what and when used to strictly reside in the riders, but now with race radios and live feeds of the race being beamed in real time into the team cars which follow the races, it has largely shifted to team directors like Jackson. Not just who the team's leader is for a given event (though such things are usually obvious), but also when to attack and how, and which of the other riders are in difficulty are all broadcast into the ears of the riders from the almost omniscient vantage point of the team car.

A long tradition on any group ride is to sprint for city

limit signs, and as our small group approaches the final kilometer before the green sign which designates Santa Cruz proper, I wonder if that will be a game we play today. I look around for telltale signs: the repositioning of the hands, taking a sip from a bottle, or the shaking out of thighs, but see nothing. As what's called a pure sprinter – an explosive rider who struggled to even make it to the finish if there was a single hill – it was the final focused minutes leading into a sprint that I enjoyed the most.

As a sprinter, you learn to be patient. You watch and wait, biding your time as the race unfolds over the span of hours – breakaways going clear and being caught, selections being made – all the while attempting to preserve your energy for the all-out frenetic effort of the final sprint. You seek shelter in the field and intuitively know that every bit of energy you expend not only risks your being dropped, but also saps some unknown amount of power from your sprint.

Once the desperate clawing of simply staying with the group is behind you, you begin to smell the finish line and the roles are reversed. The tactics of attacks and breakaways having already played out on the road, prey becomes predator, and if the legs are good and you know you are in contention for a victory, a switch is flipped. In the closing kilometers, your awareness both widens and narrows, pain lessens as adrenaline floods your bloodstream. Focused intently on the wheel in front of you, the distinctive sound of gears being shifted under heavy pedaling is amplified by the deep section carbon rims of race wheels, and even if you can't see them, you learn to sense the riders around you – turbulent air over your arms, or a shadow under your elbow. Fully present, you adapt to the flux of the situation, surfing from one wheel to the next and guided primarily by instinct, you carefully measure your effort such that you have nothing remaining at the precise moment you cross the finish line.

As the city limit sign comes into view, I estimate that it's about 250 meters away but we're riding into a slight headwind, so it's best to wait as long as possible before starting to sprint. Biding my time, 200 meters quickly becomes less than 175. Suddenly, Zach stands and starts to accelerate, and for a stroke or two I match him, but rather than sprint, I begin to laugh at the pantomime of our former seriousness. I feel another rider on my hip – Jackson, or maybe Matt – but overcome by laughter, I sit up as the playful sprint unfolds in front of me. The rest of the group rolls by me, sprinting like we had so long ago, but now understanding that none of it had ever meant what we'd once thought.

Φ

Although Jean-Paul Sartre and Albert Camus are often lumped together by the broad brush strokes of posterity, it was the striking differences between their approaches and temperaments, which began to reveal to me the true limits of philosophical thought.

Beginning in the late 1930s, the pair began to review one another's work admiringly before meeting for the first time during the summer of 1943. A friendship born of mutual respect quickly developed between the working-class, Algerian-born Camus and the *haut bourgeois* Sartre. Though both nominally existentialists – with the requisite shared concerns for freedom, agency, and the creation of meaning in the face of life's absurdity – in many other regards, the two men couldn't have been more different. While Sartre is noted for physical unattractiveness, Camus was dashing and well dressed. Bogart-esque, in photographs he can be seen flashing a warm, knowing smile as a cigarette dangles from his mouth. Unsurprisingly the media adored Camus, and along with Sartre and de Beauvoir, he came to represent existentialism in the popular post-war mind.

Some five years before the two first met, Camus concludes his largely positive 1938 review of Sartre's novel *Nausea* in a fashion which foreshadows the future differences between the two men, writing that the various threads, 'don't add up to a work of art: the passage from one to the other is too rapid, too unmotivated, to evoke in the reader the deep conviction that makes art of the novel.' Here, one senses Camus' awareness that, though undoubtedly well crafted, Sartre's fiction merely exists in order to illustrate his abstract philosophical thinking, whereas Camus – though certainly philosophically educated, was first and foremost a novelist and prose stylist. Rather unlike Sartre, Camus' primary concern wasn't untying the Gordian knots of metaphysical philosophy, but rather with explicating the irreducible contours of the particular.

This difference in approach is as significant as it is because, following both Nietzsche and Heidegger, I was left with the sense that any future attempt to unwind the rational, metaphysical project on its own terms – from within – would have to successfully deliver me from the false and destructive promise that rationality alone could save me. It appeared that for the philosophers who came after Nietzsche and Heidegger the 'answer' lay not in more philosophical thought as I found in Sartre, but in a new kind of art or poetic practice grounded in a deep reverence for the particular. It seemed that after the self-described 'dynamite' which was Friedrich Nietzsche, a new definition of what philosophy is and seeks to accomplish was required. Counterintuitively, in the wake of Nietzsche and Heidegger, Camus is a successful 'philosopher' precisely by no longer trying to work directly within the traditional limits and terms of philosophical thinking.

Even beyond these matters of philosophical approach, Sartre and Camus also had wildly differing emotional sensibilities and as clichéd and exaggerated as it is, it's largely owing to Sartre that you find the existentialist trope of sadness as a badge of honor – a sign of resistance against the stupidity and cruelty of the world. From the frontman of The Cure, Robert Smith, to the wisdom that *alles ist scheiße*, there's the pervasive thought that if this state of grinding misery is what modern society has delivered us to, then it's only responsible to want no part of it. Somehow implicit in saying yes – in being happily an insider – is a lack of awareness, a tacit acceptance of not just stupidity, but even the world's cruelty which to me often felt like a betrayal of the suffering which was everywhere for those with eyes to see it.

In the face of this crushing weight, cycling often seemed superfluous and silly. How utterly pointless that I'm paid to ride my bicycle along with a hundred or so other people and, moreover, that we all so badly want to complete an arbitrary distance before the others.

Stripped of the thin veneer of its socially given meaning, much of the world becomes not merely pointless, but in the fullest sense of the word, *absurd*. I bristled against all the lives I wasn't living – the innumerable versions of myself I'd sacrificed on the mantle of becoming a bike racer. However, while it's easy enough to say that you don't want to piss your life away on nonsense, far more than Sartre, Camus emphasizes that the more difficult task is that of determining for yourself what exactly *isn't* nonsense. In some ways everything is, and there's a deep wisdom – and even bravery – to embracing frivolity rather than standing in the corner and rejecting life out of principle; it's this key difference of temperament, even more so than their relative literary merit, which seems to distinguish Camus from Sartre.

Tellingly, by 1951 with the publication of Camus' *The Rebel*, the two friends split once and for all – Sartre feeling that Camus' nonviolent political commitments were insufficiently radical and that for the far left to succeed, violence would be a necessary step in the path towards the sort of social justice and freedom which both men craved so deeply. Even in this split, we can discern the same fundamental contours of their differences: on the one hand, the humane Camus, and on the other, Sartre's uncompromising commitment to certain ideological positions which from beginning to end characterized his life and work.

The two men would never communicate again and, only nine years later, at forty-six years old, Albert Camus was killed in a car accident – having decided at the last minute to travel to Paris by car rather than by train. In a stroke of cruel absurdity, his unused train ticket was found in his pocket. Also in the car was the beginning of a sprawling autobiographical novel which Camus anticipated would be his finest work. Upon his death, his former friend Sartre wrote affectionately of him:

He and I had quarreled. A quarrel doesn't matter – even if those who quarrel never see each other again – just another way of living together without losing sight of one another in the narrow little world that is allotted us. It didn't keep me from thinking of him, from feeling that his eyes were on the book or newspaper I was reading and wondering: 'What does he think of it? What does he think of it at this moment?'

Inescapably alone, we're always asking the world who and what we really are while not fully trusting its answers. Like being trapped within the confines of a language which only you speak, we're never able to fully grasp the emotional experience of any other person except by imperfect analogy. No matter how much you love someone, you're at best clunkily translating their sufferings and joys in terms of your experience rather than theirs. However, the greater your emotional imagination, the more this solipsistic gulf is bridged. Only empathy of this sort can hope to blot out the otherwise intractable horror of the loneliness from which so many spend the better part of their lives attempting to flee.

Φ

As both an athlete and an individual I gradually came to understand my every action in the light of not merely seeking validation, but as a plea for insight as to the very nature of my existence. My desire to be something or someone written in my ambition on the bike and off, it seemed apparent that there is no such thing as knowing either yourself, much less someone else, disinterestedly – as they 'really are' – and everywhere I turned, it felt as if I was in a hall of mirrors not of my own making. Yet, it still felt that deep down I was *something* or *someone*, and while I couldn't bring myself to subscribe to the notion of creating or finding some true self, at least there was some part of me which remained just substantial enough to resist such vapid solutions.

Some thinkers deliver you to new ways of framing your very existence, but for me, Sartre only articulated my greatest fears without offering a glint of hope for even temporary redemption. Even though Sartre's *diagnosis* of the experience of what it is like to live in a world which has been stripped of meaning seemed accurate, his *reaction* – to recoil in nausea at the bare facts of existence – has always struck me as merely a matter of temperament. If the role of the philosopher is not to just diagnose, but to treat spiritual sickness, then Sartre seems sorely lacking. Perhaps in my Americanness, I continue to see freedom and possibility as inexorably intertwined and, because of this, have difficulty in traveling fully down Sartre's path; or perhaps I remain, to my core, too committed to the Nietzschean ideal of being someone who can look existence in the eye in all of its horror and still say *yes*. Rather than succumb to the seeming nihilism and intractable solipsism of Sartre's way of thinking, it seemed possible that with a different, more optimistic, outlook, one might interpret his diagnosis not as the curse Sartre describes, but as a gift which would have been inconceivable to any past generation.

In sharp contradistinction to Sartre, in Albert Camus we find *joy*, and Camus concludes what is perhaps his most well-known nonfiction work, *The Myth of Sisyphus*, with exactly this sort of 'happiness in spite of':

I leave Sisyphus at the foot of the mountain. One always finds one's burden again. But Sisyphus teaches the higher fidelity that negates the gods and raises rocks. He too concludes that all is well. This universe henceforth without a master seems to him neither sterile nor futile. Each atom of that stone, each mineral flake of that night-filled mountain, in itself, forms a world. The struggle itself towards the heights is enough to fill a man's heart. One must imagine Sisyphus happy.

Here, Camus' Sisyphus doesn't merely endure his fate of never-ending futility, but in the most radical act of self-creation imaginable, finds a way to do so *joyously*.

It seemed that this was the only task – the only sort of understanding – which was truly worthwhile. With this feat of joyous acceptance, all the tensions and contradictions would resolve and, like Dante emerging from hell, I'd be able *to once again, behold the stars*.

Chapter 7

The Retreat of Perfection

> *Philosophy: a route of many roads leading from*
> *nowhere to nothing.*
>
> —Ambrose Bierce

Once we reach Santa Cruz, Highway 1 turns into a crowded surface street, filled with cars, stoplights, and pedestrians. Located on the northernmost crescent of land which forms Monterey Bay and cut off from the Silicon Valley by a winding mountain highway, Santa Cruz feels a world away from the rest of the Bay Area. While the University of California sits on a hill high atop the city, along the main drag of the downtown, Pacific Avenue, nestled among artisanal coffee shops and boutiques, are head shops that sell bongs, tie-dyed tee shirts, and black-light posters of Jim Morrison and Bob Marley. During the summer and through the fall, the echoes of bongo drums reverberate through narrow alleys infused with the acrid stench of urine. In every way, and for reasons both good and bad, people find their way to West Coast cities like Santa Cruz.

This isn't just the city where I met Denika and went to university, it's also where, when I was no more than six or seven years old, I met my paternal grandfather for what was both the first and the last time. We only called him Ed. Now all I can recall are fragments: a long, unkempt beard, a homeless shelter, seeing my father cry for the first time, and what I know now is the smell of alcohol on the breath of an old man I'd never met before. My family rarely spoke of the details but I've always imagined the worst when it came to my father's childhood. Perhaps, given everything, my father had done the best he could, and I wondered if what they say is true – if pain could be inherited. If trauma could be passed down not just through emotional habit, but more literally imprinted upon the DNA which moves from one generation to the next. Ed died shortly after I saw him in Santa Cruz. And while I know that as his only surviving child, my father had dealt with the logistics of having his body cremated, to say anything more would be melodrama, speculation, or both.

Our small group of cyclists briefly skirts an industrial area of the town before turning onto West Cliff Drive, which circuitously traces the irregular contours of the eroding coast. On one side, tall two- and three-story beach houses rise to overlook the ocean, while on the other, a broad strand is filled with walkers, surfers, and people precariously piloting rented beach cruisers. Looking inland towards the neighborhood, I'm able to ever so briefly glimpse the street where Denika had lived when we first met. Like it was yesterday, fragments come rushing to me: kissing her under the yellow light of a streetlamp; and how, dressed up like an angel for Halloween with white muslin wings against her olive skin, she'd pushed through the throngs of people who'd crowded the downtown, glancing back over her shoulder expectantly to check that

I was still following her. The early, electric months, during which we'd discovered one another had all taken place here.

With smiles and waves, the other riders who've joined us turn off into a parking lot to meet the family or friends waiting to drive them home. Fully trusting in how Jackson and Zach ride, I relax slightly now that it is just the three of us. Without so much as applying pressure to the pedals, we easily glide by the slow-moving stream of cars – weaving in and out as if we're making our way back to the peloton through the race caravan. Gauging my reflexes, I can sense that I'm too tired and not as mentally sharp as I want to be. Before I can see it, I hear the sound of the roller coaster at the Boardwalk, the rhythmic clickety-clack of it climbing the wooden trusses, followed predictably by the riders' screams.

Riding quickly, we make our way past the beach volleyball courts and the electronic thumps and chirps emanating from an arcade. Embedded in the road are train tracks which I'm mindful to avoid. Another road converges with ours and we merge in with the steady stream of cars and buses filled with tourists. My attention elsewhere, I forget about the tracks and allow my narrow tires to become lodged in the channel where the rails run. I try to shift my weight on the bike in order to change direction, but it's too late. Unable to remain balanced on the bike, time seems to slow down as I realize what is happening. As the ground approaches, I have time to run through a series of thoughts: *disbelief, annoyance*, but more than anything else, *not this shit again* – and still clipped into my pedals, I come crashing down on my hip, knee, and elbow. My body pulses with adrenaline. I can't remember the last time I've fallen – at least ten years ago. Ahead of me it takes several seconds for Jackson and Zach to realize what's happened. I stand and assess the damage to my bike and body. My shorts are torn and my hip and elbow have begun to bleed. My shift lever, saddle, and shoe seem to have taken the worst of the impact and are now disfigured from their previously pristine state by the rough pavement. A skateboarder with long blond hair calls from the sidewalk – asking if I'm okay before offering the obvious advice that 'you need to watch out for the tracks.' Before they even reach me, I remount my bike and rejoin Zach and Jackson. My left shifter has been pushed over by the impact, and as I reach down to bang it back into place, I realize that the palm of my left hand is also covered in blood.

'Fuck this,' I think. What am I doing here rather than at home with Denika and Graeme? I feel as if I've let my friends down – none of this was supposed to be dramatic or difficult precisely because we all – at least in theory – know what we're doing. Just as I had when I was hurting the worst in a race, I suddenly want out, and I contemplate calling Denika and going home. Logistically it wouldn't be hard, we've ridden back south and from where we are, she's less than an hour away by car.

Surprised, but without reproach or admonition, Jackson and Zach ask if I'm okay. I tell them I am, but we've all been here before and they know I'm lying. 'Less than twenty more miles,' Zach says encouragingly, 'no problem.' And so I do the only thing I know how, I keep riding. This ride no longer holds the promise of being as I'd imagined, but I'm also not going to allow myself to give up.

Φ

Superficially, the concept of *perfection* as something to strive for and work towards seems straightforward enough, invoking images of gleaming *concours* cars, flawless gymnastics routines, and picture-perfect families. Throughout much of my life I've been at once spurred on and plagued by notions of the perfect. A handmaiden to America's Horacio Alger myth of self-betterment, wherever the idea of perfection has taken root, it posits that there is a gulf between the world as it is, and the world as it *should be* which can be traversed by one's unwavering grit and tenacity. It's easy to believe that there will be some point in the future when the internal tension is resolved – when at long last the ideal of who and what you want to be will square with reality. It is here, on the matter of material success and perfection as they relate to pressing spiritual and existential questions, that the great American Jazz Age novelist F. Scott Fitzgerald was at his most perceptive – perhaps more so than many philosophers.

Often derided for his apparent obsession with the rich, for me – even more so than his contemporary, Hemingway – Fitzgerald remains the quintessential American novelist. Throughout his work, he understands that it is only after having achieved material success that the American psyche is willing to confront the deeper issues of what a good life might consist of. In a nation which has always been obsessed with doing, progress, and achievement, existential questions are held in a strange sort of abeyance – *After x, y, or z has been achieved, then I can think about what my life has meant.* By depicting the affluent however, Fitzgerald removes all of the practicalities and material striving which stop so many from ever confronting ultimate issues. Revealing himself to be an existentialist on par with de Beauvoir or Camus, Fitzgerald writes of the autobiographical protagonist

Amory Blaine in his 1920 debut, *This Side of Paradise*, 'it was always the becoming he dreamed of, never the being.'

Wanting for little materially, Fitzgerald's characters are forced to face the basic facts of their existential condition in a fashion that we see repeated throughout American celebrity culture. From Jim Morrison to Marilyn Monroe, to Kurt Cobain, there's a telling and uniquely American fascination with those who seem to 'have it all' and yet still self-destruct, which shatters the pervasive fiction – the lie that so many of us use to get through the day – that happiness lies on the other side of achievement. What did they see, we are all left to wonder – those who 'had it all' and still said no to life? And, though I grew up far from the affluence portrayed in Fitzgerald, as I thought about my attraction to perfection, this desire to transcend the burdensome decay of the material world was something I understood to my core.

Overwhelmed by the ephemeral beauty of life, it felt as if everything I cared for most was always slipping through my fingers. I pined for the permanence of perfection, for a protected and unchanging life under museum glass. I didn't just intellectually understand philosophy's enchantment with the rarified and abstract, but also the emotional pain which underpinned the entire idea of metaphysics – of unseen and intangible things and ideas, forever safe and more perfect than that which we can see, hear, or touch. Caring about the state of material things never felt like an end but a means – a way to make the stuff of the world go away so that I could finally devote all of my attention to the transcendental things which truly mattered. Seduced by the promise of thought, I imagined perennially clean houses, immaculate bikes, and gleaming cars – a material world so perfect that it would never trouble or distract me from what truly mattered. As the river of life rushed by, perfection stood on the bank like a fiery beacon of salvation and I longed to one day relax into its calm embrace.

Scratches, flaws, imperfections, and decay were all hallmarks of not just my own failings, but the ultimate futility of life itself, and I remember the elation when in late December or early January I'd walk into a hotel room at the first training camp of the year and see bags of new clothing, helmets, and luggage at the foot of my bed as gleaming new bikes were being assembled outside by the mechanics. Perfection held the hope of a certain sort of calm completion and there were many days when, after a hard morning of training, I'd return home, clean the house, wash my bike and kit, and it was then and only then – with crumb-less countertops and a chain that sparkled – that I could truly feel at peace. At least for a while, I'd held the chaos of the world at bay. As the saying goes in German – tellingly evoked for everything from calming a crying child to consoling a friend, 'Alles ist in Ordnung' – literally, 'Everything is in order.' Once I developed eyes for it, imperfection was everywhere, and I had the feeling that only my unremitting vigilance stood between me and the world as I knew it falling apart. Letting go meant decay and chaos – nothing less than the death and rot of everything I had and was.

However, there was always a fine line to be walked between striving to be perfect without going too far – without becoming *a perfectionist*. One had to aim towards perfection without the pursuit turning on itself, and like many traits – particularly 'neurotic' ones – I sensed that there was also something very gendered about being a *male* perfectionist which I disliked and actively wanted to resist. Among men, perfectionism seemed cold and sterile in its valuing of things over and above not just ideas, but people. Emptiness is filled with spotless garages, shiny but impractical cars – perhaps a watch collection – and in its performative predictability and seeming lack of insight, this was a stock figure I desperately wanted to avoid becoming. I wanted perfect things not as an end, but as a means to never have to worry about things again.

It was more than mere control over things I craved, and I wondered what exactly this thing was that I wanted so deeply? Just what was *perfection*? Was a chip in the paint-work the point at which I deemed something 'imperfect'? What about a bit of lint embedded in the clearcoat of an otherwise pristine frame? Deep down I knew that the very idea of visual perfection was a perspectival fiction. Under a microscope or in the right light, no matter how seemingly flawless an object, there were faults to be found. In reality, nothing is in fact perfectly ordered and uniform on every level; perfection was only an arbitrary demarcation – not a state, but merely a matter of degree and vantage point.

The more I tried to truly understand what perfection even was, the stranger and more elusive it appeared. As we've already seen, to the Platonic mind, the perfect ideal exists only in the realm of the forms. Removed from time and space, the forms remain forever the standard for not just all objects in the world, but for all concepts. Aspiring towards 'goodness,' 'truth,' or 'beauty,' one had to have an ideal of perfect goodness, truth, or beauty as their ultimate standard or the very notion of these concepts collapses. More than simply being separate from the visible world, ideals are north stars which will forever guide humanity towards an ever-retreating horizon of perfection.

Much of this thinking was taken over by later Christian theologians and philosophers for whom the very idea of perfection was inexorably bound up with the being who is lacking in nothing and thus the embodiment of every conceivable sort of perfection: God. Here perfection isn't simply that which is free from error, it is also entirely *complete*: deficient in nothing and wanting nothing more. There is the idea that perfection isn't just removed from a sloppy contingent reality, but also self-sufficient. What does 'self-sufficient' mean in this context? It means that at the end of all the contingent events which have led the world to exist as it does – the chance meeting of one's parents, stretching back to the formation of the universe itself – there was something, some preceding cause, which allowed these events to take place: C following B following A in an endless regress. But among medieval theologians and philosophers (who were essentially one and the same) perfection – and thus God – is that which requires no other cause, the *un-caused cause* which set in motion all that is and could ever be.

At this point, it would be easy to object – to see discussions of God and perfection in the same light as the famously derided medieval question as to how many angels can dance on the head of a pin, but I found that precisely because it was so foreign to me, stepping into the logic of these figures was enticing. Like playing intellectual dress-up, attempting to truly comprehend the medieval and early modern ways of understanding the world induced a strange vertigo which revealed the true force and possibility of ideas and showed that in another life my ways of seeing the world might have all been otherwise.

This linking of God and perfection is most clearly expressed in what is commonly termed the 'ontological argument' for the existence of God. Derived from the Greek, ὄντος, ontology is the study of existence in the broadest sense, and the ontological argument is among the many so-called rational proofs (which as purely logical, don't require investigation in the world) put forward for the existence of God. Most famously formulated by Saint Anselm of Canterbury, the ontological argument attempts to rationally demonstrate the existence of God by claiming that God is the most perfect being conceivable and that human beings innately possess such a notion of perfection. From this definition, Anselm makes the case that existence is more perfect than nonexistence, and therefore if we have an idea of God in which God doesn't exist, we have introduced an internal contradiction of logic: if God doesn't exist, this means that we still retain a notion of a being more perfect than this nonexistent God – namely, one that exists. To avoid logical contradiction in terms of our idea of perfection, Anselm thus 'proves' the existence of God.

There are no two ways about it – this logic is exceptionally foreign to our sensibilities. However, on its own terms, it also remains oddly difficult to fully refute. The ways of understanding reality implicit to the ontological argument serve to illustrate the full extent to which the concepts of perfection, truth, and goodness are all comingled, stretching deep into the recesses of Western thought and continuing to shape how we make sense of the world.

Φ

As the adrenaline wears off, my wounds begin to throb with pain. After what feels like an eternity, we turn onto the street where we have a small guest house booked for the night. A gentle afternoon breeze is blowing and mottled light filters onto the dark pavement through the trees that soar above us. I've ridden down this road before but now, as we look for the address, it seems interminably long. We'd been told that the driveway was steep, but when we turn onto it, we see that it's at least a 30 percent grade and that to simply make it up without falling over will require a final desperate push. We sprint in an attempt to try to run into it with some momentum, but quickly slow to a crawl on the steep pitch and are forced to stand out of the saddle in our smallest gear ratios. Our bikes swaying beneath us, we move to the left and right with the action of our pedaling, all the while trying to keep both enough weight on the rear wheel to maintain traction and enough on the front so that it doesn't lift into the air.

Once we reach the top, we meet the house's owner and are taken to the small suite adjacent to the main residence. It's quickly agreed on that, having fallen, I should shower first. I make my way down a dark hall and into a small bathroom. For the first time I fully survey my injuries. My socks, bib shorts, and arm warmers are all torn and bloodstained – my jersey the only article of clothing that's unscathed. I turn the water on in the shower, strip off my clothes and, with a feeling of satisfaction, throw everything but the jersey into the trash can next to the toilet. Like that, the most glaring hallmarks of the crash are gone. I step into the warm steam and look closer. My hand, knee, and hip are all bloody and as I examine the hip I realize that it has begun to swell, stretching the skin like a sausage in its casing.

I remember Harvey telling me that, as a sprinter, if I didn't crash hard at least once a year then I simply wasn't taking enough risks. For all the pain that had come when I'd stopped racing, I'd at least imagined that I'd never again be in a shower other than my own scrubbing out my wounds – but here I am. I quickly find that I remember the routine of scrubbing out road rash all too well. I wish I had a brush, but my nails will have to do. The important thing is to get the dirt and the tiny black flecks of pavement out of the wounds. I take a deep breath and as I start to scrub the raw flesh, I realize that this fall has ground off a keloid scar from another long-ago crash which up until this afternoon had cut across my hip like the spine of a mountain. Now only a smooth patch of skinless flesh remains and I know I'm done cleaning it out when it begins to weep a combination of dark-red blood and an amber secretion which resembles the nectar of an overripe apricot. Once I've repeated the process on my palm, elbow, and knee, I let the warm water run over my back. In the next room I can hear Jackson and Zach talking and laughing. Long before cycling, I'd been a sickly child who'd spent many days and nights with the shower running in a steam-filled bathroom so as to lessen my bronchitis and even now, more than anyplace the shower feels safe. I take a deep breath and allow the moist air to fill my lungs. I think of texting Denika and telling her but decide against it. I'm continuing on so there's simply no point. I think of my bike with its scratched levers and torn saddle and remind myself that nothing has happened that can't be fixed.

I dry off, join my friends and, for a moment, I feel like I'm sixteen again.

Φ

There is no more central an idea to Judaeo-Christian thought than that of *the fall* – the implicit belief that while life as we know and experience it is painful and flawed, there once existed a primordial moment of perfection and unity. The idea of this original, tragic separation and the longing for a way back permeates Western philosophy. And it was against this backdrop that many philosophers and scientists during Europe's Scientific Revolution came to view the world as having been constructed by a sort of divine and infallible watchmaker who revealed him or herself through the perfection and consistency of the scientific laws which were being discovered at a rapid pace.

From the newly uncovered mathematical order which dictated the motions of physical bodies, to the interactions of substances, and the movement of the stars, the discovery of so-called *natural laws* revealed the fingerprints of an infallible divine creator who had established the order which governs the universe. In figures as diverse as Sir Isaac Newton, Rousseau, and Descartes – who described 'the cosmos as a great time machine operating according to fixed laws' – for this generation of thinkers, nature was simply too elegant to not imply some sort of perfect divine intelligence lurking behind the natural order.

Within this context, religion and science – faith and rational inquiry – weren't at odds as many see them today, but intimately linked. Understanding the world mechanistically didn't reduce it to dead matter; instead each successive discovery illuminated a path back to the mind of God. In this light, even those things and events which appeared evil were accounted for and understood as perfect within a scheme which was incomprehensible to the finite and imperfect human intellect.

However, as early as the French philosopher Blaise Pascal, who lived from 1623 until 1662, what Nietzsche would later call science's 'drive to truth' began to outstrip religion. In practical terms, the idea of a watchmaker made no difference, and as a result it gradually fell away as an unnecessary construct, paving the way for the sort of alienation which would become the central theme of so many existentialists.

As Pascal wrote with a degree of clarity and sober beauty which cuts across the centuries:

> When I consider the short duration of my life, swallowed up in the eternity before and after, the little space which I fill, and even can see, engulfed in the infinite immensity of spaces of which I am ignorant and which know me not, I am frightened, and I am astonished at being here rather than there; for there is no reason why here rather than there, why now rather than then. Who has put me here? By whose order and direction have this place and this time been allotted to me? The eternal silence of those infinite places frightens me.

Pascal was prescient in his insight, and from Copernicus to Darwin, as science slowly edged human beings from any position of primacy, perfection gave way to randomness; to the 'infinite monkey theorem' of the twentieth-century French mathematician Émile Borel, which famously states that given an infinite amount of time, a monkey hitting keys at random on a typewriter will almost certainly produce *Hamlet* before once again returning to gibberish.

From the perfection of ideals standing outside of an ever-changing and corruptible world, we are delivered to a vast and indifferent universe, governed by nothing more than chance selection across incomprehensible swathes of time and space, until the very notion of perfection comes to appear less and less relevant. Perfection gave way to pragmatism – to 'whatever works' – and as we saw in Nietzsche, Heidegger, Sartre, and other existentialists, we are thrown back on ourselves without recourse to ideals.

In all of its forms and permutations, metaphysics is a theme which haunts Western thought, and yet there is no external standard to measure life by – no way for the proverbial cartographer-cum-philosopher to sketch a map of existence which fails to account for him or herself – and suddenly the emotional stakes present themselves in stark relief. Every sunset, every dying flower and lover's embrace is rendered incomprehensibly poignant. Although it appears cloaked in the cool indifference of logic, perfection offers not just a rational standard to aspire to, but an escape from what is perhaps the cruelest fate which befalls each and every one of us: *the passage of time*. Separate and distinct from the changing world, perfection holds the promise of releasing us from the painful, unremitting cycle of birth and death, and it's not an overstatement to say that at its core, perfection's greatest wish is to stop time.

Both standing at what they regard as the end of metaphysics, Nietzsche and Heidegger regard the pre-Socratic philosopher Heraclitus of Ephesus, with his concern for *Becoming*, rather than the fixed abstractions of *Being*, as the touchstone for how the modern individual might overcome thinking which seeks permanence and perfection by locating itself outside of time and space. Unlike other thinkers of his period who sought principles which were independent from the flux of life, Heraclitus saw life as nothing but change, famously saying that 'no man ever steps in the same river twice.' This opposition between the fixed principles of Being and the flux of Becoming reveals both the unique genius of Western metaphysical philosophy as well as its tragic flight from the everyday world which has come to inform the way nearly all of us understand reality and ourselves.

Φ

By the time the three of us start back down the long, steep driveway on foot, the sun has already dipped behind the mountains across the valley. We're all tired and hungry, but with only spotty cell phone service, none of the cars that we've booked to drive us into town for dinner have actually arrived. Once we reach the street, Jackson takes his phone from his pocket and looks down the dark road. He shakes his head momentarily and walks several steps before motioning for Zach and me to follow him.

'Wait, so what are we going to do – just walk to town?' I ask Jackson.

'How long was the road? Couple of miles? We're bound to find one of the guys,' Jackson replies confidently. From his expression, I can tell that Zach is also less than sure, but with limited options and our judgment dulled by our hunger, we begin to walk towards town. In the cheap flip-flops that we've both sent ahead to ourselves, every step is painful for me and Zach, and within minutes Jackson in his sneakers is several strides in front of us. On one side of the road is a dry creek bed lined with ferns, thick brush, and redwoods and on the other, small houses with dirt driveways, and land that was long ago cleared for horses and cows to graze. Within minutes, darkness falls quickly and completely and as we continue on, I realize I can't recall the last time I've been out walking after dark.

Unlike me, Zach's spirituality has coalesced into the vessel of Christian practice and belief. Like all genuine faith, I know he didn't arrive at it easily and, as we walk, we talk about ideas that I understand only in the abstract – grace, forgiveness, and the hand of something or someone benevolent lending purpose to events large and small. In his knowing sort of melancholy, punctuated by humor, I've always understood Zach, and I remember sharing a room the night before a race when we were still teenagers and talking for hours about everything that we already knew we didn't understand and that seemed impossible to ever make sense of. All these years later, I wonder if he's been able to find meaning and peace in a way that I haven't.

As we walk, I think of love and friendship. I try to imagine what Denika looks like, but like everyone I love the most, I find it strangely difficult. I can hear her voice in my head but can only picture a hazy image that I know isn't right at all. Zach turns to me and laughs about what compelled us to follow Jackson, and as a car drives by he sticks his thumb up hoping to hitch a ride, but unsurprisingly the car simply speeds by. More destructive than imposing ideas of perfection on ideas or things is imposing them on someone else. From within the prison of your own concepts, you always see the other not as they truly are but through an idealized lens of your own making, never bridging the gulf that makes life bearable and real love possible. Sartre famously said 'Hell is other people.' I'm sure he was wrong though. I'm certain that if there is a hell, it's being forever trapped in yourself.

Ahead of us, we can occasionally make out Jackson, his silhouette a dark penumbra in the flood of light from the oncoming cars. I'm hungry, my hip is so swollen I walk with a slight limp, and with every step I feel the plastic thong of the sandal dig into the soft flesh between my toes. Above us the stars shimmer in the autumn air owing to some phenomenon which I suspect has a name – but which I'm pleased to find I don't know. I'd always thought that the way towards faith was through thinking but now I mostly know better. Zach and I walk in silence for a moment – but for the crickets – and then overhead we hear the distinctive sound of large wings flapping through the air. Above us, an owl glides across the road and lands stealthily on the branch of a redwood. We stop and look at it looking at us so intently that it's as if the entirety of life itself is gazing back at us through its electric-green eyes. As a car approaches, the owl takes flight again with several powerful flaps of its broad wings, and as we continue to walk, I turn over perhaps the only verse I know by heart, T.S. Eliot's 'East Coker':

Wait without thought, for you are not ready for
    thought:
So the darkness shall be the light, and the stillness
    the dancing.
Whisper of running streams, and winter lightning.
The wild thyme unseen and the wild strawberry,
The laughter in the garden, echoed ecstasy
Not lost, but requiring, pointing to the agony
Of death and birth.

I think of the happiest I've ever been; throwing Graeme in the air in the swimming pool on a hot summer day or the feeling of Denika's warm brown hair against mine. Everything that matters most remains forever shrouded – forever unspeakable. Things rarely teach you what you imagine they will but that's not to say that their lessons are without value. There is no seeing around or over or through. *Things merely are.*

From around a bend, a car approaches and comes to a stop next to us. The window is rolled down and the driver cranes across the passenger seat towards us.

'You Jackson?' the driver asks.

'Yeah,' Zach says, 'you our Uber?'

'Glad I found you. Hop on in.'

Zach and I slide into the back seat of the car. It smells of gum and pop music is playing on the radio.

'Our friend is walking up ahead too,' I say, just as Jackson's figure comes into view through the windshield of the car.

Φ

From gleaming white handlebar tape, to the shiny team cars that followed the peloton, cycling is a thoroughly aesthetic phenomenon. The beauty of the sport is first and foremost visual and predicated not simply upon bravery or athletic prowess, but just as much by the spectacle of the field of riders aboard their perfect, gleaming machines. Upholding this tradition is tantamount to respecting not just the sport in some abstract way, but even an indicator of respect for your competitors. You simply don't show up at a race – no matter how insignificant – with your kit dirty or your equipment in need of maintenance. The day before races, bikes are scrubbed, bar tape changed, race wheels fitted, and new white socks pulled from their packaging with the thought that looking professional is one controllable step in the tenuous path towards actual success.

However, everything looks perfect from far away, and up close I was beginning to see the flaws. I was a bike racer and not a bike collector, and while equipment flowed in a steady stream from sponsors and was well cared for, it was far from unblemished. In Heidegger's sense of the *ready-to-hand*, bicycles came to be tools. The logos of old sponsors were blacked out with Sharpies, shipping and travel left paint marred and scuffed, and my tangible ideas of perfection began to transform into ideas about perfect *races*: technically flawless team pursuits with perfect exchanges and criteriums where not a watt of energy was wasted. This was a sort of perfection that wasn't deadening, abstract, and divorced from life but fully involved. Rather than futile attempts to preserve objects under museum glass or make claim to an ideal conceptual realm which is immutable and immune from the ravages of time, this sort of performative perfection – while ephemeral – was in some ways far more *real*. Like building sandcastles on the beach at low tide, with athletic perfection there is little prospect of fooling yourself into believing that it will last as anything more substantial than a memory.

Slowly, rather than scratches and blemishes, I began to concern myself with diets, with the height and width of my time trial handlebars and the position of my cleats. With analytical decisiveness, I told myself that for every facet of the sport there had to be a *right answer*, and it was easy to believe that there was an ideal position on the bike or a perfect training program.

Step by step I improved but I also realized that it was easy to go too far – to allow an ideal to rule you. Just as I had with philosophy, I was forever searching for something to hold on to and I came to be known as a rider who was 'in my head,' and someone who could easily sabotage himself. Circumstances were never as I imagined – they were always contingent, filled with late flights, rain delays, and lost equipment, and the best riders navigated this uncertainty with an ease and calm acceptance which I was rarely able to emulate. However, it was on those rare instances when I gave up trying to control what happened that I came closest to perfection on a bike.

Now demolished, the National Sports Center Velodrome in Blaine, Minnesota was built for the 1992 Olympic Trials. Every track has its own character, and Blaine, as we called it, with its smooth hardwood surface and elegant transitions from the straight to steep, wall-like corners was the most beautiful velodrome I ever competed on.

It was late spring and the air was already warm and humid when I arrived for a stop in the national series of track races – then known as EDS Cups. My bike bag had been briefly lost by the airline and the trip to the race had felt chaotic, but I'd still been calm throughout the long week of racing. On the next to last evening of racing, we lined up for the finals of what was always my favorite event, the team pursuit.

Four kilometers long – sixteen laps of a 250-meter velodrome like Blaine – each of the four team pursuit riders takes a turn at the front of the group, before slotting back into the final position by steering up the steep track and then back down onto the final wheel. A bit of rest in the shelter of the draft of the riders in front of you and then you hit the front again.

The four of us – with matching bikes, wheels, and skin-suits – take deep breaths on the start line before a series of tones begin which indicate that the countdown has begun. A final higher-pitched beep signals the start. Heart rates skyrocket with the violent standing start, and we quickly form a single-file line low on the velodrome. As we circle the track, the primary sensation is speed. I fixate on the wheel of the rider in front of me and the black measurement line that's the shortest way around the track. In spite of being at my physical limit, in the immediacy of the task at hand, time seems to slow down. Each lap, we hear our time splits called out to ensure that we're riding to our schedule. Colby Pierce – the rider in front of me – is small and folded over into a seemingly impossibly low position which provides me only the smallest of drafts. He pulls off and I take my turn at the front only to swing up through the steep corner and time my descent back down perfectly to re-enter Colby's slipstream, now the last rider in the group. The sensation of speed is amplified by the reverberation of our hollow, drum-like disc wheels and, as we enter each corner, the steep, 45-degree banking pushes us into our saddles and aerobars, and we have to crane our necks against the G-forces. Fourteen laps to go suddenly turns to just eight – only two more kilometers. Still no mistakes from any of us – no stalling out at the front, no sloppy exchanges. As the team circles the track, the hidden trusses which support it flex under our weight and the sound has the quality of an impending wave breaking over the surface of the velodrome. With three laps to go we lose a rider, and I hear my teammate Dave McCook call out 'three, three' so that the next rider can time his exchange and not come down too late. Here was a sort of perfection that wasn't divorced from life – that didn't grasp so tightly that life is turned to stone. Without the anxiety which comes from thought or anticipation, I simply react. Squarely situated in the here and now and deep in the stream and flux of becoming, rather than fearing its impermanence, I enjoy it precisely because it is so temporary. I hear the bell signaling one lap to go and come to the front and give one last pull, pedaling as hard as I possibly can. It's the time of the third rider across the line that counts, so in the final straight we finish in formation – Colby drifting up to my right hip while Dave comes under me. A gun fires as we cross the line and as I ride around the apron of the track, I glance up at the digital scoreboard and see that we've won. Poetry in motion – there is no perfection, only life.

Chapter 8

The Seen and the Known

> Conclusion: The faith in the categories of reason
> is the cause of nihilism. We have measured the
> value of the world according to categories that
> refer to a purely fictitious world.
>
> —Friedrich Nietzsche

As a matter of temperament, I've always been attracted to certain ways of thinking, preferring the sweeping, romantic, and artistic to the more precise work of clarifying language, formal logic, or the elucidation of how it is that scientific modes of inquiry are able to function as they do. For me, philosophy offered not merely the hope of greater intellectual clarity, but of seeing the world anew: flight from – or at least a way to tolerate – the pain of existence. If depression was a function of how I *understood* the world, then the best way to escape it seemed to lie in dispensing with the notions which had brought me such pain and adopting an entirely new – and perhaps less painful – way of understanding existence.

Going back at least to Aristotle however, there's a parallel tradition in philosophy of more analytically minded thinkers who prefer meticulous systematic distinctions to sweeping insights. Motivated by intuitions vastly different from my own, this style of thinking, guided by the north stars of clarity and precision, seeks to distinguish problems which in theory can be solved from those which as a matter of logic cannot, and it becomes a question of intellectual disposition if one prefers to say something limited about a small portion of what it is to be alive, or a great deal more – perhaps too much – in a less exacting fashion.

Although metaphysical ways of thinking are exceptionally tempting, conceptual, abstract ways of understanding ourselves and the world come at a high cost, and the 2,500-year story of philosophy is also one of the discipline's ever-diminishing scope. Time and again, philosophy has been forced to evaluate its reason for being in a way which is unlike any other field, drawing each generation back to the central, swirling question: what is this thing called *philosophy*? What does it propose to know or help one to understand, and by what standard is this understanding valuable? The sciences all have their discrete domains of inquiry, and while there may be territorial squabbles, fundamentally there is little question as to the purpose and scope of chemistry, physics, or biology. Likewise, while art may attempt to speak to the universals of the human condition, it never makes the audacious claim that its insights are once-and-for-all structures which are baked into the very fabric of reality.

As I worked my way through the history of philosophy it became increasingly apparent that among those thinkers who resonated with me most, there was only the thinnest of lines separating the literary artist from the philosopher, perhaps little more than the megalomaniacal desire to universalize his or her vision of the world – to transfigure their idiosyncratic reaction to life into a certain historically determined schema which endows the merely personal with the credibility of universal truth. Unlike science or art, philosophy sought to get behind the world and say something about knowledge and understanding – to articulate existence *in general*, and more and more I wondered if perhaps in attempting to do so, it was unable to really say anything at all.

This picture of philosophy as nothing more than the arc of the metaphysical tradition is far from complete. Running parallel with the rationalist, metaphysical tradition is another, more grounded and tangible understanding of philosophy as a tool to ensure the veracity of what we know, and which sought to explain the explosion of science and our ability to investigate the world. In order to understand what's at stake in these two views of philosophy, it's necessary to return to the seventeenth century and a decidedly British philosophical school called *empiricism*.

Derived from the Greek, *empeiria*, empiricism is historically bound to the idea of practically derived experience which is free from theory and abstraction. Largely associated with the Englishman John Locke (1632–1704) and the Scotsman David Hume (1711–76), British empiricism rejects Descartes' fundamental conclusion that the senses are unable to provide a sound basis for knowledge. From its high regard for plain language to its commonsense practicality, there's perhaps no philosophical movement which so accurately reflects the character and temperament of English-speaking peoples.

Born just outside of Bristol and educated at Christ Church,

Oxford, John Locke not only wrote broadly on philosophy, but was also trained as a physician, and in his political writings provided the conceptual basis for much of modern liberal democracy. Locke's probing intellect was far-reaching and inventive while still remaining grounded in a way which was almost entirely antithetical to his Continental counterparts.

In his 1690 treatise, *An Essay Concerning Human Understanding*, Locke describes human consciousness as an 'empty cabinet' which is furnished only by way of sensory experience. Born blank, we start with sensory input – embodied data – and it is only after experiencing something that we begin to draw abstract conclusions about what we have encountered: that frogs tend to jump or that the sun rises and sets. In contrast to Descartes and the so-called 'rationalists,' who believe that we move from the general to the particular, Locke claims that we move from the particular to the general – that experience leads to abstraction rather than the other way around. While Descartes sought a solid, *rational* foundation for knowledge, for Locke and the empiricists, it's not rational principles which are primary, but *experience*. In Locke's account, the 'self' is fundamentally receptive – a product of the innumerable experiences and sensations of existence but with nothing fixed or substantial beyond that.

Though still nominally religious, for Locke, it's our role as perceivers of the world which births our ideas and hence our very identities. In Locke, there is scarce discussion of the soul or any God-given identity and the self is little more than a combination of sensory knowledge and one's reflections as they relate to that experiential knowledge. Here, for a certain type of modern individual who subscribes to a particular materialist, scientific belief set, this may appear to be a far more 'accurate' worldview than the idealist, metaphysical one. But, as we shall see in the case of Locke's fellow empiricist, David Hume, a generation later, without the mind bringing something to the proverbial party, the seemingly commonsensical empiricist position is ultimately unable to account for the very scientific insights that it initially appears so amenable to.

Born in 1711 in Edinburgh as David Home (a surname which he would later anglicize to Hume), Hume began university at just twelve years of age. Although cryptic as to the precise nature of the experience, when he was eighteen the precocious Hume is said to have experienced a philosophical insight so profound that he elected to apply himself entirely to the discipline.

Following the path of Locke, in his 1739–40 masterwork, *A Treatise on Human Nature*, Hume argues against the rationalist, Cartesian concept of innate ideas, understanding the mind as a *tabula rasa* or blank slate, and the self as little more than what Hume termed a 'bundle of sensations,' which, as a matter of logical necessity can never perceive itself. For the almost areligious Hume, the material world is all there is, and in the most fundamental sense, it is the experience of sensory reality which *orders the human mind*. Neither Platonic ideal nor some fundamental self stands outside of space and time. There are no transcendental ideals to aspire to or measure the world against, only the unremitting stream of our sensory information.

For Hume, these impressions of the world and even one's own body are discrete and atomistic – 'I see a chair,' or 'I feel cold' – and it is the very fact that one's impressions are disconnected which leads to Hume's radical skepticism about causality, and doubt as to our ability to justify the most basic prerequisite for scientific investigation, namely that one event can be said to necessarily follow from another.

Commonly known as the 'problem of induction,' for Hume, causation itself – that one billiard ball colliding with another will cause the other to move – cannot be justified through experience. No number of instances of A 'causing' B can allow us to conclude with the sort of certainty Hume demands that one event *caused* another. As he writes, 'Objects have no discoverable connexion together; nor is it from any other principle but custom operating upon the imagination, that we can draw any inference from the appearance of one to the experience of the other.' According to Hume, so called causation is little more than a 'mental habit' to which we become accustomed – not any sort of fixed law which can be proven through the empiricist standard of experience. There is no reason that in the future, two events which appear to be related (one billiard ball striking another and causing it to move) ought to forever remain in their current configuration. As the British analytic philosopher Bertrand Russell – no friend of idealism or existentialism – says of Hume's position on causality in his sweeping 1945 book, *The History of Western Philosophy*:

Hume's philosophy, whether true or false, represents the bankruptcy of eighteenth-century reasonableness. He starts out, like Locke, with the intention of being sensible and empirical, taking nothing on trust, but seeking whatever instruction is to be obtained from experience and observation. But having a better intellect than Locke's, a greater acuteness in analysis, and a smaller capacity for accepting comfortable inconsistencies, he arrives at the disastrous conclusion that from experience and observation nothing is to be learnt. There is no such thing as a rational belief . . .

Thus, we are faced with the fact that while it might seem that the empiricists with their emphasis on experience and observation are far more scientifically minded, as the mechanistic and often counterintuitive nature of the universe began to reveal itself, the rigid empiricist position that all we know and understand is derived from the senses, in fact becomes less and less tenable.

In spite of the best efforts of the empiricists, the world is once again divided between the conceptual and the sensory – between commonsense, everyday experience, and the unseen but 'really real' world of science and physics comprised of atoms – of planets orbiting and bodies moving according to fixed laws.

In the wake of Hume's seemingly devastating impasse, the problem becomes how to both justify science and allow for the free will of moral action; the answer will come shortly, in the form of a Prussian professor of philosophy living in Königsberg named Immanuel Kant.

Φ

The next morning, I wake up before dawn. The window next to my bed is open and from the redwood forest below I can hear the gentle coos of a morning dove. I try to roll onto my back but find that overnight my wounds have dried and become stuck to the clean white bed sheets. A pang of guilt passes over me with the thought that someone else will have to clean up my mess. I get up and go to the bathroom where I wet a washcloth and try to dab off the amber-colored Rorschach blots left by my road rash, but even with scrubbing, I'm only able to make them ever so slightly fainter. From the living room, I can hear the inflectionless drone of the news reader as Jackson sits listening to the BBC news on his phone. Wars and bombs in places I've never been are followed by the abstraction of all abstractions, financial markets. The Dow, the DAX, and the FTSE up, down, or flat, and I'm reminded that having essentially lived and worked in Europe for more than a decade, Jackson's head remains on two continents.

In the comfortable silence of friends, the three of us shake off sleep, shower and begin to pack our things. There is a thick layer of fog and I step onto the porch feeling the air and peering skyward.

'Legwarmers?' Jackson asks.

'And probably a jacket and full-fingered gloves,' I reply. 'It'll be annoying once it warms up, but it's just too cold.' We kit up, fill our bottles, and methodically stuff a day's worth of bars and gels into our jersey pockets. With a final check that we have everything, we survey the space one last time, get on our bikes, and roll back down the steep driveway. I'm stiff but don't feel as bad on the bike as I'd feared. The road that had seemed so long last night on foot quickly disappears beneath our wheels and we emerge into the town of Soquel.

We find the post office and drop our overstuffed envelopes of dirty clothing in the mail before making our way to a crowded café. Out of place in our cycling kits, we order and eat leisurely at a table next to a window so we can watch over our unlocked bikes. As we eat and sip coffee, Jackson tells us about a rider under his charge – a Kiwi who'd narrowly missed the podium at the World Championship time trial and the sort of numbers he was producing in training for it, wattages that would have been unimaginable to any of us. This elite echelon of the sport is what Zach and I aspired to, but never quite achieved.

The riders that he's worked with on Tour de France-winning World Tour cycling teams exist in a rarified world of Italian sports cars and flats in Monaco, and hearing about this version of the sport is akin to a report back from the moon. As Jackson talks, occasionally sipping his espresso, I'm struck by how abstract my interest in the sport has become. Growing older within the context of a sport is a strange experience, and in what seems like the blink of an eye, the sport's top riders – who for so much of my life were older than me are now for the most part ten or even fifteen years younger. More than talent or luck, its work ethic that Jackson respects, and I'm reminded that he's perhaps the hardest working person I've ever met – someone who was mostly raised by his single father, he's been handed nothing and through sheer force of will has been able to provide for his family through cycling.

In the years after I stopped and Jackson was still racing, I'd often motorpace him through the late winter and into early spring along the back roads that crisscross the rolling hills south of San Jose. With Jackson almost always wearing his national team kit in order to help talk our way out of any chance encounters with patriotically minded police,

I'd drive as Jackson rode only inches from the rear tires of the silver Honda motor scooter. Like tubular tires and riding the rollers, among professionals motorpacing is sacrosanct – its benefits undoubted – but for obvious reasons it's also dangerous, and you have to have total trust in your driver. With a single lapse of attention, you at best ruin a workout, and at worst can cause a catastrophic crash such as the one that killed Eddy Merckx's driver in the late 1960s.

Above the roar of the scooter, everything becomes a matter of instinct, and while sometimes the rider communicates to the driver by yelling 'up' for faster or 'down' for slower, with Jackson there was no need for words, I simply looked in the mirror of the scooter and read his expression and body language with an understanding which was the result of thousands of hours training together. Intuitively knowing just how hard he could go over a given grade, I'd smoothly relax my throttle hand to ensure that I didn't force Jackson over his limit and ruin the effort. The combination of trust, skill, speed, and the success of my friend brought me to the verge of joy; burned into my memory is the strange, redoubling echo that is self-consciousness – not just happiness – but an awareness that in this moment, on this rural road on a beat-up scooter with the wind in my face, I was happy.

It's starting to get late, and with at least seven hours on the bike still in front of us, we take our final sips of coffee, walk past the crowd of families gathered near the door, put on our helmets, and set out for the ride south towards today's destination: Big Sur, California.

Φ

Here it is worth pausing and thinking critically about how the average individual in a modern industrial society conceives of the basic terms of their existence and the strange extent to which this aligns with the sort of naïve empiricism that we encounter in Hume.

Born with a blank slate of a mind encased in a bag of skin, our hypothetical modern person attempts to make his or her way in the world by learning enough about how things function and what actions result in what consequences so as to survive in a hyper-competitive society. The basic conceptual demands placed on an average citizen in an industrial society are not to be underestimated: paying one's bills and taxes, safely operating a car, and somehow earning enough income to survive are far from trivial matters, and in response to these demands a certain worldview is fostered. Implicit in this arrangement is the belief that sensory reality is accurate – that it is *really real*, and the words and images we ascribe to the world correspond to it in some less than arbitrary way. In keeping with Hume, we learn through both our experience, and that which we call *education* – namely the formal, codified experience of others. In a deep sense knowledge *is* power – the ability to predict and understand the behavior of things in the world, and the more you learn about reality, the more apt you are to be 'successful' in every sense of the word. The world orders the human mind, and the more accurate a picture you have of the external world, the more likely it is that you'll be able to exercise control over it.

However, this view of the world – no matter how prevalent or seemingly 'obvious' it may appear – fails under the weight of its own terms; experience alone turns out to be insufficient to account for how we learn and make predictions about even the most fundamental aspects of the world, and it becomes strangely difficult to demonstrate something as basic as one event 'causing' another. Moreover, not only does modern science not operate with the hope of getting at some 'really real' reality, but on a more personal level, I found that conceiving of myself in these reductionist terms left me feeling alone and isolated – in every sense *decoupled* and alienated from the world and my existence – and the question of how it is that we can know what we know comes to the forefront.

Metaphysics isn't simply an escape hatch from an obvious and given reality, but in fact turns out to be necessary for so-called everyday reality to function as it appears to. Thus far we've traced the arc of philosophy through metaphysics, but like two sides of the same coin, it would be equally possible to tell the story of Western philosophy guided by the framing question: *How is it that we can know anything about the world?* It was this question, of knowledge, control, and the extent to which the world corresponded with our perception of it, which in many ways forced philosophy into the abstract, metaphysical back roads and impasses that Nietzsche was so critical of; ironically, getting at the 'really real' quickly leads the rigorous mind away from the sensory world, and as we saw in Descartes, there is the lingering fear that the senses can't be trusted – that it all might be no more substantial than a dream.

In his precision and logical rigor, David Hume brings this tension to a head, showing that a scientific worldview which is grounded only in our senses fails to provide a sufficient explanation for something as basic as causality; in so doing, Hume paves the way for arguably the single greatest philosophical mind to have ever existed, Immanuel Kant.

Standing at the crossroads of modern science and religion, Kant sought to account for the so-called laws of nature while still allowing for the autonomy of individual moral choice. Familiar with British empiricism and Hume's impasses when it came to providing a viable explanation of causality, Kant famously credited Hume with waking him from what Kant called his 'dogmatic slumber.'

Attempting to overcome Hume's so-called problem of induction, Kant inverts the basic formulation of how it is that our perceptions correspond with the world, proposing that the mind is not a blank slate which is ordered by the world, but rather our perceptions of sensory reality are ordered by the mind. For Kant, our brain is always filtering the world through not only our senses, but also through modes of understanding – including causality – which are neither found in the world, nor derived from our sensory experience.

This inversion, which places the human mind at the forefront as an active shaper of reality was nothing less than revolutionary – akin to Copernicus' revolution which placed the Sun rather than the Earth at the center of the solar system; as Kant writes in his 1781 opus, *The Critique of Pure Reason*:

> If intuition has to conform to the constitution of the objects, then I do not see how we can know anything of them *a priori*; but if the object (as an object of the senses) conforms to the constitution of our faculty of intuition, then I can very well represent this possibility to myself.

Certain given forms of human sensibility dictate how we understand reality itself, and it is only with the guidance of the concepts which we bring to the table – what Kant terms 'categories of understanding' – that we're able to make sense of our perceptions and create what we call 'reality.'

Here a thought experiment is useful to help comprehend Kant's radical move. As we know, our vision and hearing are both limited to only narrow wavelengths, but had these organs evolved differently – allowing us to see infrared light or hear higher frequencies – we would have very different ideas about the nature of reality. So too with the categories of understanding through which we make sense of the world. Reality is not fixed, not something 'out there', but something constituted – in the most literal sense, 'informed' – by the structures of the human mind.

For Kant, there is thus no way to get at the 'really real,' and yet he concedes that there indeed are things which exist in the world of space and time that are the root source of our sense perceptions. Kant termed these inaccessible and forever unknowable objects 'things-in-themselves' (*Ding an sich*) writing that, '. . . though we cannot *know* these objects as things in themselves, we must yet be in position at least to *think* them as things in themselves; otherwise we should be landed in the absurd conclusion that there can be appearance without anything that appears.'

In the process of overcoming Hume's skeptical empiricism while still accounting for scientific progress, Kant delivers us back to a cleaved, bifurcated world. On the one side is the seen, phenomenal world of our senses, while on the other are the *things-in-themselves* of what he calls the 'noumenal' world – forever not simply unknown, but in principle *unknowable* objects, which exist, but which we can never have any direct experience of.

In order to understand Kant's position (and not conflate his metaphysics with Platonism) it is critical to keep in mind that Kant's noumenal world is inaccessible to either thought or perception and thus can never serve as any sort of ultimate standard or ideal as Plato's forms had. For Kant, nothing intelligible can be stated about the perception-independent *things-in-themselves*. The rational, knowable world is thus bounded and circumscribed, and in splitting the world as he does, Kant establishes the limits of rational thought and inquiry. As we can never have direct contact with the 'really real' objects of the world we are left with only our limited modes of perception, and as a result must make sense of the world not on ultimate terms, but on all too human ones.

Even more so than other thinkers, encountering Kant changed how I experienced the world. An academic through and through, Kant's writing might be dry and precise, but his central theme is one that felt attractive in its rebellion: *not only are your conventions worthless, none of what you claim as important is even real in the most basic sense*. With the sort of 'nausea' that Sartre describes, the world becomes *weird* in the best sense of the word as you realize that you're not a mere observer but have the power and freedom to be an active shaper of reality; though he predates even the earliest proto-existentialists it's difficult to imagine existentialism without Kant's Copernican revolution which placed the human mind at the forefront. You are not only the world, but the world – as much as we can ever comprehend it – is each and every one of us.

Cutting against understandings of Kant which portray him as an unfeeling Teutonic systematizer is an episode which took place shortly before his death, recounted in Erwin Panofsky's essay, 'The History of Art as a Humanistic Discipline':

> Nine days before his death Immanuel Kant was visited by his physician. Old, ill and nearly blind, he rose from his chair and stood trembling with weakness and muttering unintelligible words. Finally his faithful companion realized that he would not sit down again until the visitor had taken a seat. This he did, and Kant then permitted himself to be helped to his chair and, after having regained some of his strength, said, '*Das Gefühl für Humanität hat mich noch nicht verlassen*' – 'The sense of humanity has not yet left me.' Both men were moved, almost, to tears.

Like the melodic refrain of Beethoven's 'Ode to Joy,' just when it seems that chaos might win out and render all actions futile and all choices relative, the same ancient dualities emerge again and again in the trajectory of Western thought.

Standing with Kant at the edge of modernity, metaphysics reappears like a specter, forever beyond the pale of human comprehension. And, as we regard the arc of metaphysics with Kant, in all of his humanity and pathos, it's worth recalling Schiller's words to the final, choral refrain of Beethoven's 'Ode to Joy':

Do you sense your Creator, O world?
Seek Him above the canopy of stars!
He must dwell beyond the stars.

Life it seems is not just transitory, but fundamentally *incomprehensible*. Always elsewhere. Always 'beyond the stars.'

Φ

From Santa Cruz through the small, farming town of Watsonville, Highway 1 is a proper freeway and too dangerous to ride, so we traverse surface streets and narrow farm roads as we make our way south along the arcing crescent of Monterey Bay. Just south of the town of Carmel-by-the-Sea, we'll rejoin Highway 1, which by this point has once again become a mere two-lane highway, and ride the final forty or so miles into a place which verges on the sacred to me: Big Sur.

As we pick our way through the coastal neighborhoods south of Soquel, I feel a strange sense of intimacy with the families out playing – with the joggers and people mowing their lawns. I'm able to project myself into these lives – to decode the thousand unspeakable signs and symbols adorning things and people I've never met. As we pass a man washing his car, I feel the dizzying 'what ifs' of all the lives I'll never live. The very idea of myself, of the identity I have done so much to cultivate is nothing more than a series of innumerable accidents and feedback loops not of my own making and, for a moment, I feel afraid. Ahead of me, I hear Jackson laugh at something Zach's said but I can't hear what, and seconds later he points out a pinecone in our path and yells 'Hibbs!' to me before deftly flicking it away with his front wheel without so much as slowing down. And, as easily as that, I'm drawn back to the familiar terrain of myself.

Soon enough, the well-kept neighborhoods of Aptos and Seascape give way to a deserted road which skirts the ocean before cutting inland and then delivering us to a broad expanse of freshly tilled fields. But for the occasional tractor, these roads are nearly devoid of traffic, and I find that I'm able to relax, confident that even if we encounter a car, owing to the flat, treeless landscape it will be easy to see and hear it approaching.

We encounter a small ascent and, nearly in unison, all tap our shifters and stand out of the saddle. We'd all grown up with the same cycling heroes, absorbing their movements through countless videos and photographs, and even now, we still move like them on our bikes. Low over the bars with wrists tilted inward just ever so slightly, Jackson and I like Vandenbroucke, and Zach, coiled up – with a lower heel – more in the style of the Swiss time trialist Fabian Cancellara and the powerful German, Jan Ullrich.

The grid of farm roads at an end, we turn right and are thrown onto a busy two-lane highway. Only feet from us cars zoom by, and we intuitively form a single paceline and begin to ride faster simply in order to spend as little time on the road as possible, each of us taking quick, team pursuit-style pulls to maintain our speed. With a slight downhill and a stiff tailwind at our backs, we're traveling at almost the same speed as the cars in the lane next to us. Among nearly every racing cyclist I've ever known, there's a deep affinity for speed and it's impossible not to think of Lawrence of Arabia aboard his motor bike, the Italian

Futurist, Filippo Marinetti – a fan of cycling – who wrote in the movement's manifesto, 'We affirm that the beauty of the world has been enriched by a new form of beauty: the beauty of speed,' or even Aldous Huxley who famously quipped, 'Speed, it seems to me, provides the one genuinely modern pleasure.'

And yet, it's all too easy to take speed for granted. The sort of speed most people experience is mediated – rendered non-threatening by well-appointed trains, jet liners, and luxury cars, which are designed to shelter you from speed's dangers. But on the bike, the sensation of speed is immediate and visceral. Faster and faster, the road disappears beneath my narrow tires as the roar of the wind drowns out everything else. I glance at Jackson's handlebar-mounted computer as he drifts past me and see that it reads 76 kilometers an hour. Coming to the front of the group, I scan the road for debris. Seeing only smooth, black pavement, I shift into my smallest cog, lower my back, and push on. Akin to Graham Greene's account of playing Russian roulette as a teenager simply to feel alive, the risks I once took on descents and in the closing kilometers of races dislodged me from the deadening assessment of life which I seemed to slip into so easily. Lulled out of my complacency by a brush with an oncoming car or nearly falling from a mountain road, my heart would heave in my chest with adrenaline and the whole of the world would suddenly glow with previously unseen possibility.

The descent steepens and, with our largest gear ratios spun out, we all crouch into our top tubes and place our hands on the bar tops going into a 'death tuck' akin to that of a downhill skier. Aerodynamic but with our hands far from the brakes, suddenly we're traveling faster than the cars next to us. I feel the top tube between my knees as I tightly grip the handlebars right where they meet the smooth carbon of the stem. Just after the steepest point I hear Zach yell over the roar of the wind, '94k an hour.'

As we near the ocean, rolling hills give way to the sprawling marshland of the Elkhorn Slough. Graceful, pure-white cranes with stick-thin legs dot the expanse and reeds rise from the darkness of the shallow brackish waters alive with fish and insects. Named after wives, lovers, and mothers, on the ocean side of the road are weathered fishing boats with peeling paint which evoke a bygone maritime culture that's slowly dying out. The shoulder of the road widens, and the tarmac turns to smooth grey concrete as we cross a bridge that spans the mouth of the estuary as it meets the ocean. We round a bend, and the towering smokestacks of the Moss Landing Power Plant come into view – looming like giants over the landscape.

The small towns that run along Monterey Bay – Seaside, Pacific Grove, Carmel, and Monterey itself, feel suffused with history. Compared to the Bay Area they're only sparsely populated, and rather than the business parks and housing tracts of the Santa Clara Valley, the canneries, farms, and back alleys chronicled by John Steinbeck comingle with affluence which has fled the Bay Area in search of solitude. Here the fog creeps inland and cool ocean air drifts through the delicate branches of cypress trees that crane longingly towards the dark waters of the Pacific.

After riding on a frontage road next to the highway for about an hour, we find a bike path that runs parallel to the ocean. Meandering through Monterey proper, we dodge walkers and joggers as we make our way past parks with barbecues and the sounds of children playing, before reaching a harbor with sailboats moored in tidy rows. The air is thick with the smell of stagnant ocean brine and rotting kelp and as we pass a golf course, I glance up: in the distance, the vapor trails of two jet liners have intersected, forming an X in the sky above us – linear and inorganic against the backdrop of wispy white clouds.

At an intersection, we turn off the path and head briefly inland in search of food and something to drink. The fact that Monterey is a former military town brings a calm sense of institutionalized order. The wide streets are quiet, and among the low-slung buildings dressed in muted greys and greens, there's the sense that from taxes, to dental work, to psychotherapy, for those with the means, this is a place where everything is conducted in hushed, assured tones: *Don't worry, we can take care of that*, in a manner so full of sincerity and competence that it can't help but be believed.

Block after block, we pass small office buildings, but nowhere to buy food, until at last we reach a gas station with bathrooms and a small convenience store. We ride into the driveway and dismount – leaning our bikes against the wall that faces the pumps. Hungry but not famished, I watch the bikes while Zach and Jackson go into the store.

'You want anything?' Jackson asks.

'Sure, maybe a Snickers and a Gatorade,' I reply. Jackson nods as he roots through his jersey for his credit card and rambles in, each step resonating through the stiff, carbon fiber soles of his cycling shoes.

While different sorts of people shop at different sorts of stores, go to different schools, and live in different neighborhoods, gas stations remain the great equalizer in America. I stand and watch as people come and go: gardeners in a white pickup truck, a concrete crew, and a woman in a Mercedes with thick dark hair and sunglasses like Jacqueline Onassis. Smelling something, I look down and see a cigarette, its tip still smoldering in the black sand of the ashtray on top of the trash can next to me.

Jackson and Zach return and we fill our bottles and empty the day's wrappers from the pockets of our jerseys into the trash. The familiar sweet citrus taste of Gatorade in my mouth, we get back on our bikes and ride away – once again returned to our own insular world of cycling.

Φ

Kant's Copernican revolution exemplifies why the counterculture found philosophy appealing. When confronting a post-war America which had become stiflingly conformist, the most radical move conceivable was to claim that the very terms of reality itself are far from the givens that they profess to be. Psychedelic drugs were a shortcut to the realization that reality itself is little more than a social construct into which one is indoctrinated, and Timothy Leary's enjoinder to 'Turn on, tune in, and drop out,' suddenly appears to have the backing of an entire philosophical edifice which justifies the assessment that things are not as they appear – that in a very fundamental sense the world is all in your head.

Borne out by modern physics which demands that the observer be taken into account, self and other – observer and observed – always imply one another, reality being far stranger and more counterintuitive than we are led to believe. As an active shaper of reality, we are freed from the common feeling of being a mere cosmic accident, forever separate and destined to roam the face of a foreign planet. Unmoored from convention which demands that we view ourselves as separate and alienated, the social games which had appeared to be reality itself suddenly fall away and new possibilities of living present themselves.

For Californians – both in idealized theory and practical reality – the place which was perhaps most central to ideas of how to live differently was Big Sur. A half-day's drive from both San Francisco and Los Angeles, the nearly ninety-mile stretch of rugged coast where the Santa Lucia Mountains plunge into the Pacific – collectively called Big Sur – came to be a stand-in for escape; a place where, free from the trappings of society, artists could create and people could live simply and sincerely.

For thousands of years, El Sur Grande, as the Spanish came to call it, had been home to Native American tribes – Esselen, Ohlone, and Salinan – and though there was no port and little overland access to the narrow band of coast, it was first chronicled by the Portuguese mariner Juan Cabrillo in 1542. Cabrillo's pilot, Bartolomé Ferrer, wrote of the nearly vertical Big Sur coastline, 'The land is very high. There are mountains which seem to reach the heavens and the sea beats on them. Sailing along close to land, it appears as though they would fall on the ships.' It was owing to this precipitous topography that, but for some sporadic logging and homesteading, Big Sur remained nearly cut off from the outside world well into the nineteenth century. In typically American fashion, it was the construction of a road – in this case, the Big Sur Highway, which later became Highway 1 – which made the area what it is. Completed in 1937, it stretches from Malpaso Creek in the north to San Carpóforo Canyon, near the town of San Simeon, in the south. Cutting into the near vertical cliffs and reliant upon numerous bridges to span creeks and ocean inlets, the winding two-lane road is the only way in or out of this long stretch of coast which lies at the westernmost edge of the North American continent.

By the late 1930s and early 1940s, Big Sur began to attract a new creative class of artists, bohemian intellectuals, poets and musicians, the most famous of whom was the American writer Henry Miller. Miller first rented a cottage in Big Sur in 1942, and in 1944 moved into a cabin on Partington Ridge Road in the heart of Big Sur with his young wife, Janina Martha Lepska – a philosophy student thirty-one years Miller's junior who'd turned down a graduate fellowship at Yale in order to marry him.

Epitomizing the ideal of the simple, bucolic life which Big Sur would come to represent in the popular imagination, Miller described his life there in a 1945 letter to fellow writer Lawrence Durrell:

> I have a wonderful cabin, you know, dirt cheap – ten dollars a month. I have a young wife (21), a baby on the way probably, food in the larder, wine *à discrétion*, hot sulphur baths down the road, books galore, a phonograph coming, a radio also coming, good kerosene lamps, a wood stove, an open fireplace, a shower, and plenty of sun, and of course, the Pacific Ocean, which is always empty ... This is the first good break I've had since I'm living in America. I open the door in the morning, look towards the sun rising over the moun-

tains, and then bless the whole world, birds, flowers and beasts included.

A precursor to the Beat generation of Jack Kerouac, Miller saw American conformity and capitalism as crippling – not just socially or politically, but *spiritually* – and regarded Big Sur as nothing short of sacred, a space free from what Miller termed the '*Air-Conditioned Nightmare*' which he chronicled in a memoir of his cross-country road trip by the same title. Big Sur was an alternative to the vapid capitalist ecosystem comprised of meaningless work and comfortable distraction which was robbing the best and brightest of their very souls. Echoing what Nietzsche with his contempt for the so-called 'herd' might have thought of modern life, Miller bristles at the insipid squandering of vitality that he sees among young Americans:

> Most of the young men of talent whom I have met in this country give one the impression of being somewhat demented. Why shouldn't they? They are living amidst spiritual gorillas, living with food and drink maniacs, success-mongers, gadget innovators, publicity hounds. God, if I were a young man today, if I were faced with a world such as we have created, I would blow my brains out.

And the solution? – to simply opt out of the game that one had deemed a spiritual nightmare. A healthy sense of agency and purpose coupled with the insight that it is society that is sick and not you, compels an escape back to an original, unsullied Eden.

For generations of Californians – myself included – Big Sur became an ideal just as much as a physical place, and the 1960s brought not just Kerouac, but poet Lawrence Ferlinghetti, the famed Esalen Institute – a locus of the Human Potential Movement which focused on the intersection of Eastern and Western religions – as well as Tassajara, the first Zen monastery in the United States.

As both Nietzsche and Heidegger understood, abstract thinking is strikingly devoid not just of the thinker, but also of place, and Big Sur became the Californian equivalent of Thoreau's Walden Pond, Nietzsche's Alps, or Heidegger's famed Black Forest hut in Todtnauberg – a place which was sought out by those who'd come to see through so called 'objective reality' and were now confronted with the stark question: *who am I really?*

But what happens when you realize that the truism holds – that wherever you go there *you* are? Or, even more radically, that there is no self to even discover – that your identity is little more than a hall of mirrors, a conglomeration of all that you've been forced to believe about yourself from others. Stripped bare, it depends on one's temperament if it is horror or elation when you discover that in a fundamental sense it's your mind that's shaping reality. Faced with freedom and terror in equal measure, in the loneliness of alpine passes or along the ragged Pacific, the noise of what Heidegger calls *das Man* – the anonymous, unnamed mass of society which believes that reality is 'out there,' which worships wealth and lives for distraction – retreats into silence.

In many ways less cynical than Miller, it was Kerouac's *Big Sur* – an autobiographical novel written about his escape from the literary spotlight after the resounding success of

On the Road – which has always resonated with me. Cutting against the abstract, detached sort of knowledge which characterizes philosophical thinking, Kerouac writes, 'On soft Spring nights I'll stand in the yard under the stars – something good will come out of all things yet – And it will be golden and eternal just like that – There's no need to say another word.' Later, in a revelatory sentence which shows just how important and sweeping Kant's Copernican revolution was for the counterculture, Kerouac writes even more pointedly, 'because to me the only thing that matters is the conceptions in my own mind, there has to be no reality anyway to what I suppose is going on.'

Big Sur, and all it came to represent, was where I imagined that one could truly be free; a place where all the trappings of society fell away and with a simple pre-reflective elegance, I'd be like a child again. Among the melancholic cries of seabirds, the day would come when I'd slide into what I really was just as naturally as one falls into the gentle embrace of sleep.

Chapter 9

Thinking Through Thinking

> *Thinking only begins at the point where we have*
> *come to know that Reason, glorified for centuries,*
> *is the most obstinate adversary of thinking.*
> —Martin Heidegger

South of Monterey, we enter the small coastal village of
Carmel-by-the-Sea. Full of art galleries, restaurants, and
quaint stone cottages which look plucked from England's
Cotswolds, the actor Clint Eastwood was famously once the
mayor, and from the European cars parked on its streets,
to the stylish couples eating at sidewalk cafés, ostentatious
out-of-town affluence tentatively comingles with the well-
heeled locals – trying to adopt the airs and graces which
seem to assure that come what may, they too will maintain
their slice of the ever-diminishing 'American dream.'

After climbing the steep grade that leads out of the downtown, we're delivered back to Highway 1 which, south of
town, gradually gives way to an open, tidal lowland. Only a
handful of scattered oaks dot the landscape, and a stiff ocean

breeze sweeps through the expanse of golden grass. The road is wide and desolate but for the occasional car which glides by us with a palpable lack of urgency; this isn't a road that leads to jobs, shopping malls, or airports and ahead of us, the dark tarmac extends until disappearing into the haze of the shimmering horizon. Roads like this – where you're able to see unending pavement unfurling in front of you – can sap your morale. In bike racing as in life, there's a certain self-protective wisdom to not knowing what's ahead – to simply dealing with each moment as it comes – and here too much is revealed all at once

Since leaving Carmel behind, we've been talking and laughing. But now, the three of us grow silent and settle into the work at hand at a pace that while not uncomfortable, is just strenuous enough to discourage the additional effort required for conversation. Distance becomes time and, my eyes fixed ahead, I can see the hours stretched out in front of us. Pedaling at the same cadence, my back low and hands on the brake hoods, my lungs fill and empty rhythmically in time with my pedal stroke; a sip of water or a shift in weight on the saddle, but little else as we tap out mile after mile. There remains something highly instructive about the way in which boredom forces you to confront yourself, and these long, prayer-like stretches of doing nothing more than pedaling were once part of my life, honing and strengthening my capacity to be fully absorbed in what I am doing.

Zach comes to the front and, feeling the wind shift, Jackson and I stagger to the far side of the road. I feel the soft handlebar tape under the palms of my glove-less hands and notice that the pavement has changed – at some point smooth black tarmac has given way to the sun-bleached grey of older, rougher chipseal. No matter how hard I try to relax into the sea of reality which surrounds me, my consciousness remains a filter, omitting far more than it takes in, and as the hours pass, we say little to one another. Potholes and glass are pointed out, but each of us is left alone with his thoughts and sensations as we carefully dole out our energy, fully immersed in the task at hand.

In the silence, internal landscapes – ghost towns which I'd long ago vacated to make space for the distractions of everyday life, creep back into my consciousness and I wonder why I ever abandoned them – what, and more importantly *who* had I given up by so doing?

The story of modern life is the slow but relentless spread of the all-devouring logic of capitalism. At first, only things were commodified; later the logic of markets and progress spread into art and culture, until finally it became our very attention which was being bought and sold. Measured by clicks and likes, we flee from ourselves, but these hidden places – reclaimed by the sustained silence of so-called boredom – are nothing less than the mystery of life itself, and as we approach the northern edge of Big Sur, the world once again grows enigmatic.

Φ

Imagine that in the darkness of the night some god or monster who was capable of answering every conceivable question stole into your consciousness and you asked: *Why do I exist? What does life mean? Why is there something rather than nothing at all?* Taking at face value that this being is omnipotent and omniscient, what sort of answers would suffice to make the world *make sense* – to make you feel at home in the world again? Assuming every question was answered, would you still feel in your bones that some sublime mystery remained outside the bounds of what can be put into words?

Cycling had already shown me that when you bring enough care and attention to any task, you realize that what it is to be alive is far more complex than can ever be expressed with words alone, and it became apparent that for me the 'questions' that mattered most were precisely those that were not only unanswerable, but perhaps not even *ask-able*.

Throughout twentieth-century philosophy, we see versions of this divide as to what is worthy of rational discussion play out again and again as the limits of intelligibility are vigorously contested and it's Martin Heidegger's famous 1929 claim that *'Das Nichts selbst nichtet'* – that 'the Nothing itself nothings,' which establishes many of the battle lines. In saying 'the Nothing itself nothings' is Heidegger stating something profound about the nature of existence – about how in our rush to investigate the things of the world we have passed over the most basic question – why is there something rather than nothing at all? Or are such questions merely nonsense masquerading as profundity?

One of Heidegger's most articulate and brilliant critics was the German philosopher Rudolf Carnap. Roughly a contemporary of Heidegger, Carnap became the standard-bearer for a school of philosophy called logical empiricism, and Carnap's conflict with Heidegger exemplifies the differences between the existentialist, romantic worldview, and a more scientific one which has its roots in British empiricism and is oriented around ideas of utility, precision, and progress.

Greatly influenced by Bertrand Russell and Gottlob Frege's

advances in formal logic, Carnap – as well as the other logical empiricists of a group which came to be known as the Vienna Circle – married the clarity of formal mathematical logic with a strong belief in empirical, scientific investigation. With these tools at their disposal, the members of the Vienna Circle aimed to distinguish *sense* from *nonsense* in an attempt to once and for all turn philosophy into a rigorous science and clear from the table so-called 'pseudo statements,' metaphysical speculation which by definition can never definitively be deemed either right or wrong. As Carnap wrote:

> The metaphysician tells us that empirical truth-conditions cannot be specified; if he adds that nevertheless he 'means' something, we know that this is merely an allusion to associated images and feelings which, however, do not bestow a meaning on the word. The alleged statements of metaphysics which contain such words have no sense, assert nothing, are mere pseudo-statements.

For Carnap and other members of the Vienna Circle, it was a travesty that philosophy had failed to make progress for some two and a half millennia, and they sought to transform the field by designating those matters which would, at least in principle, be *solvable*. Their criteria for this – for something to make sense and thus either be affirmed or denied – was twofold: it either had to have logical meaning which could be deemed true or false, or it had to have the possibility of being tested in the world of experience.

Owing to what were then recent advances in logic, Carnap

understood all logical statements as either true or false based on their logical *form* alone – having nothing whatsoever to do with the facts of the world. Here, the classic example of a true statement being, 'all unmarried men are bachelors,' and a logically false one being, 'all married men are bachelors.' The first statement, called a tautology, is true by virtue of only its form – all As are A – while the second is patently false.

Unlike those statements which are either logically true or false, or those claims which can be investigated by science, Carnap claims that statements of metaphysics are simply *meaningless*. Neither true *nor* false, metaphysical statements such as Heidegger's are the result of slippage in language which allows them to take the form of a logical claim without actually being one.

By Carnap's standard of philosophical meaning, Heidegger's assertion that, 'the Nothing itself nothings,' is thus little more than an idiosyncratic bit of poetry which muddies the waters of philosophical inquiry. Tellingly derided by Carnap as a 'musician without musical talent,' he believes that Heidegger and other existentialist thinkers who speak to areas of human experience which are better expressed in music, art, or literature, only distract philosophy from its lone legitimate task: distinguishing sense from nonsense. Had Heidegger presented his work *only* as poetry, Carnap may have an aesthetic judgment as to its quality, but for Carnap and the logical empiricists, the real problem with Heidegger and other metaphysical philosophers isn't one of aesthetics, but that their work is presented in the philosophical form which, by its very nature is making a claim not simply to beauty, but to truth.

When I first encountered Carnap's criticism I didn't know what to make of it. On the one hand, it was compelling in its lucidity, but on the other it seemed to leave so much of what mattered most to me unaccounted for. Perhaps with my interest in questions which I was slowly coming to realize were unanswerable, whatever it was I was seeking was, as Carnap suggests, properly outside the domain of philosophy.

Φ

Once we're past Point Lobos, the vegetation grows denser and the flat, sandy beaches gradually turn to jagged rocky outcroppings that look like something from Bergman's *The Seventh Seal*. Inviting in its silent darkness, a thick pine forest bounds both sides of the road. Years ago, I'd been to this very spot with Denika, and as we ride past, I remember the sweet smell of the pines, the sound of the waves as they crashed against the rocks, and how the sensation of the soft needles underfoot had made the world itself seem far more gentle than it is. As I see it now, I realize that in some ways my fondest wish has always been to disappear into something or someone else – into the darkness of the forest, into the person I love, or to be consumed entirely by the pattern of how someone other than me thinks.

I look down at my legs as they turn the cranks and realize just how little I'm aware of at any given moment. Just as it rains, *it* seems to pedal – and I regard my own body like a spectator. The game that we're all taught to play isn't simply predicated on assuming that you're a passive, receptive subject in a world of objects, but just as much on certain ways of distinguishing the voluntary from the involuntary. We internalize the voices of stern parents and punitive coaches – in both ourselves and others, demanding responsible agents to praise and blame. Right or not – alienating or not – for the game to go on, the conscious and voluntary which we ostensibly control, must thus be differentiated from the involuntary.

At first, the difference between the two seems obvious; we neither consciously beat our heart nor digest our food, but as we consider the arbitrary line between *doing* and *knowing how*, this distinction slowly begins to blur. In strange motels that still vaguely smelled of cigarette smoke, I used to lie on the bed with a heart rate monitor on, slow my breath, and watch my pulse fall – 62, 58, 49 until my heart, with its stroke volume increased because of training, was beating scarcely more than once every other second. Certainly, we can control our heart or breath, but what about blushing or falling asleep? What about loving?

The harder you try at many things the worse the result. Will and consciousness expand and contract until the very idea of agency and volition is drawn into question. The beating of our hearts and the shining of the sun bleed into an undifferentiated field of existence which we're not alien to, but a part of. Recalling how in Sartre's *Nausea* Roquentin recoils at the naked 'is-ness' of the roots of the chestnut tree, at the point where the ordering ego disintegrates, you can react with either terror at the apparent loss of self, or with elation upon discovering that, being everywhere there is in fact no self to lose.

We hit a short, steep descent and I stop pedaling. My freewheel disengages, clicking more and more rapidly until the individual clicks merge into a single unwavering monotone. Almost imperceptibly, a cool headwind kicks up and as I begin to pedal again, I shift into a larger cog to maintain my cadence. Without thought, heels drop on the down stroke only to lift again at just the right moment in a gentle arc akin to the flapping wings of a seabird.

Miles ago, Zach settled into a rhythm at the front and never pulled off, so we've made more progress than we would have otherwise. As I watch him, metronome-like turning over a gear, I'm reminded exactly why Zach was once such a strong time trialist. The dense pines now behind us, we summit a short climb and the ocean reveals itself again. Mountains rising high above us, here the highway is cut into the steep hillside. The afternoon sun hangs low over the ocean, bathing the landscape in the warm, cinematic light of late fall. Sensing that I need food, I take a gel and banana from my jersey and eat them, washing the sticky remnants in my mouth with a sip of water.

The traffic is now mostly tourists in rented cars with out-of-state license plates; a couple in a white convertible has been leapfrogging past us as they stop at every turnout to take photos of themselves with the ocean as a backdrop. Having raced on this stretch of road when it was a stage in the Tour of California, Jackson knows it the most intimately out of the three of us. It's been years since I've been this far south on Highway 1, and while I've driven it, I've never ridden it before, and every rise, pothole, and gust of ocean wind that you're blind to in a car is now inscribed into my legs and body. Jackson is silent for a moment as he stares at the road:

'I remember the year I had the jersey for most aggressive rider, this stage was so freezing it was unbelievable. Hour after hour – I just couldn't keep warm. This stretch up here,' Jackson says, motioning ahead with his chin, 'this exposed one – I remember every inch of it. I've never been so cold in my life. Nothing else I could have done, I guess . . .'

'There wasn't,' Zach replies unequivocally. 'That was a great stage though. Against that field . . . ' Everything between us is loaded shorthand. We know what '*that field*' means in a race that was won by a Tour de France champion who would later be banned for doping.

As we approach it, the graceful arch of the iconic Bixby Canyon Bridge comes into view. The road narrows, and once we're on the other side, I glance back and am able to glimpse the creek and sandy cove hundreds of feet below. Like anything sacred, the landscape here has two faces, and as we ride south, the mountains that loom above our narrow shelf of a road rise ever more skyward – their verticality highlighting the endless horizon to our west where the expanse of blue stretches so far that it remains indeterminate – sky and water never fully resolving into a definite horizon. The indifference of the world is reflected back to me in every jagged rock and lonely windswept cypress.

My energy begins to wane and, with the dying light casting long, disfigured shadows on the pavement, the landscape that had seemed so strikingly beautiful is slowly transformed into something more malevolent. We push on, but with every sheer cliff or rocky outcropping looming over the dark painted waves, the thought appears from the hidden recesses of my mind: *was this it?* – was this where my aunt had jumped?

Φ

I never knew her, but I knew the aftermath. Sending ripples through the decades and across generations, once someone in a family takes their life, suicide becomes an option in a way that it otherwise never would have been – one possibility among others. Her name had been Lenore – Lenore *Hibbard* – but somehow I'd never even attached my surname to her and doing so brings with it a strange pit-of-the-stomach sadness. As we ride past a dirt pull-out, hundreds of feet above the Pacific, I think of her – of *it* – and how she must have driven to the ocean alone. Car tires over gravel, she'd set the parking brake, walked to the edge, and jumped. Had she decided that morning as she'd gotten dressed – telling her daughters goodbye for what she already knew would be the final time? Rather than having to imagine or empathize, I know first-hand what it's like to be in so much pain that the prospect of continuing to be alive is simply unbearable. Rather than having death imposed upon you by fate owing to accident or sickness it's an act grounded in inconceivable pain, but also *autonomy* – in the choice to foreclose the possibility of all other choices – *I no longer want to exist* – and she slowly became an explanation for both my father's unspoken trauma and my own pain; depression lurking in my genes as an inevitability.

My father had gone as far as to call killing yourself a 'family tradition,' and when he spoke of the shock treatments which had robbed his sister of her memory and how it had fallen on him to arrange her funeral only to discover that as a suicide, no priest would officiate it, his tone was so detached – the events so abstract – it was as if it had all happened to someone else. And I slowly came to understand that there had been a version of my father – perhaps one who'd been even more like me – whom I'd never met.

As is the case with many family tragedies, I know few details. This is not to say that I want to, or that knowing would somehow make it better or more comprehensible. Of all conceivable human choices, killing yourself defies comprehension, and no amount of knowing can bring it into the light of understanding. Nothing can ever be said which truly makes either the act itself – or the depression which precipitates it – *make sense*.

Before my worst episode of depression, I'd had the ability to make sense of almost anything – to make it fit into some schema or context – but somehow after, nothing ever again felt as solid as it once had. All my judgments were now shaky and preliminary. It seemed as if I'd run into a brick wall beyond which thought simply no longer applied. Rationality felt like a cruel joke of sorts and I realized that I had been a victim of my own thoughts – that I'd backed myself into a series of conclusions about the world from which 'depression' flowed almost as a matter of consequence.

For years, cycling forbade me from being what I was: deeply sad. I trained. I toiled, I barfed by the side of the road as I tried to outrun it, but at base, I suffered, feeling the pain not just of my own life, but the universalized and abstracted pain of existence itself.

I wondered what it would mean, what it would say about me to not be depressed – to say 'yes' and positively affirm a world so replete with suffering. Perhaps it was best not to *understand* anything, to realize that rather than being reve-latory, knowledge of certain aspects of what it is to be alive and what human beings are capable of is simply crippling. Here there is no intellectual response. No consolation to be found in philosophy or literature that doesn't besmirch – just unending rage and sadness beyond all words and logic for which there is simply no 'why.'

Although Nietzsche famously derided the pathos and empathy of Christian morality which he argued turned the instincts of the strong and innately noble against themselves, it's worth recalling the event which preceded Nietzsche's final breakdown. Shortly after leaving his room in Turin on the morning of January 3rd, 1889 the forty-four-year-old Nietzsche emerged into a piazza where he saw a cabbie mercilessly beating his horse. Overcome with compassion, a tearful Nietzsche is reported to have tenderly wrapped his arms around the neck of the exhausted animal in order to protect it, before himself collapsing to the ground – precipitating the final psychotic break from which he never recovered.

Say what one will of Nietzsche, blind to the overwhelming pain of the world he was not. Creeping around and behind the superficial surface of life reveals not merely elation, but the unspeakable suffering suffusing all of existence such that it becomes impossible to avert your gaze. As the saying goes, *one death is a tragedy; one million deaths is a statistic*, and to draw all of the small things near – to follow Nietzsche's teacher Schopenhauer and truly feel yourself into the existence of every tree, of every bird, mite, and passerby on the street – is to feel yourself into the sort of pain which in its particularity defies all logic and intelligibility.

Φ

Working in the long shadow cast by Nietzsche, Heidegger also wished to 'overcome' 2,500 years of Platonic metaphysical thinking. While he believed that with his radical inversion of metaphysics, Nietzsche was indeed 'dynamite' – the final coda of the metaphysical arc – Heidegger is quick to point out that inversion isn't overcoming, and that in many ways

Nietzsche remains the 'last man,' still trapped by the terms of the system which he sought to transcend. 'Thinking,' Heidegger writes, 'does not overcome metaphysics by climbing still higher, surmounting it, transcending it somehow or other; thinking overcomes metaphysics by climbing back down into the nearness of the nearest.'

With more than a bit of grandiosity, Heidegger thus places himself at a new beginning, suggesting a way of thinking which doesn't merely attempt to redeem the world from our deadening abstractions, but even more fundamentally, considers the seemingly unthinkable question which is present at both the birth and death of metaphysical philosophy: *Why is there something rather than nothing at all?*

Taking Nietzsche's pronouncement that 'God is dead' one step further, Heidegger claims that not only have the gods fled, 'defaulting on their return,' but that humanity has become so enchanted by material progress and technical thinking – 'so destitute' – that we now fail to even recognize this abnegation of the holy as the momentous event it was.

With the great German poets and thinkers as his guides – Herder and Rilke, but most of all the Romantic poet, Friedrich Hölderlin – Heidegger attempts to trace a path back to a beginning which isn't rationally determined, but poetically felt, and which returns us to a relationship with the primal wonder and unity which once enchanted all existence – invoking Pascal, what Heidegger calls '... the logic of the heart as over against the logic of calculating reason.'

Both logically and temporally, *thinking* always comes before logic – before the rationality of Carnap and the logical empiricists who, in their rush to understand the things of the world, have once again passed over the impenetrable mystery that there should be something rather than nothing at all. In Heidegger, philosophy is shifted from a game of distinctions – of this and not that – to one of preconceptual wonder that anything at all should be. 'Making itself intelligible,' Heidegger wrote, 'is suicide for philosophy. Those who idolize "facts" never notice that their idols only shine in a borrowed light.'

I've now spent more than half of my life trying not just to understand Heidegger's words, but to feel them sufficiently such that they redeem and re-enchant my everyday reality with the simple wonder that anything should exist. These glimpses are only fleeting and ephemeral though, and like a symphony or work of art brimming with impossible possibility, Heidegger's thought can birth moments of elation and insight which later disappear like a phantom. Akin to the ecstatic moments on the bike when everything seems possible, Heidegger's way of thinking can lead to false hope which can never be cashed out in the workaday reality of everyday life.

The question quickly presents itself: how does one live with this insight? How does one act or live better or differently for it? Perhaps these are the wrong sort of questions to even be asking – still too willful and calculative – and yet I persist: '*What shall I do now?*'; here I have no answer or way forward, only the distinct feeling that not knowing – not feeling this – would be far worse.

My relationship to philosophy remains forever bound up with my father. With a knowing wink and nod – *You understand none of this is really real?* – philosophy was our secret language and in many ways my father *was* philosophy. Understanding it was understanding him, and when we talked about feelings, they were always distant and abstract, but when we talked about *ideas*, they were immediate and palpable. The only way for me to make sense of him – and thus myself – wasn't by bypassing ideas, but by working *through* them, and Heidegger's story of returning home – of thinking through thinking so as to start anew – was thus perfectly in tune with my own emotional life. Heidegger's clarion call to overcome the chains of mere reason was charged with my desperation to beat back all the words and intellectualization and feel my way back into the graces of my father who at once seemed so near, and yet so far. Heidegger's thought is suffused with a longing for all that might have been – for all the paths that philosophy might have taken – and as I think about my life and my childhood, my attraction to this impulse to return anew seems almost inescapable for me.

Where words fail, poetry – the art of saying the unsayable – begins. Banned by Plato in *The Republic*, it's no accident that both Nietzsche and Heidegger invoke poets and the poetic to help us transcend our current epoch. 'To be a poet in a destitute time,' Heidegger writes, 'means: to attend, singing, to the trace of the fugitive gods. This is why the poet in the time of the world's night utters the holy.'

Like any story, the purpose of philosophy isn't for it to be *true*, but for it to make life just that little bit more bearable. No poem of Dante or Hölderlin, Rilke, Plath or Eliot, is less true now than it was when it was written, but can the same be said of philosophy? What of philosophical thinking so self-aware that its only ultimate claim is the utter impossibility of all ultimate claims?

Carnap and the logical empiricists may have been wrong in

their understanding of Heidegger, but in a more fundamental sense, I've slowly begun to think they were right – that philosophy has indeed been populated by 'musicians without musical talent.' When you attempt to say something about everything you end up saying nothing, but when you poetically articulate the contours of the particular, it can become a stand-in for all that is and ever was.

In the wake of Heidegger's thought, it seemed that the only way forward was through art in the broadest sense – a deep concern for something – a practice which brings consolation, forcing you to be totally absorbed and engaged in the world. As Nietzsche writes of the poets:

> to feel thus *squandered*, not merely as an individual but as humanity as a whole, in the way we behold the individual fruits of nature squandered, is a feeling beyond all other feelings. – But who is capable of such a feeling? Certainly only a poet; and poets always know how to console themselves.

In the end was it truly possible to overcome philosophy from within? Perhaps the whole edifice of rational arguments about the fundamental nature of existence was limited? Imagine if the poets hadn't been banned; if salvation was instead sought in all that's near and particular in the so-called little things, in landscape and the warmth of a summer evening.

Written during the final months of 1888, shortly before his breakdown, we find Nietzsche's mind at its clearest and most profound on the matter of these 'small things':

One will ask me why on earth I've been relating all these small things which are generally considered matters of complete indifference: I only harm myself, the more so if I am destined to represent great tasks. Answer: these small things – nutrition, place, climate, recreation, the whole casuistry of selfishness – are inconceivably more important than everything one has taken to be important so far.

Precisely here one must begin to *relearn*. What mankind has so far considered seriously have not even been realities but mere imaginings, more strictly speaking, *lies* prompted by the bad instincts of sick natures that were harmful in the most profound sense – all these concepts, 'God,' 'soul,' 'virtue,' 'sin,' 'beyond,' 'truth.' 'eternal life.' – But the greatness of human nature, its 'divinity,' was sought in them. – All the problems of politics, of social organization, and of education have been falsified through and through because one mistook the most harmful men for great men – because one learned to despise 'little' things, which means the basic concerns of life itself.

Φ

The sun has begun to set by the time we near the outcropping of buildings that are the nearest thing to a downtown Big Sur has, and as we ride the final few miles to the cabin where we'll be staying for the night, the dense redwood forest which bounds the highway gradually grows darker around us. Once we arrive, we leave our bikes outside and walk into the small market which doubles as the check-in, before making our way to cabin number ten just across the highway.

Outside, a single bulb casts a forlorn yellow glow across the dark-green door and cement stoop of the structure. A light breeze carries the faintest hint of smoke from a campfire which mixes with the earthen sweetness of the forest, and for the briefest of moments, I'm nostalgic in a way I don't fully trust. Inside we find that the space is tidy but spartan with three single beds, a wood fireplace, and a narrow galley kitchen. It smells musty, and with its fixtures and well-worn linoleum floors from the 1950s, it's not hard to imagine Kerouac or Miller in a space like this. The past is never just the past; always just below the surface it infects us, coloring our judgments of reality, and as I shower, I remember the home movies I'd found of my father and his sister as children after my grandmother died. There was Lenore with my father – both no more than eight years old. In a blue dress with a smock, she takes my father's hand dotingly and leads him towards the camera – smiling and happy in the saturated colors of Kodachrome. In a way that now seemed to defy all logic and rationality, somehow *this too had been.*

Jackson, Zach, and I change into our street clothes and begin to walk up the road to get dinner. After riding for most of the day, walking seems foreign and unnatural compared to pedaling, and my first few steps are stiff and deliberate. For the first time in a long time, I look up. Glittering swathes of the Milky Way are spread out above the towering canopy of redwoods. Standing at the end of billions of years and innumerable cosmic events – a product of the Big Bang itself – I'm aware that I'm aware; nothing less than the energy of the universe staring back at itself.

An unspeakable ocean inside me, all I'm able to bring to

words is an approximation of an approximation – shadows comparing notes in the darkness of a trapped-in existence. As we walk, I recall other dark nights long ago lying next to my father on the warm cement of the driveway and how as we'd looked up at the stars, he'd explained that the light we were seeing had traveled so far that the star could already be long dead, and I wonder how someone this sensitive – someone so like me – could have left my mother, sister, and me?

Once we round a bend in the road, the trees clear and a small moonlit cove comes into view. In and out, the waves rhythmically crash and spread across the smooth sand only to withdraw again. When he was a baby in his crib, Graeme's belly would rise and fall up and down with this same rhythm as he drifted into sleep – in and out and in – his trust in the world total and unbroken. Undifferentiated, he was the world and the world was him. It's *more* life I've wanted all along, not *less*, and afraid that if I start, I'll never stop, I hold back the tears.

Zach looks over and asks if I'm all right. 'I am,' I tell him, without lying.

Chapter 10

Nothingness and the World Beyond Words

A Zen teacher saw five of his students returning from the market, riding their bicycles. When they arrived at the monastery and had dismounted, the teacher asked the students, 'Why are you riding your bicycles?'

The first student replied, 'The bicycle is carrying this sack of potatoes. I am glad that I do not have to carry them on my back!' The teacher praised the first student. 'You are a smart boy! When you grow old, you will not walk hunched over like I do.'

The second student replied, 'I love to watch the trees and fields pass by as I roll down the path!' The teacher commended the second student, 'Your eyes are open, and you see the world.'

The third student replied, 'When I ride my bicycle, I am content to chant nam myoho renge kyo.*' The teacher gave his praise to the third student, 'Your mind will roll with the ease of a newly trued wheel.'*

The fourth student replied, 'Riding my bicycle, I live in harmony with all sentient beings.' The teacher was pleased and said to the fourth student, 'You are riding on the golden path of non-harming.'

The fifth student replied, 'I ride my bicycle to ride my bicycle.' The teacher sat at the feet of the fifth student and said, 'I am your student.'

—Zen proverb

The next morning, I'm gently roused from sleep by the chirping of birds emanating from the dense redwood forest which surrounds the cabin. My head still on the pillow, I watch as flecks of dust float in the shafts of bright morning sunlight which stream through the streaked window. In the bed beside mine Jackson stirs, but with nothing to rush to, the three of us remain in leisurely silence. Deep and dreamless, sleep had come easily, and I'm conscious of just how clear-headed I am – the world itself seemingly at peace.

Last night, we'd walked back from dinner along the pitch-black highway to the sound of crickets, talking and laughing about long-ago races remembered by no one but the people who'd ridden them, and riders who'd disappeared into the recesses of time: the junior from Oakland who'd raced costly custom framesets which had been hand-made for him in France, and the brothers from Los Altos who'd always ridden road races in their time trial helmets and skinsuits. To anyone else it would have sounded like nothing more than reminiscing, but somehow we still needed each other's memories to make sense of why cycling had once been so important to us. We're old enough now to know that ultimately it was insignificant, and yet inexplicably *it wasn't*, and we wonder out loud to each other in a thousand different ways: *what was this thing that had once enchanted us so – and why?*

I get up from bed and silently make my way into the small back room which overlooks the forest and sit down on the worn couch next to the dusty wood stove. It's only been two hard days, but all the old sensations are beginning to return – the same familiar stiffness when I walk, and the uncanny feeling of cleanliness that comes with being fit. I can feel that my resting pulse is already lower, and with each passing day, the bike has felt more and more natural as my body adapts to the workload and absorbs my newfound fitness. Looking down at my legs, I see that, like ripples in a pond, bands of green and purple now radiate out from where I fell on my hip, and dark tan lines from my shorts cut across my thighs. Today's ride will be our longest: nearly 200 kilometers with a few punchy climbs in the first couple of hours as Highway 1 takes us from Big Sur through the coastal village of Cambria, just south of which we'll cut inland to our hotel in the university town of San Luis Obispo.

When I return to the kitchen, Zach and Jackson are awake and we dress and walk across the street and eat breakfast at a small café tucked next to the town's only gas station. Over coffee and talk about the route, I notice aging photos on the wall from Big Sur's heyday in the 1950s. In one, a happy family stands next to a cargo helicopter which has just landed with supplies. In another, the building in which we're sitting is being constructed. The same man who was with his family next to the helicopter stares confidently into the camera, a sincere smile across his face and a hammer in his hand. America is a nation which lives in the present tense, idealizing the past while being careful to never fully metabolize it, and California has come to mean everything precisely because it actually means so little.

In both Hollywood to the south, and Silicon Valley to the north, it is a place which remains forever nascent – a fantasy defined more by an inexplicable combination of nostalgia and hope, than for what is or ever truly was. California's is a nostalgia which dislocates. A discordant pining, not for the actualities of the past, but for the once plausible hopes for a future which never came to be.

The waiter returns with our food and my glass of orange juice, placing it on the table deftly before retreating to the kitchen. As I look down at the pale-yellow eggs and too-dark bacon on my plate, I suddenly find it inexplicably sad and strange to be living at a point in time when even hope is only either second-hand or steeped in the stench of irony.

Φ

In cycling, almost everything is a matter of managing highs and lows – the frenetic storm of all-out effort followed immediately by the calm respite of recovery. In order to perform, a cyclist's body and mind need to be either on or off – either sprinting inches from other riders at 70 kilometers an hour, or half asleep on the massage table – and beyond a certain threshold of physical talent, it's regulating these highs and lows which becomes one of the primary jobs of any elite athlete.

For the 2001 season, I was reunited with Jackson and Zach on a team which was built around young riders and sponsored by The Olympic Club. Competent but not among the chosen, I'd tried but largely failed to transition my finishing speed to the road, and had settled into a schedule that mostly comprised of the national calendar of track races. Too good to quit, but also not living up to the trajectory I'd established as a junior, in order to get my career back on track, I obsessively sought to optimize every last bit of my equipment and training. From the footbeds in my shoes to weightlifting and diet, no stone was unturned, and Harvey and I tried to approach my preparation and training with fresh eyes – without regard for what had worked in the past or for what other people thought best. Things had fallen into place before, and I tried to trust that they would yet again.

Observing the unflappable ease with which the best riders dozed, played video games, or stretched in front of the television when they were off the bike, I came to realize that more than anything else, it was the ability to let go and relax that I lacked. Unlike me, the most successful were able to leave the day's triumphs and failures behind so that their body and mind could recover. However, in my case – to paraphrase Oscar Wilde – I found that doing nothing at all was somehow the most difficult thing in the world. During stage races and hard blocks of training, there were long nights of staring at ceilings and trying to force rest that never came. Full of adrenaline and knowing what the next day would bring, I'd plead with myself to just settle down, but more often than not it didn't work, and I'd find myself at a velodrome infield or crowded start line blurry-eyed with exhaustion and already at a disadvantage.

Just as music isn't merely sound, but sound followed by intervals of silence, improvement isn't work alone, but the right amount of work followed by rebuilding through rest and recovery. As the years went on, I realized that although I knew exactly how to will and push myself to the peaks, much to my detriment, I never mastered letting go and sliding into the valleys of recovery. Like a Gordian knot, trying to think myself out of thinking or will myself into relaxation, everything tightened upon itself until I felt trapped by my own thoughts.

Bored with myself, anxiety quickly bled into despair. And, as I began to discern the trajectory and limits of both will and thought, increasingly it was Eastern – rather than Western – philosophy which seemed most applicable to the life of an athlete, and I was forced to confront the central question which could no longer be side-stepped: how to let go?

Φ

Long before I was a bike racer – and before I'd ever heard of Kant or Nietzsche or Heidegger – on lazy weekends when I'd go with my father to do errands in his rattly diesel Volkswagen pickup, we'd listen to lectures by the Anglo-American popularizer of Zen Buddhism, Alan Watts. At once erudite and roguish in the best sense, it was Watts who made thinking seem exciting and even dangerous, and helped me to realize that the schoolboy version of reality which I'd been fed was merely one choice among many.

Born to middle-class parents in Chislehurst, England in 1915, Watts had an early interest in mysticism and Eastern religions, and while still in his teens he became a member of the London Buddhist Lodge. After undertaking Zen training in New York, Watts attempted to reconcile his spiritual interests with his childhood Christian faith and attended seminary outside of Chicago – becoming an ordained Episcopal priest in 1945. However, finding church orthodoxy both dogmatic and dour, Watts resigned from the priesthood in 1950.

Relocating to California, Watts took a teaching position at the American Academy of Asian Studies in San Francisco, shortly thereafter beginning a popular weekly radio program in which he sought to articulate the basic tenets of Eastern philosophy to an American audience. Although a well-educated academic, in the spirit of the burgeoning counterculture, Watts' talks were informal, and rather than 'scholar,' 'philosopher,' or 'guru,' Watts described himself as a 'spiritual entertainer,' often erupting into infectious laughter at the precise moment that he'd led his listeners to the threshold of insight.

Properly more a contemporary of Kerouac and the Beats than of 1960s hippies, Watts' message aligned perfectly with a receptive San Francisco Bay Area looking to throw off the shackles of post-war conformity. Formally associated with the San Francisco Zen Center, for periods of his life Watts lived on a houseboat moored in Sausalito which overlooked the Golden Gate Bridge, as well as a small cabin in the bohemian community of Druid Heights on the slopes of Mount Tamalpais. In no sense a proselytizer, Watts expounded the teachings of Eastern philosophy not with the goal of conversion in any sort of religious sense, but with the aim of liberation – of showing a way out of the social game which for many had come to be taken so seriously that its terms came to be confused with reality itself. As Watts writes with his typical lucidity, 'the game of Western philosophy and science is to trap the universe in the networks of words and numbers so that there is always the temptation to confuse the rules, or laws, of grammar and mathematics with the actual operations of nature.'

Central to many of the Eastern wisdom traditions which interested Watts is the idea that prior to all of the differentiations and the distinctions which are the product of language and abstract thought, the world – unparsed and undifferentiated – simply *is*. Writing in the sixth century BCE, Lao Tsu begins the *Tao Te Ching* with the following lines:

> *The Tao that can be told is not the eternal Tao.*
> *The name that can be named is not the eternal name.*
> *The nameless is the beginning of heaven and earth.*
> *The named is the mother of ten thousand things.*
> *Ever desireless, one can see the mystery.*
> *Ever desiring, one can see the manifestations.*
> *These two spring from the same source but differ in name; this appears as darkness.*
> *Darkness within darkness.*
> *The gate to all mystery.*

Not only Watts, but also D.T. Suzuki, Eugen Herrigel, and other early popularizers of Eastern philosophy in the West often appear enigmatic by the standards of logic. They speak of 'effortless effort' and, 'thoughtless thought,' in a way that seemed to describe the best days on the bike when the pedals felt as if they turned on their own accord, emphasizing a way of confronting the world which is fundamentally preconceptual and thus avoids the knots of anxiety and alienation which are the result of thinking which, as Watts puts it, 'confuses symbols for reality.'

Without becoming mired in the same intractable dualities present in Western philosophy from the ancient Greeks onward – subjects and objects, perceiver and perceived, phenomenal and noumenal – Zen Buddhism, Taoism, Hinduism and any number of Eastern philosophical traditions don't regard human beings primarily as knowing subjects attempting to gain access to an external world. Instead, human beings are understood as an outgrowth of a primal unity which lies beyond language and rationality of which each and every one of us is inescapably a part.

After traversing the byzantine missteps, dead ends, and distinctions without a difference of Western philosophy, Eastern philosophy was refreshing in its clarity. And, in the writings of the Zen scriptures, the Upanishads, Zhuangzi and the *Tao Te Ching*, there is little sense of the tragic originary separation between creator and creation – between knower and known – and rarely (if ever) are unseen metaphysical realms posited or deferred to.

With the limits and utility of abstract thought circumscribed from the outset in these traditions, the rational subject of Plato, Descartes, and Hume retreats to the background, and that which is beyond words and rationality – beyond what is called *Maya* or illusion in Indian philosophy – presents itself. Going by many names – God, Brahman, Ultimate Reality, Nirvana, the Tao, and Being itself – regardless of what it is called, the experience remains the same: in a sudden burst of insight, the veil of individuation falls away and one comes to realize, *I am that.*

On the most fundamental level, each of us isn't an isolated ego, but instead a glimmer of a far greater, universal consciousness which, as Watts describes it, is 'playing a game of hide and seek,' taking this form and that, becoming self-aware in slightly different ways through each and every sentient being. As the dancer Nijinsky – the physical outsider par excellence – wrote in his diary:

> People must not think me. They must feel me and understand me through feeling. Scholars will ponder over me, and they will rack their brains needlessly, because thinking will produce no results for them. They are stupid. They are beasts. They are meat. They are death. [...] Man is God and therefore understands God. I am God. I am man. I am good and not a beast. I am an animal with reason. I have flesh. I am flesh. I am not descended from flesh. Flesh is created by God.

And then tellingly – heart-wrenchingly – Nijinsky simply writes over and over, 'I am God. I am God. I am God ...'

Here however it's critical to point out that this experience isn't one of mere megalomania. In Nijinsky as well as Nietzsche – who shortly before being committed, signed letters as 'The Crucified' or 'Dionysus' – the dissolution of the ego which blurs the boundary between the self and ultimate isn't about having the power of the godhead, but speaks to the legitimate insight which lies at the root of all mysticism: namely that each of us is indeed nothing other than the ultimate reality of Being gazing back upon itself – the universe made self-aware.

Φ

After breakfast, we return to the cabin. Inside, our bikes line the wood-paneled walls, and jerseys, shorts, and helmets are scattered haphazardly across the couch and small tile countertop which divides the kitchen from the living room. Already nearly ten o'clock and with limited daylight, we each begin to prepare our equipment. Tires are pumped, bottles filled, and the familiar smell of the camphor and capsaicin in the embrocation that riders apply to their legs permeates the cabin as we stuff the pockets of our jerseys full of energy bars and gels.

In a society almost totally devoid of ritual, the way a cyclist pumps their tires, adjusts their helmet, or even carries a bike, takes on a graceful elegance which is charged with significance. From Catholic mass to the Zen Buddhist tea ceremony, ritual with its aim of making the invisible visible, always outstrips the actual objects involved. And, as banal as getting ready for a ride might appear, at the lowest points in my life the well-worn rituals around the bike have felt nothing short of sacred – serving as an unfaltering reminder that *this too shall pass*.

As I remove the head of the pump from the valve it lets out a brief gasp and I feel the tire with my thumb one last time before buckling my helmet and tightening the ratchets on my shoes. After one final walk through the cabin to check that nothing has been left behind, we lock the door and set out. It's a Monday morning, and as we head south, the highway becomes quieter with each passing kilometer. High above us, the bright light filters through the branches of the redwoods, casting shadows which play across the tarmac as it disappears beneath our wheels.

For the first hour we climb at a steady tempo up a slow drag of an ascent with a consistent grade that allows me to settle into a rhythm – what riders call a 'racing climb,' where even the sprinters can typically stay in contact with the group. In front of me Jackson stands out of the saddle for several pedal strokes before turning back to Zach and me.

'Man, my legs aren't feeling the greatest. You guys remember how much further it is to the top?'

'Around another 2k to the summit I think,' Zach replies between breaths.

As Jackson drifts to the back, I become aware of the force I am putting into the pedals and slow down ever so slightly. With each passing day I've felt stronger, and within the first five minutes on the bike, I knew that today I'd have good legs. We round a bend. Ahead of us is a long straight section of road, and gradually the summit comes into view. Cognizant of the long day still ahead of us, we roll over the top of the climb easily. I zip my jersey back up and take a sip from my bottle and as the road falls steeply away, the Pacific comes back into view. Framed by an outcropping of weathered shale and grey siltstone rising to my right, the dark water is all the more expansive and, for the first time, the abstract fact that Asia lies somewhere out there feels like first-hand knowledge.

Quickly gathering speed, I feel the air as it rushes over my skin and roars in my ears. Like water flowing down a mountain, we intuitively find the fastest way through a series of technical corners. Braking early, we set up wide before sweeping across the apex and reaccelerating. In the unflinching immediacy of the present, future and past dissolve into the periphery, and as we approach an S curve – a right and then an abrupt left with decaying pavement along the ideal line – I feather the brakes. Through the steel cable

I can feel the brake blocks make contact with the carbon surface of the rim and then snap back as I release the lever. Once we're through the final bend, I see an aging Ford pickup truck approaching from the other direction – it's faded red body linear and inorganic against the blue, brown, and green of the landscape. As we blast by, I make the briefest of eye contact with the grey-haired old man driving it, but by then I'm already shifting my weight in anticipation of the next corner and, however brief, I'm granted a respite from all of my words and thoughts.

Establishing the contours and texture of reality itself, we're taught that existence is spoken into being. Language however isn't merely incomplete, but passes over all that's both literally and proverbially *unspeakable*. Whatever meaning there is seemed to appear at all the points where words fail. A gentle, arcing left and then a hard right and as the radius of the corner tightens, I'm surprised that Jackson's taken the line he has and to stay on the road, I have to push the bike over far harder than I'd anticipated.

I want to take Denika in my arms and tell her that I'm sorry, that I've made it all too complicated and that I want to start all over again. I'm ready to live simply, cleanly, and easily – here among the ocean and the trees or someplace like it. I've felt this way before – this feeling of an escape so close I can taste it – however I'm old enough to know that a thousand little things always get in the way. Things I detest but should love. I want to be rash, but I've also slowly learned to never fully trust this inclination.

Φ

Season after season, I looked for problems to solve and things to optimize – a tiny, half percent improvement in my pedaling efficiency or reduction in my aerodynamic drag. For athletes of a certain temperament however, this scientific, analytically minded approach to improvement which seeks to isolate and optimize this or that weakness – let's call it the modern Moser approach – only works to a certain point.

Derived from the Greek, the word *analysis* literally means to loosen or tear apart, and while this way of seeing the world as a discrete set of problems can be fruitful, it can also introduce a sort of conceptual feedback which hinders the instinctual spontaneity required to be an athlete. And, as my improvement stalled and my disenchantment with Western philosophy increased, I began to wonder more and more about those who approached cycling not as a series of problems to be overcome, but as a state to be attained.

While their personalities and backgrounds varied widely, the riders who'd been able to carve out long-lasting professional careers all shared not just an ability to relax and recover, but also a sort of mental flexibility that allowed them to adapt. Sickness, missed training days, or travel hiccups were brushed off as part of the process, and there was a lack of rigidity which I struggled to emulate. Perhaps unsurprisingly, Zen, with its clear emphasis on the preconceptual 'beginner's mind,' held enormous appeal for someone as perfectionistic as me.

Validating my own hard-won experience, Zen conceives of conceptual thinking as limited, and rather than a positive correlation between conscious, willful effort and a desired result, trying too hard at anything means that you miss the mark. From the symphony violinist, to the race car driver, to the archer, among the most skillful at any activity there is always graceful ease which occurs as a result of conscious will and intellect stepping aside.

As Awa Kenzô, the Zen teacher at the center of *Zen in the Art of Archery*, tells his German pupil:

> The more obstinately you try to learn how to shoot the arrow for the sake of hitting the goal, the less you will succeed in the one and the further the other will recede. What stands in your way is that you have a much too willful will. You think that what you do not do yourself does not happen.

Through a sincere, lasting engagement with nearly any activity or practice, you come to realize that in order to progress further, you must relinquish control. The idea that you are a thinking, rational actor who can impose your will only works to a certain point. As the willful striving of a subject set against a world of objects reveals its limits, you come to understand not just abstractly but *intuitively*, that ego-driven notions of the self don't simply have intellectual limits but also practical ones.

Translated into the terms of modern sports psychology these 'peak experiences' took place when I let go – the race that I was just 'training through,' or that for some reason or another didn't matter was almost always when the sensations were the best. Indifferent to the outcome, the calm of my well-worn warm-up routine would give way to legs that turned the pedals with such inexplicable effortlessness that it felt as if I had been made to ride a bicycle. This isn't to say I always won – that the sensations always correlated to the external result – but on race days like this I at least never got in my own way. On days like this I loved racing my bicycle.

Rather than the mind–body dualism of Descartes, Zen emphasizes the lived and embodied. Any human activity can be seen as an opportunity to cultivate a stillness of mind which, like the stillness of calm water, is able to reflect the world rather than impose concepts on it. In keeping with Nietzsche's damning critique of metaphysics, Zen makes no recourse to anything unseen or metaphysical. Squarely situated in the here and now of *this* world, Zen still accounts for the glimmers of insight which point us towards the mystical truth that in the very midst of the 'little things' of everyday reality there exists something wondrous. As Alan Watts writes:

> the spiritual is not to be separated from the material, nor the wonderful from the ordinary. We need, above all, to disentangle ourselves from habits of speech and thought which set the two apart, making it impossible to see that *this* – the immediate, everyday, and present experience – is IT, the entire and ultimate point for the existence of a universe.

Rather than clinging to life, Zen practice and poetry finds beauty precisely in its materiality and transience. There is no place to stand but where you are – no way to step outside of the stream of life in order to understand it once and for all, and, atypical for a spiritual practice, rather than the melancholic ideas of abandonment and sacrifice which suffuse Western philosophy and theology, Zen is humorous and playful – as Alan Watts says, 'sincere without being serious.'

Unlike the written word, there's something uniquely intimate about listening to the human voice as I did with Watts. Even now, I can recall the cadence of his speech and timbre of his voice, and all through my years of trying to unravel and think through Western philosophy, Alan Watts was with me – offering an alternative and laughing at the self-seriousness of my efforts.

While I've come to admire Zen greatly, it would be an oversimplification to say that having reached an impasse in Western thought, the solution had been as simple as finding salvation in the wisdom of the East. My experience with Zen is – and continues to be – far more ambiguous. Even though on many levels the answers seemed 'more correct' than those of Western philosophy (and in some ways strikingly similar to those of Heidegger), rather than liberating, Zen has always felt dangerous. Try as I might, I have remained stuck on my way to living the insights of Zen. Just what was stopping me? What was I so afraid of and why?

Latent in nearly every Western philosophical system of thought is the powerful and pervasive idea that, but for our will and volition, the world would descend into chaos. Goodness itself is light, order, and rationality – goodness is *doing* – activity rather than passivity. To see how deep this conception of *nothing* runs in the West, one only has to think of the Latin dictum, *ex nihilo nihil fit*: 'from nothing comes nothing.'

However, nothingness isn't understood as a mere neutral absence, but as an immediate threat against which each of us must be ever-vigilant in order to stave off the nullity which would otherwise overwhelm us. It's exceptionally telling that in Dante's *Inferno*, the space occupied by the most depraved of sinners – the pit of hell – is characterized not by the active aggression of the punishments which take place there, but by the ice-bound stillness of its all-encompassing negation.

If each and every one of us is an active, Kantian shaper of reality, what would happen if our rational imposition were to cease? Who or what would come to pass? Recall the opening lines of the Gospel of John, 'In the beginning was the Word, and the Word was with God, and the Word was God.' Here we see in stark relief the underlying belief that cognizing the world doesn't simply bring order to it, but in fact *creates* it even, and several lines later we encounter the moral consequences of loosening our grip on the rational and abstract: 'And the light shineth in darkness; and the darkness comprehended it not.'

Deeply embedded in my psyche is the idea that words and thoughts speak a shared reality into being and, by so doing, stave off the naked terror of existence which we saw earlier in Sartre. Light – the light of *logos* and rationality – is all that stands between us and nothingness, and slowly I came to realize that for me the idea of 'letting go' – however tempting – felt like nothing short of annihilation. In fully embracing Zen, it felt as if I risked becoming a detached observer who, in my attempt to assuage my own suffering would be doomed to look upon both life's ecstasies and tragedies from behind a plate glass window of indifference.

For Zen practitioners, this is precisely the point – you

relinquish your small, willful, ego-driven self, and come to understand that in the most basic sense you are the world and the world is you. The union between subject and object complete, suffering and anxiety fade as mere ego-driven fictions. There is no fixed self, rather the self is always contingent – located only within the ever-flowing stream of life.

With cycling, music, art, and anything so absorbing or transcendently beautiful that it makes me forget about myself, in flashes and glimmers, I'm on my way towards Zen, but I'm far from having arrived and I don't know if I ever will. While the idea that I can know and maintain some fixed self seems a dubious proposition, I remain bound to something I can neither articulate nor relinquish. Forever blind to my motives, perhaps I love myself too much; perhaps the world.

Inexorably linked to the nullity of death, passivity is at once my greatest fear and my fondest wish. Exhausted by myself and the world, I've often imagined floating on my back in a swimming pool on a summer's night high on psychedelic drugs. Under my eyelids, shapes and colors would tessellate against a backdrop of finality and resolution. No need for words, very little of me would remain – almost nothing. As the cool night air moved rhythmically in and out of my lungs and the water lapped at my ears and chin, everything would at long last make sense. I'd only hear the beating of my heart, just as I'd heard my mother's when I was still inside her – before I knew that I was an I. As insignificant as a shadow, simultaneously everyone and no one at all, Pascal emerges onto the stage of my consciousness, whispering words so poignant and human that through the centuries I can still feel his warm breath on my cheek: *The silence of these infinite spaces frightens me.* Where is Graeme, I wonder? Denika? The uncertain divine nipping at my heels, ever so slowly I allow the unthinkable question – the terror from which I've always fled – to present itself fully: What will it be like to go to sleep and never wake up?

Φ

For hours we pedal along the narrow shelf of a road carved into the rocky grey earth of the cliff side. Further south, the landscape has gradually become more arid – the canopy of redwoods replaced by sage scrub and stoic oaks, one gnarled, moss-covered limb springing forth from the next in haphazard organic perfection. The highway is desolate, and the smattering of houses are nearly all invisible from the road – their existence inferred only by the occasional ocean-weathered mailboxes that we pass. His shaggy blond hair peeking from underneath his helmet, as we approach a climb Zach rides up behind Jackson and stealthily grabs the rails of his saddle to slow him down, but Jackson quickly feels that something's amiss and looks down at the drivetrain of his bike before turning around, cursing in Italian, and starting to laugh along with Zach and me.

The afternoon sun high overhead, a gentle ocean breeze kicks up, becoming visible as it makes its way through the golden grass which covers the rolling hills. On the expanse of horizon, it's possible to spot the occasional fishing trawler – a speck of humanity in the vastness. It's already midday and with more than a hundred kilometers to go we realize that we're racing darkness and pick up the pace. As we make our way past the Tassajara Zen Center and the Esalen Lodge, where Alan Watts lectured so many years ago, I think of days spent with my own father – of days when things had once been simple.

Where we'd been hundreds of feet above the crashing waves, we gradually start to descend closer to sea level, and just north of Ragged Point, come to a makeshift stoplight hastily mounted on a crooked pole beside the road. Ahead of us, I can see where the highway has eroded into the water, and past the long line of stopped cars, workers and heavy machinery are cutting into the rocky hillside in order to rebuild the road. The light changes from red to green and we tuck into the slipstream of an old minivan with rust creeping up its wheel wells. Next to the single, narrow lane of pavement, a new roadbed – pristine and pitch black – has been laid and workers mill about in orange vests and hard hats pointing and talking over the roar of equipment. Hours from any town, I wonder how they get here each day. As I glance at their faces, each seems to have a look of self-possessed determination, of destiny even – *there is a road to be built* – and I try to imagine what it must be like to inhabit the world with such clarity of purpose. Where I am nothing, in their hard-hat swagger they seem to be *something*.

Less and less do I believe in being great at anything – in notions of being smarter, stronger, or better. On a long enough timeline, any success turns into its own sort of failure. All that matters is small and near – pulsing against the backbeat of its own finitude; dancing in the first rain of the season with Graeme or lying in the darkness next to Denika.

I know enough to realize that it's no coincidence that all of my heroes ended up alone, and all I can do is try to do better.

Chapter 11

You're Not Merely This

Sometimes it's strange being me. I travel the world meeting people, I'm surrounded with friends and my life is full, but all the time I am confronted by a young man I have nothing in common with. He is me, but he is not me now. In fact, I have been me now for longer than I was him, but no one wants to know about me.

—Eddy Merckx

I must love being nothing. How horrible it would be if I were something! I must love my nothingness, love being a nothingness.

—Simone Weil

In the West there's a long tradition of the self being conceived of as tripartite – the ego, superego and id; the Father, the Son and the Holy Spirit – and perhaps most importantly, the notion that within each of us there resides not just one, but three selves: the public, the private, and the secret.

However, in our modern quest for so-called authenticity these three domains have increasingly bled together. And, rather than the promised unity, there has instead only been ever greater confusion around the basic question of identity – of who any of us is *really*. Not only has what was formally hidden and private become aired in public through social media, but the once private language of fulfillment and self-actualization has become co-opted. From the fast-food worker to the executive, the public self of your profession is increasingly also supposed to be a genuine private passion and, particularly in the United States, the prevailing expectation is not simply that one is paid for their skill or labor, but that the entirety of your identity is in alignment with your professional role in an organization.

With this blurring of spheres in mind, what does it mean on the most fundamental level to be recognized as an athlete? Who or what is it about *you* that's being validated and by whom? Is it something that matters – an element of character or work ethic which can be controlled and is thus worthy of praise – or in reality is a successful athlete merely being lauded for something as indiscriminate and transitory as their genetic propensity for strength or endurance? Perhaps for something even worse – for something not merely incidental, but ultimately even destructive?

The idea that sport serves to establish identity and build character is ancient, and an entire industry exists around the premise that lessons from the bike, pool, or tennis court, can be taken into the boardroom or applied to this or that challenge after your career as an athlete has come to an end. To me, this white-collar mythologizing of athletic success has always felt like so much trite doublespeak. Unrealistic for both athletes and those who would seek to emulate them, an athlete's identity is reduced to being nothing more than their sport for the rest of their lives and – perhaps worse – life itself comes to be framed as a series of challenges to be overcome in the pursuit of 'success.' Rather than leading towards any sort of true insight or authentic self-understanding, this way of conceiving what it is to be an athlete instead only perpetuates the unremitting competitiveness of twenty-first-century capitalism and distracts from any hope of 'becoming what one is.' As Nietzsche writes of the path towards selfhood:

> To become what one is, one must not have the faintest notion of *what* one is ... The whole surface of consciousness – for consciousness *is* a surface – must be kept clear of all great imperatives. Beware even of every great word, every great pose! So many dangers that the instinct comes too soon to 'understand itself.'

All too often, the notions of self which compel success 'come far too soon' – born from wounds and desires only hazily understood and on some level, ambitious people always believe that there will be some point in the future when the internal tension is resolved and the ideal of who they want to be will square with reality. More often than not this point never comes. The tension continues from one goal to the next, until one of two things takes place. The first – far rarer – comes under the heading of success. You win an Olympic gold medal or the Tour de France and, for better or for worse, become the thing you always imagined. Perhaps more fortunate are those for whom 'self-understanding' arrives neither too soon nor too late, and the entire spell of achievement constituted on terms not of your own making is broken.

Whenever I tried to peel away the layers of my own pretense, the swirling question – unanswerable and enigmatic – loomed larger and larger: *Who am I really? Just what is this thing about which I care so much that the mere prospect of relinquishing it engenders abject terror?* And rather than providing any sort of answers, my identity as a cyclist only served to muddy the waters of understanding.

At the highest levels, sports aren't healthy. They don't as a matter of course prepare you for business success, for more fulfilling personal relationships, or to better deal with corporate 'teammates.' In reality, the analogy is far closer to having been an addict, and most of the former riders I know have spent the better part of their lives *getting past* having once been successful cyclists. Time and time again, I saw that the path away from cycling was far more perilous than the one which had led to it.

Φ

By the time we're through tiny Ragged Point, we've already been on our bikes for more than five and a half hours, and I can feel that my body is starting to consume itself. Gradually my consciousness has narrowed to a pinpoint of immediacy: food, water, and simply controlling my bicycle. The most basic of sensations are at once rote and novel as my perceptions are filtered through the translucent muslin of exhaustion. As I stare at Zach's rear wheel in front of me, I take my hand from the handlebar, remove a berry-flavored energy block from my jersey, put it into my mouth, and allow it to slowly dissolve against the flesh of my cheek.

Now, more than a decade since my childhood cycling hero, Frank Vandenbroucke, died alone in a hotel room after having been banned for doping, long gone are the days of imagining that I'm racing towards glory. Nothing more than a tired, out of shape version of myself, I think of little more than trying to be present and doing what's necessary to make it through the rest of the day.

Well south of Big Sur, the road is flat and straight – vertical cliffs replaced by long stretches of sandy beaches – and in the distance, the sun already hangs low over the dark Pacific. A group of motorcyclists who we'd seen stopped at a dirt pull-out miles ago fly past us aboard gleaming BMW motorbikes, waving to us casually as they pass before disappearing over the crest of a rise. My legs are tired and drained and, sitting last wheel, I unclip from my pedals and shake each leg in turn, hoping to revitalize them, but when I resume pedaling, find that it's not helped one iota.

The palm trees which distinguish Southern from Northern California begin to dot the expansive floodplain between the ocean and the mountains as we make our way into the tiny coastal town of San Simeon – best known for being the former home of the billionaire newspaper magnate William Randolph Hearst.

Perched high atop a hill overlooking the Pacific, from miles away I begin to discern the silhouetted outline of Hearst's sprawling 1920s estate. Growing clearer with every pedal stroke, its white Spanish-style buildings are dressed in the warm, yellow glow of the autumn light. Before she'd died, my grandmother and I had visited the mansion which had been turned into a historical landmark. Making our way up the long driveway, to piped-in recordings of jazz and ragtime, we passed the peacocks and zebras that still roamed the property. Inside – from the wood-paneled library where Charlie Chaplin and Winston Churchill had once sat, to the expansive indoor pool with its blue and gold mosaic of Neptune – the entire estate seemed designed for tourists to indulge not merely their historical curiosity, but the hidden hope that with enough work, perhaps anything was possible.

Ahead of me, Jackson pulls off – momentarily coasting with his leg locked at the bottom of the stroke as he drifts back onto my wheel. His sunglasses off, his eyes are sunken and, reading the fatigue on his face, I feel better knowing that it's not just me who's tired. As we ride past the gated entrance to the long, winding drive that leads to Hearst Castle I think of the old adage – American to its core in its dismissive cruelty – *if you're so smart then why ain't you rich?*

If the world of professional cycling taught me anything, it's that more often than not, life's so-called winners are just the ones who've gotten away with the most.

Φ

As the trajectory of my racing career stalled, praise and criticism alike came from people who had never been in my position – managers, so-called coaches, and hangers-on, who opined from the proverbial sidelines on my training, my psychological state, and my equipment choices.

When I was racing well, I craved for it to be noticed, but when I was riding poorly, the criticism cut deeply. People I'd never met, and journalists I'd never spoken to, wrote about how I was performing and what I deserved in a way that felt deeply personal. What, I'd think, entitles you – someone who never made it out of the category threes – to comment on how I'm racing? How small is your life that what I am doing in a bicycle race would even cross your mind? Even though I resisted being reduced to a cyclist, the sport remained my world – my wellspring of identity and worth. What I'd failed to understand were the sort of people to whom I'd relinquished so much control; perhaps they weren't so much like me as I'd once believed.

While some involved in the sport were well-meaning and saw me as a person and not just a commodity – people like Terry Shaw, my first coach Christopher Campbell, former pro Craig Schommer, and of course Harvey – many others were desperate, delusional, or both. Believing that any number of young riders were their ticket to being someone of importance, there were innumerable people involved in the sport who would attach themselves to upcoming riders as agents, managers, or advisors of some sort in an attempt to gain the power that life had withheld from them in other arenas.

Here you might rightly wonder why the culture of the sport would be so hostile when the stakes are, relatively speaking, so low? The simple answer is desperation.

Cycling – in particular American cycling – has always been by any standard a poorly funded sport. In American professional cycling, everything is in a perpetual state of crisis and those that survive in any capacity for any period of time typically only do so because of a willingness to do whatever is necessary to make ends meet. For a rider, a six-figure salary is entering exceptionally rarified space, and in reality, most make no more than one or two thousand dollars a month. Financial backers come and go and teams are always teetering on the verge of insolvency. Wealthy phantom sponsors lure riders to teams that never actually materialize. Some contracts are honored, and others aren't and – perhaps most significantly – desperate riders were willing to dope not just to win as professionals, but even to merely make it into the domestic professional ranks.

While I understood and came to accept that I was an expendable marketing commodity, as I saw the underbelly of cycling in the early 2000s, I couldn't tolerate the stories sold to outsiders of purity and simple hard work. From the lowliest domestic pro on down, we all understood to varying degrees that the game was rigged from the outset. The air having been sucked out of the room by the Armstrong generation which had preceded ours. In the late 1990s and early 2000s, Grand Tours and Olympic gold medals weren't won as the saying goes, 'on bread and water,' and while some continued in spite of this knowledge, I had a great deal of trouble squaring my *Chariots of Fire* idealism with the reality that a large percentage of riders were cheating, and as I became more outspoken on the topic of drugs, I watched as my opportunities in the sport evaporated.

As the philosopher Judith Butler writes, with biting psychological insight, 'You only trust those who are absolutely like yourself, those who have signed a pledge of allegiance to this particular identity,' and as the curtain was slowly drawn back to reveal what cycling really was, the less I cared about being validated by a system which I now had so little respect for. Gradually realizing that I'd brought a knife to the gunfight of professional cycling, rather than athletic success, I slowly started to envisage a different, deeper sort of belonging: being welcomed by artists, writers, and academics – by people whom I imagined *felt as I did*.

Momentum is a funny thing though, and so despite my doubts, when I received an offer from the top-ranked American professional team, HealthNet, I thought it just might be a new beginning for my cycling career, but it turned out to merely be the beginning of the end.

While still far from consistent, I'd ridden well the previous season, finishing third at the Collegiate National Championship points race behind Bobby Lea and Mike Friedman, both of whom had already qualified for the following summer's Olympics. I was never going to be anything of note on the road, but I'd had flashes of my junior success in mass start endurance track races. By this point I'd been racing full-time for the better part of a decade and I felt that I largely understood what worked for me and what didn't and so, just as I had so many years before, in late fall I began training again in earnest for the upcoming season.

More than ever, I felt the weight of the fact that after this year, there would be no more chances. Wanting to be certain that I could look back on cycling without either remorse or regret, throughout the cold, unusually dry winter I settled into a routine which involved little more than training, going to the gym, eating, and sleeping. Knowing that I needed the autonomy and focus afforded by training alone, I'd set out from where I used to live in the Seabright neighborhood of Santa Cruz, past the yacht harbor, and along crowded beaches until I was delivered to the open farm roads of Watsonville where I could undertake my long-tempo intervals unencumbered by stoplights or traffic. Aboard my new team bike emblazoned with sponsor logos, everything felt simple again. The variables were known; all I needed to do was to produce a certain wattage for a given amount of time, and just be left to train hard, and recover well – surely this was possible. From equipment, to coaching, to stress, everything seemed within my control.

Calories were measured, data collected, and the long aerobic rides of November and December were gradually replaced by more intense intervals as spring approached.

However, from the very first early season races, I could tell that something wasn't right. My body simply wouldn't respond; at race pace my legs were dead, and my heart rate refused to rise with the intensity. I was tested for things ranging from Lyme disease to anemia, but everything came back normal. Desperate to succeed, rather than rest, I began to train even harder which only dug my hole of fatigue deeper and deeper, and try as I might, the results simply never came.

In what would turn out to be the last road race I would ever start, I made the winning breakaway only to feel so nauseous I had to drop to the back in order to throw up. In the no man's land between the breakaway and the peloton I climbed off my bike and stood in silence next to an orchard waiting for the broom wagon – the car that follows races, 'sweeping up' the riders who've dropped out – and when I climbed inside, I knew that my time as a professional cyclist was effectively over.

At the end, I thought of the beginning – of the day on the schoolyard so long ago when I'd laced my fingers through the chain-link fence during lunch and watched transfixed as the cycling team had ridden past. I'd felt trapped and they – pedaling effortlessly in the slipstream of their team car – had seemed free, and I wondered how it had come to pass that the thing that had once felt like the epitome of freedom had turned into its own sort of cage.

I'd been training full-time since I was fourteen years old, and my body had simply had enough. Convinced that this chapter of my life had come to an end, I sold all of my equipment, took a job in marketing and, with an eye towards becoming an academic, began applying to graduate programs in philosophy.

Φ

Just south of the village of Cambria, a light but constant rain begins to fall. Wipers chatter across glass, and one after another, car headlights are switched on and the three of us sit up, remove our black rain jackets from our jerseys, and pull them on. In the rain, the ambient noise of traffic is muffled, and I become aware of the distinct sound of our narrow bicycle tires running through the thin layer of water which sits atop the dark pavement. Mile after mile it's mostly the same: a landscape comprised of condominiums on the inland side and sprawling lots full of camper vans and RVs facing the ocean on the other. In the cold and wet I almost always feel stronger, and inexplicably hitting green light after green light, we take smooth, steady turns at the front. I reach down, take my water bottle from its cage and pull its valve open with my teeth. Feeling the fine grit of the road spray in my mouth, I take one swig and then another until my mouth is once again clean.

As we round a bend, the road rises, and towering Morro Rock gradually comes into view. Lonely and dark, it looms above the ocean at the entrance to the small bay. Rather than mortuaries and funerals with their grotesque parodies of everlasting life, this was where we'd scattered my grand-mother's ashes when she'd died – the wind gently taking the ashes from my father's hand into the Pacific. I think not just of her, but also of her only daughter – of Lenore; both together and not, something and nothing at all, amid the same infinite, swirling waters.

I've never been able to find who wrote it – almost certainly a German Romantic poet – but on a night long ago, my father had read a poem to me which had likened every living soul, in our journey from birth to death, to a single drop of rain falling through the sky. Not knowing where it came from or where it was going, but eventually returning to the vast sea of the collective unconscious, only to repeat it all again and again until the end of time. Ahead of us, the dark sky is full of seagulls and, as we pass the imposing grey rock, I feel a wave of sadness or something like it washing over me. Zach pulls off and as I come to the front, I push harder, waiting for relief – for the pain to arrive searing and visceral in my legs and lungs. Now old enough to have witnessed the way in which all things come and pass upon the stage of existence, Nietzsche's sublime insight which had once seemed the stuff of madmen – the idea of the eternal return – has come to feel as certain as my own hand: This life isn't the first time.

The wind shifts as we start up a shallow grade, and as I pull off, the metallic taste of exertion lodges itself in the back of my mouth.

Once we're through Morro Bay, we turn inland. The rain now past, long shadows play across the darkening hills populated only by power poles, and the occasional grazing cow. It's still rural, but here the road leads towards cities and towns, and a steady stream of cars streak past us. After a long hard turn at the front that I feared would leave me behind, Zach drops back and, as we start to ascend a small rise, Jackson stands and begins to muscle up the grade.

Elbows bent and his eyes resolute, he still looks just as powerful as when he was a pro. As he drifts past my hip and onto my wheel, I'm reminded of the fact that – with a degree of dramatic irony worthy of Greek or Roman tragedy – Jackson, one of the best American riders of my generation, had been relegated to being Lance Armstrong's body double for Nike commercials. When Armstrong had been too busy, it had been Jackson they'd called. His legs and body a stand-in, splashed across the television screen when Armstrong had been at the peak of his fame – inspiring old and young alike to be like him with a voiceover espousing the virtues of hard work and determination.

It's often argued that doping was victimless – that the choices made were all those of consenting adults – but the reality was murkier and more destructive. There was no way to know at fourteen or sixteen years old the choice which would confront us; only slowly and once we'd gone too far to turn back, did it become apparent: dope or walk away.

Moving in micro-generations, the door had been largely shut for American riders born in the early 1980s – riders far more naturally talented than me – who, based on their physical talent and work ethic should have had long, successful careers; a laundry list of riders who were robbed of opportunities – Ryan Miller, Skyler Bishop, John Hygelund, Matt Dubberley, and John Rutherford – people who had the moral fortitude to simply walk away from the sport when the true stakes became apparent.

Becoming *a winner* – being on the cover of *VeloNews* and leading namesake *Gran Fondos* – meant not only doping, but also assuming a certain double identity: one, secret and private, and the other public, which were in direct conflict; I disliked not just what I would have to do, but who I'd have to become in order to progress any further and understood that if I had chosen to dope, the shame would have outweighed any perceived success. However, I was far from alone in this choice: irrespective of being discovered, there was an entire group of riders for whom a doped victory would have been pyrrhic – who also intuitively knew that they would have seen themselves not as winners, but only cheaters.

None of us will ever know who the real champions might have been. The apparently successful ones – the ones you've heard of – were simply those most willing to sacrifice their very identity for the validation of a thoroughly corrupt system. I used to be angry, but now I'm mostly sad – cheater and cheated alike – for everyone who had the misfortune of being involved.

For all of our sakes, the sport should have been something better.

Φ

By the time we enter the outskirts of San Luis Obispo it's already dark, and gradually all the things that a city wants to forget about begin to appear: a sewage treatment plant, some sort of an electricity substation, and then, nestled into a hillside, the distinctive bright lights, razor wire, and rectilinear brutalism of a sprawling prison complex.

Like everything terrible in modern America, its reality is shrouded in language designed to obscure and the green road signs leading to the gate call it either a 'Men's Colony' or 'Correctional Facility.' It takes little perspicacity or empathy to see through the abstractions – to comprehend the reality of what this place is, and as we ride by the gate, my freedom feels all the more contingent. Certain things are invisible only to those who lack sufficient powers of imagination. So much of what seems civil, decent – heroic even – depends on a sort of willful blindness that makes me distrustful of every righteous claim to power or truth.

As we limp into downtown San Luis Obispo, every pedal stroke is a labored effort requiring all of my remaining will and volition and I desperately just want off my bike. Hoping to draw on some untapped, recondite source of energy, I take the pair of headphones I'd put in my jersey this morning with the thought of perhaps needing them at a moment of desperate exhaustion just like this. I insert them into my ears and press play, but, from the first notes, I realize that I'm too tired for even music to have its usual effect. Over a small rise, Zach begins to pick up the pace and I yell 'off,' but my plea is drowned out by the wind. I grit my teeth and do all I can to remain in Jackson's slipstream, until finally I can do no more.

On the bike, as in life, you're ultimately alone, and meter by meter, I watch as my friends disappear up the road. In the distance they grow smaller and smaller, and my mind begins to turn frantically – not only do I not have a phone, I don't even know the name of the hotel that's booked for us. Suddenly Jackson looks back and realizes I've been dropped. He whistles to Zach, and they slow and soft-pedal, waiting for me to catch back up. Once I rejoin them, they start to push on again after giving me a knowing nod that means everything – not merely waiting, but more significantly, *not leaving me alone.* At once collective and lonely, adversarial and cooperative, both cycling and life are enigmatic and fraught with contradiction and, like anything or anyone that you love with all of your heart, it has loved me back – not as I might have wanted it to, but the best it can.

In the final tedious miles, we make our way past shopping

centers and strip malls anchored by convenience stores and dry cleaners, before turning into a residential neighborhood full of tidy bungalows.

One window after the next illuminated by the blue glow of television screens, the smell of dinners wafts into the street. Here there are fewer lights than the main drag we've just turned off and in the darkness, my black bike disappears beneath me – making it feel as if rather than riding, I'm floating. After skirting the downtown, we finally turn up a quiet one-way road which leads to our hotel. At long last, rest.

Chapter 12

Things Merely Are

I am an unthinking philosopher. I am a philosopher with feeling.

—Vaslav Nijinsky

As we carry our bikes up the flight of concrete steps that lead to our hotel room, a sense of happy relief cuts through the haze of our shared exhaustion. What was most important was that none of us had let ourselves down – we hadn't given up or complained – at no point had any of us violated the unspoken pact that we'd long ago established with ourselves and each other to be the type of person who doesn't quit.

At the top of the stairs, we make our way past a bank of vending machines and I see that in spite of the dressings of fresh paint and carpet, the building is laid out in typical roadside motel fashion with the three stories of identical maroon doors all facing a central pool, and as we approach our room the sounds of people splashing and laughing in the water echoes in the confines of the bounded space.

Everyone here, including us, will move on – maybe tomorrow, maybe the day after – but as long as you can pay, for now at least, there's a ready-made, impersonal sort of belonging which you can leave behind entirely at any moment. As vacuous as it may be, this itinerant, Las Vegas sort of acceptance without risk has always held a certain allure. In spaces and places like these, identities can be tried on and shed with a cinematic ease which makes anything feel possible.

Zach inserts the keycard into the slot in our door and the deadbolt retracts with an electronic click. Inside, the hotel room smells of cleaning solution and the air conditioner drones in a steady monotone. After our rustic Big Sur cabin, the room feels spacious and the beige walls, crisp white sheets, and stone vanity seem clean and modern. We arrange our bikes in a tidy row against the dresser, unbuckle our cycling shoes from our swollen feet, and sit on the small couch staring at our machines for a moment before Jackson breaks the silence with what we're all thinking, 'That's a good bike,' he says definitively as he motions towards his mud-splattered bike, 'better than I'd thought.' And, as exhausted as I'd just been – as much as I'd wanted to get off it – as I regard my bike now, I somehow only feel an even greater affinity for the thing which has delivered me here. Its lines are more graceful than I'd realized before – more organic and somehow more a part of me – and as we begin to unpack and get ready to go to dinner, I can't help but turn my gaze towards it. As the saying goes in the U.S. Marines about one's rifle, but equally applicable to mass-produced bicycles – *there are many like it, but this one is mine.*

Once I'm alone in the bathroom, I flick on the fluorescent light and glimpse myself in the mirror. Weary, and cheeks sunken, I haven't shaved in days and a beard has begun to creep across my face and neck. My arms – stick thin – are slightly sunburned, while my legs are coated with dirt and road spray which stops abruptly where my socks and shorts had been. My hip, knee, and elbow – now scabbed over – are slowly beginning to heal. Except as they relate to the bike, I somehow feel as if who I really am has very little to do with this face or these limbs which reside in the world – a place I've always struggled to exist and be fully present in.

Φ

It was late August of 2009 – and still stiflingly hot and humid – when Denika and I moved to Chicago so that I could begin graduate school. My cycling equipment had nearly all been sold, and when we arrived, I hadn't so much as ridden a bicycle since the last time I'd raced some four years prior.

We lived walking distance from the university – on the city's North Side – in a neighborhood full of well-kept grey stone buildings. Bounded by Lake Michigan and a rolling swathe of park, the rumble of the elevated train over its aging wooden trusses spilled through narrow alleys and onto the tree-lined sidewalks. Public and private spaces alike weren't simply older than those of California, but built with an impractical attention to detail and beauty which infused the city with a certain melancholic sense of an industrial past that no longer was. In every delicate cornice and precise bit of stonework, I felt the oppressive passage of time. *Someone had made this once – someone who without doubt no longer exists.*

Having received a teaching fellowship from the department, I was no longer an American cyclist, but a philosophy graduate student. While I led discussion sections, and kept office hours, nearly every waking hour was spent reading.

In my silent corner on the third floor of the library, I was outside of time and space, and at the end of the day I'd emerge hungry and blurry eyed into the twilight, passing throngs of well-dressed commuters returning home from their jobs in the downtown. Where I'd imagined like-minded peers, for the most part I only encountered a neurotic, hyper-competitive environment fueled by the scarcity of university teaching positions. Intellectual affinities and interests bled into personality and demeanor, until nearly every interaction was colored by the single looming question which quickly became both tiresome and painfully isolating: *who among us was the smartest?*

Having forced reality into submission, the so-called life of the mind which I'd pined after when I'd been a cyclist felt out of touch and devoid of emotion, and gradually I came face to face with an otherworldly dread unlike anything I'd ever known.

Drained of color and texture, the world became cinematically remote, and I looked on with a feeling of helplessness as I realized more and more with each passing day that no amount of thinking would save me. Wondering just who and what was real, I came to regard my own life with a detached sort of anthropological curiosity – uncertain if I believed in my life more or less than the people I passed on the street who all seemed so certain of the roles that they'd chosen to play.

When I think now of my time in Chicago, I still recall the view from the window of that library as I gradually sank into a deeper and deeper depression: oppressively low clouds like a blanket over the monochrome expanse of brick buildings which stretched unbroken towards the flat horizon. Consumed by ideas, it felt as if everything tangible and real had been swept out to sea, and I spent the little free time I had wandering through the nearby zoo and arboretum staring at rare orchids, monkeys, and a sad, solitary sun bear, trying to feel their existence sufficiently to push against my own and make life feel like something more than a mere abstraction.

It seemed to me that to understand philosophy in any real sense meant to leave it behind. Whatever they were – poets, thinkers, or perhaps Heidegger's 'shepherds of Being' – those who truly understood certainly weren't academics.

Just as the snow finally began to melt that spring was when the depression became so severe that it was clear to Denika and me that our only option was to return home to California to treat it. As we left Chicago, I told myself that perhaps I'd go back once I was better, but like cycling, deep-down I knew that this chapter in my life was over.

Φ

As we wait just outside the hotel lobby for the cab which will take us downtown for dinner, the three of us peer down the dark street expectantly. Above us there is only the faintest sliver of a moon, and as a cool evening breeze begins to kick up, it makes its way through the fronds of the up-lit palms in front of our hotel and causes the metal rigging of the flag to strike the aluminum pole with a series of sporadic hollow clanks.

A short car ride delivers us to a downtown street corner. In our warm-up pants and flip-flops, we're conspicuously under-dressed but too tired to care, and after walking for a few blocks we find the steak house Jackson remembers. Inside we're quickly led through the main dining area, past the kitchen, and onto a large patio with olive trees protruding through the wooden decking. Having now lived more of his adult life in Continental Europe than America, Jackson is adamant that we eat not just well, but with a leisure that's decidedly un-American; after exchanging a knowing smile of resignation with Zach which says, *I guess we're having a nicer dinner than we'd anticipated,* the three of us settle into friendship and the calm grace of a shared meal.

As we eat, we talk about America and Europe – about place, and how in the traditional cycling nations of France, Italy, and Belgium you see family farms and notions of *terroir* which tie people to a particular plot of land. It's not mere coincidence that a number of successful European pros come from farming families where hard physical labor – be it in the field or on the bike – is a way of life. And among most European riders, there's a sense of grounding owing to the fact that even if they're poor and desperate to succeed, they're still inscribed in certain patterns of family and tradition which take the pressure off each successive generation to create itself anew.

Having grown up together – having loved and lost the same sport together – the three of us are forever bound in the never-ending process of American self-creation. I wonder how something as seemingly solid as fate could be so unbearably light in its contingency; chance encounters with teammates who became my closest friends – with a sport that became my life.

Lurking beneath all of the groping attempts at self-understanding is the psychoanalytic belief that insight – bringing the unconscious into the light of the rational – would nullify all the pain and misunderstandings, but it never seemed to work like that. In America, a true sense of finality has always been the rarest of things.

'All right, here's one,' Zach says to Jackson. 'What would you do if you weren't still working in cycling?'

'Man, I have no idea,' Jackson replies, fixing his gaze into the distance, 'No idea at all.'

Φ

Back in California, and now neither an athlete nor on the path towards becoming an academic, I assumed an identity which no one envied. In hushed, clinical tones, I filled out surveys and answered questions; *Yes, there is a family history of depression. Yes, in the last two weeks, I have thought that life has no meaning.* There were months of therapists, psychiatrists, and medicines, but little relief.

Not only was I both too physically weak and mentally agitated to ride, but all of the things that had once allowed me to escape from my own mind now felt uncannily foreign. Rather than the pleasure of losing myself in something beautiful, all that was transcendent merely threatened to swallow what little of me remained.

Here I want to be clear and unequivocal: *I'd given up on thinking* – on the notion that ideas of any sort would make life any more bearable. Amid the uncharted incomprehensibility of depression, philosophy seemed like nothing more than an artificial exercise motivated by a certain fastidious vanity in which unseen things were endlessly arranged and rearranged into different categories. Like an elaborate game of 'Animal, Vegetable, Mineral,' words piled upon words, putting things in boxes which made sense relative only to other boxes – never making contact with anything true or real. Against this backdrop, intelligence itself seemed laughably futile, and I wondered how I'd ever been so naïve as to believe that philosophy of all things would save me from anything whatsoever – much less from myself.

I'd been delivered from the spell of thinking, but to what? The world seemed sucked dry of color and purpose, replaced by an unremitting biological striving which in the most literal sense took everything beautiful and transformed it to shit. Going deeper and deeper, I stripped back layer upon layer of falseness and pretense but never arrived at bedrock. One thing neither better nor worse than any other, every sunset and blade of grass took on the unbearable poignancy of being the last of its kind and I wondered if perhaps there are some things that no one should know – if, just as the day needs the night, the subject needs objects in order to retain some sense of his or her own existence.

Having felt that I'd flown too close to the sun, I wanted nothing more than to return to the banal comfort of the inane, workaday world. Rather than being great at anything, now I merely wanted a little life – as insignificant and inconsequential as it might turn out to be.

The fall after Denika and I returned to California, we found what seemed like a promising new treatment – TMS, in which targeted magnetic pulses would precisely target the area of my brain implicated in depression in order to make it more active again. It would take a month of daily sessions, but with little relief from a series of medicines which seemed only to dull my mind, we committed to driving the hour north to Palo Alto – to the same hospital where I'd been born – for the then experimental treatments.

The doctoral student who greeted me in the waiting room

that first day was no older than me. Soft spoken and kind, I could tell that she pitied me, and I remember wanting to explain to her that I wasn't all that different from her – that like her, I was smart and ambitious – but this belied the obvious facts of the situation. I was sick, and I *needed* her in a way that I'd never needed a stranger. Blotting everything else out, I became acutely aware that my identity had been reduced to that of 'patient,' or 'depressive.'

In order to understand what had gone wrong with my brain and where to target the TMS, she explained that we'd begin with an fMRI – a scan of my brain to measure the blood flow and activity in its various regions. Led into a small changing area, I put on a hospital gown before being taken into a cool, dimly lit room dominated by a cylindrical scanner. On the other side of a glass partition, I was able to glimpse a row of computers with several doctors seated in front of them.

My head secured in a metal halo, I heard the door to the room shut and the circulating air grow still as my prone body was slid into the throat of the narrow machine. Inside, there was the distinct odor of clinical cleanliness – of rubbing alcohol and electronics – and as the machine came to life, I knew that on the bank of computers in the other room, images of my brain were appearing – blood flow rendered in vibrant shades of orange, red, green, and blue – an organ like any other and yet, somehow not. It was where *I* was. What and *who* I was. Surely there must be a cause. Maybe that was the most realistic way to see things all along: material in the world, the physical structures of my brain determining reality just as my lungs and blood and muscles had established what I was capable of on a bike. Perhaps

I'd been wrong about it all – maybe in the end everything was reducible to the stuff of the world.

In the midst of whirrs and clicks, the full magnitude of my locked-in isolation began to wash over me. *What if*, I thought, *this is all a dream?* Frightened at the idea, my heart rate rose and my body began to perspire, and it dawned on me that I could imagine no worse a horror than solipsism – nothing worse than forever being alone in your own mind – everyone and everything as ephemeral and idiosyncratic as a dream. To be sure that I actually exist in the world, I wanted to run or move – *to ride* – but in the claustrophobic confines of the machine I was forced to remain perfectly still which only exacerbated my feeling of having been unmoored from reality.

On the screen in front of me, a black and white photograph of a man with narrow eyes and a snarl of rage suddenly appeared – the 'test' I'd been told about. The image was so close to my face that at first, I had trouble bringing it into focus, but as it resolved, I was able to see that the word 'surprise' was written across the bottom of the photo. The situation felt surreal – as if it had been lifted from a science fiction film – and from nowhere and everywhere, I heard a distorted voice through a speaker.

'James, remember you touch the top button if the emotion on the card matches the face and the bottom if it doesn't.'

'Okay, I understand,' I replied – unsure if anyone could even hear me. I wanted to plead with her – with the people in the control room staring at images of my brain – to help me make sense of everything, but all I could do was play along. Image after image projected on the small screen in front of me. Exaggerated expressions of fear, happiness, and surprise spread across the faces of strangers – old and young, male and female, some mislabeled, and others not – hoping and trusting that whatever the doctors were seeing on their computers would help them understand what they needed to make the pain go away.

After that first fMRI, I emerged from the darkness of the lab into the bright afternoon sunlight and found Denika waiting for me in the car. Unflappable in her love and indifferent as to how well I rode a bike or where I published philosophy articles, her acceptance was unconditional. For maybe the first time in months, I tried to really see her as she was. Not my pain, how she might help me, or my idea of her, but her as she really was. Brown eyes, dark hair, and a faint dusting of freckles across the bridge of her nose and cheeks, I observed her observing me observing her.

In love, as in friendship, every idealization does violence to the very thing which it professes to care about most – obliterating all of the inconvenient contours and idiosyncrasies of the beloved's existence and rendering the person you purport to love into nothing more than *your* abstracted ideal of them. *What conceivable fate could be worse than this locked-in horror,* I wondered – *forever lost inside yourself?*

'Did it go okay?' Denika asked soberly.

'Yes,' I replied, 'as well as it could've, I guess.'

She'd smiled, given me a kiss and started the car before turning to me again, 'We'll get through this,' she'd assured me so sincerely that I'd believed it.

And even though there was no defining moment, no grand inflection point, ever so slowly we had gotten through it. Reality became real again, and gradually, with the strange woodpecker-like tapping of the TMS magnet against my skull, I'd gotten better where so many others hadn't.

With Denika's help, I felt my way through the darkness – towards new ideals and meanings – until almost imperceptibly, the stars once again came into focus.

Φ

Early the next morning, I'm awoken by Zach slipping out of the room in order to catch a commuter train back to his home in Santa Barbara. Slowly, I get out of bed and draw back the heavy curtains, allowing the bright sun to spill into the room. Both of us having promised to be back home by around lunch time, Jackson and I quickly shower and dress.

Outside, as we make our way past the open doors of vacated rooms that are already being cleaned and the now deserted pool, the feeling of people having already moved on is palpable. In the large hotel lobby, we eat breakfast among strangers as innocuous music plays, before boarding a shuttle to pick up the rental car that we'll drive home to the Bay Area.

In the dusty lot near the airport, we sign the papers for the car, quickly pack our bikes, and set off. A distance that had been slow and breathtaking by bike disappears quickly by car on inland Highway 101. The horses, feed stores, and wineries of Atascadero, Templeton, and Paso Robles are followed by a long expanse of barren, nearly treeless land interrupted only by railroad tracks and the decaying green barracks of a neglected army base.

Wherever it can be, nature has been put to use, and below an elevated section of freeway that runs above a dry irrigation canal, I spot the familiar outcropping of rusty oil derricks that I remember from childhood road trips – all these decades later still moving up and down endlessly in motion that looks so strikingly human that it's difficult not to pity them in their unceasing labor.

As dead insects begin to streak the windshield, we crest a small mountain range and drop into the tilled fields and dark earth of the southern Salinas Valley. I watch as rows of crops flash by, stroboscopic from the window of the car and wonder how many things – worse, how many *people* – I've looked at my whole life without ever really seeing?

Just outside of Soledad, we stop for gas off a dusty frontage road next to the freeway. Jackson inside buying water, I lean against the warm body of the car. Through my hip I can feel the fuel rushing in. A storm is approaching and to the south and west the low, dark clouds are backlit by an uncanny silver-hued luminescence. The gas pump clicks off, and in the newfound silence, I'm suddenly aware of the sound of the wind through the trees. In the distance I hear the barking of dogs and the forlorn whistle of a train and become confident – against all odds and for no real reason – that everything will be, and always has been, all right.

Closer to home, the fields of Gilroy and the sprawling suburban tract houses of Morgan Hill seem devoid of meaning – or perhaps merely so familiar that, like looking in your own eye, whatever meaning there is has become impossible to discern. Philosophy is a dead end in a culture which has little time for things which don't lead somewhere; but leading somewhere isn't the only measure of value – valuable too are journeys, and I return to where I began, perhaps changed, but in no way improved.

When we finally pull up to the house, I see Denika and

Graeme through the picture window and they emerge just as I'm unloading my bike, Graeme wrapping his arms around my legs. Kneeling next to him on the warm concrete, I watch him as he tries to tighten the front wheel of my bike.

'Like this?' he asks after a moment.

'That's perfect,' I reply.

My father once told me that I'd saved his life, and now I know what he meant.

It's not just the profane that's unspeakable, but just as much the sacred. Scattered among the remains of life's small things, the words all fail, and as I hug Graeme, I don't think of the past, but of the future. Instead of, *I think, therefore I am*, something like, *I love, therefore I'm real*. I take Denika's hand and, clasping her cool palm in mine, look her in the eye.

'How was it?' she asks, stepping back and surveying me with a smile.

'Fine,' I reply, 'really good – I missed you.'

In maturity, T.S. Eliot's, 'In my beginning is my end,' is transformed – or at least amended by Samuel Beckett. 'The end is in the beginning,' Beckett writes, '*and yet you go on*.'

If you're looking for a certain type of answer, in the end, the sound and the fury of being an athlete means absolutely nothing at all. But, if you listen hard enough – away from the cacophony of the crowd and attuned to a different, ineffable sort of murmur – you can discern something enigmatic. Something like life itself.

Acknowledgements

I'd like to thank my literary agent, Kevin Pocklington who believed in this project from its earliest stages and provided invaluable support during the long process of my writing it, as well as my editor, Richard Milner, who has both encouraged and trusted me in equal measure. I'd also like to thank PEN America for their generous financial support of me and this project – large parts of which were written during the early months of the COVID-19 pandemic in the spring and summer of 2020.

I'm also deeply indebted to the lifelong friends and mentors that I have as a result of my journey as a cyclist, including Christopher Campbell, Leonard Harvey Nitz, Terry Shaw, Craig Schommer, Jackson Stewart, Zach Walker, Matt Dubberley, Nate Shaw, Skyler Bishop, Andrew Touchstone, Ben Penner, Andrew Juskaitis, Aaron Avelar, and Julian Hickman – who as a practicing Zen monk – is also known by his Dharma name, Kazan Zenho. So much of cycling is based on the companionship of clubmates, so I would also like to acknowledge my friends and frequent riding partners, Brad Bini, Bob Graham, Matt Tamel, Jerry Kixmoeller, Bruce

Simpson, Ron Lau, Milton Kubota, Michael Wong, Mike Norris and the rest of the Garden City Cyclists for their steady wheels and laughter.

I'd also like to thank Chris Casey, Jackie Baker, Tyler Shores, Bret Luboyeski, and Paul Turner, whose encouragement, and intellectual clarity at various points provided me with both invaluable perspective as well as the necessary confidence to press on.

Nothing in my life would have been possible without the support and love of my mother Linda, father John, and sister Elizabeth, as well as my wife Denika and her family, and our son Graeme. I'd also like to thank my oldest childhood friend Tyler Lack who has seen me through so much, as well as my friend and reluctant riding partner, Ann Marie Hourigan, who not only introduced, but later married Denika and me.

Finally, because of a degenerative eye disease which required corneal transplants, in the most literal sense I would not have been able to write this book but for the generosity of donor families as well as the specialty lenses so patiently fitted by Dr. Ellin Wu, and the skill and care of my eye surgeon, Dr. Bryan S. Lee.

Selected Bibliography and Suggested Readings

Arendt, Hannah. *The Life of the Mind*. New York: Mariner Books, 1981.

Barrett, William. *Irrational Man*. New York: Doubleday Anchor, 1958.

Beckett, Samuel. *Endgame & Act Without Words*. New York: Grove, 2009.

Camus, Albert. *The Myth of Sisyphus and Other Essays*. Translated by Justin O'Brien. New York: Vintage, 1992.

Carnap, Rudolf. *The Logical Structure of the World and Pseudoproblems in Philosophy*. Translated by Rolf A. George. Chicago: Open Court, 2005.

Cohen, S. Marc, Patricia Curd, and C.D.C. Reeve, editors. *Readings in Ancient Greek Philosophy From Thales to Aristotle*. Indianapolis: Hackett Publishing, 2005.

De Beauvoir, Simone. *All Men are Mortal*. Translated by Leonard M. Friedman. New York: W.W. Norton & Company, 1992.

Descartes, René. *Selected Philosophical Writings*. Translated by John Cottingham, Robert Stoothoff, and Dugald

Murdoch. Cambridge: Cambridge University Press, 1988.

Dostoevsky, Fyodor. *The Brothers Karamazov*. Translated by Richard Pevear and Larissa Volokhonsky. New York: Farrar, Straus and Giroux, 1990.

Durrell, Lawrence and Henry Miller. *The Durrell-Miller Letters, 1935-1980*. New York: New Directions, 1988.

Eliot, Thomas Stearns. *Four Quartets*. New York: Mariner Books, 1968.

Fitzgerald, F. Scott. *This Side of Paradise*. New York: Signet Classic, 1996.

Heidegger, Martin. *Being and Time*. Translated by John Macquarrie and Edward Robinson. New York: Harper Perennial, 2008.

———. *Discourse on Thinking*. Translated by John M. Anderson and E. Hans Freund. New York: Harper Perennial, 1966.

———. *An Introduction to Metaphysics*. Translated by Ralph Manheim. New Haven: Yale University Press, 1987.

———. *Pathmarks*. Edited by William McNeill. Cambridge: Cambridge University Press, 1998.

———. *Poetry, Language, Thought*. Translated by Albert Hofstadter. New York: Perennial Classics, 2001.

———. *The Question concerning Technology and Other Essays*. Translated by William Lovitt. New York: Harper Torchbooks, 1977.

Herrigel, Eugen. *Zen in the Art of Archery*. Translated by R.F.C. Hull. New York: Vintage Books, 1971.

Hume, David. *An Inquiry Concerning Human Understanding*. Edited by Charles W. Hendel. New York: The Liberal Arts Press, 1955.

Huxley, Aldous. *Music at Night and Other Essays*. New York: HarperCollins, 1986.

Kant, Immanuel. *Critique of Pure Reason*. Translated and edited by Paul Guyer and Allen W. Wood. Cambridge: Cambridge University Press, 2009.

Kerouac, Jack. *Big Sur*. New York: Penguin Books, 1992.

Krabbé, Tim. *The Rider*. Translated by Sam Garrett. New York: Bloomsbury, 2002.

Lao Tsu, *Tao Te Ching*. Translated by Gia-Fu Feng and Jane English. New York: Vintage Books, 1972.

Marinetti, Filippo Tommaso. *F.T. Marinetti: Critical Writings*. Edited by Günter Berghaus. Translated by Doug Thompson. New York: Farrar, Straus and Giroux, 2008.

Miller, Henry. *The Air-Conditioned Nightmare*. New York: New Directions, 1970.

Murdoch, Iris. *Existentialists and Mystics: Writings on Philosophy and Literature*. New York: Penguin, 1999.

Nietzsche, Friedrich. *Basic Writings of Nietzsche*. Translated and edited by Walter Kaufmann. New York: The Modern Library, 2000.

———. *The Birth of Tragedy and Other Writings*. Edited by Raymond Geuss and Ronald Speirs. Translated by Ronald Speirs. New York: Cambridge University Press, 2008.

———. *Daybreak: Thoughts on the Prejudices of Morality*. Edited by Maudemarie Clark and Brian Leiter. Translated by R.J. Hollingdale. New York: Cambridge University Press, 2009.

———. *The Gay Science.* Edited by Bernard Williams. Translated by Josefine Nauckhoff and Adrian Del Caro. New York: Cambridge University Press, 2009.

———. *Human, All Too Human.* Translated by R.J. Hollingdale. New York: Cambridge University Press, 2009.

———. *A Nietzsche Reader.* Translated and edited by R.J. Hollingdale. London: Penguin Books, 1977.

———. *On the Genealogy of Morals* and *Ecce Homo.* Translated and edited by Walter Kaufmann. New York: Vintage Books, 1989.

———. *Thus Spoke Zarathustra: A Book for All and None.* Translated by Walter Kaufmann. New York: Modern Library, 1995.

———. *The Will to Power.* Edited by Walter Kaufmann. Translated by Walter Kaufmann and R.J. Hollingdale. New York: Vintage Books, 1968.

Nijinsky, Vaslav. *The Diary of Vaslav Nijinsky.* Edited by Joan Acocella. Translated by Kyril FitzLyon. Urbana: University of Illinois Press, 1999.

Panofsky, Erwin. *Meaning in the Visual Arts.* Chicago: University of Chicago Press, 1983.

Pascal, Blaise. *Penseés.* Translated by A.J. Krailsheimer. New York: Penguin Classics, 1995.

Russell, Bertrand. *The History of Western Philosophy.* New York: Simon & Schuster, 1972.

Sartre, Jean-Paul. *Being and Nothingness.* Translated by Hazel E. Barnes. New York: Washington Square Press, 1956.

⸻. *Existentialism is a Humanism.* Translated by Carol Macomber. New Haven: Yale University Press, 2007.

⸻. *Nausea.* Translated by Lloyd Alexander. New York: New Directions Publishing, 1964.

Styron, William. *Darkness Visible.* New York: Penguin Random House, 1989.

Wallace, David Foster. *Both Flesh and Not: Essays.* New York: Little Brown, 2012.

Watts, Alan. *Tao: The Watercourse Way.* New York: Pantheon Books, 1975.

⸻. *The Tao of Philosophy.* Boston: Tuttle Publishing, 1995.

⸻. *This is it and Other Essays on Zen and Spiritual Experience.* New York: Vintage, 1973.

⸻. *The Way of Zen.* New York: Vintage, 1989.

Weil, Simone. *The Need for Roots: Prelude to a Declaration of Duties Towards Mankind.* New York: Routledge Classics, 2020.

Wilson, Colin. *The Outsider.* New York: Putnam Books, 1982.

⸻. *Religion and the Rebel.* Boston: Houghton Mifflin, 1957.